THE LONDON ENGLISH LITERATURE SERIES
General Editor: G. C. ROSSER

LETTERS OF JOHN KEATS

LETTERS OF JOHN KEATS

Selected and edited by
STANLEY GARDNER
B.Litt., M.A., D.Phil.

University of London Press Ltd, Warwick Square, London E.C.4

FIRST PUBLISHED IN THIS EDITION 1965
Introduction and Notes Copyright © 1965 Stanley Gardner

Printed and bound in England for University of London Press Ltd,
by Hazell Watson and Viney Ltd, Aylesbury, Bucks

FOREWORD

THERE are many ways of reading literature. We can dip into a novel to pass the time away, we can give ourselves to a writer to escape from boredom or the monotony of films and television, we can read plays, short stories, and poems simply because we have developed a habit and would not be without our weekly instalment of reading. We can also read to make ourselves more mature by living through the emotional experience of other minds in this or another century. But whichever attitude we adopt, there is always one element which keeps us fascinated in literature. That element is pleasure. We read because, generally speaking, we find it pleasurable to read, and the more pleasure we find in reading the more the activity becomes part of our daily lives.

What many of us have realized, of course, is that pleasure and understanding go hand in hand—the more we possess a book, the more we come to grips with its essence, the more satisfaction it gives us. The experience becomes more relevant, more urgent. However, there are some books which we suspect contain more pleasure than we are able to extract. Their spirit seems to elude us. But with some guidance, we feel, we could possess a novel or a play or a poem and retain its genius. With such assistance in mind the present series has been edited to bring before the reader an opinion which may serve as a starting-point for discussion and fuller understanding. Each volume has a commentary or introduction which endeavours to look at a piece of literature as living imaginative experience. In this respect, therefore, it may be reassuring to find that with someone else's guidance before us we begin to see with a new and deeper perception. Our sympathy has developed, the satisfaction becomes more lasting.

G. C. ROSSER

CONTENTS

FOREWORD 5

INTRODUCTION 9

SUGGESTIONS FOR FURTHER READING 21

BIOGRAPHICAL NOTES 22

LETTERS OF JOHN KEATS 45

NOTES 237

INDEX OF LETTERS 261

INTRODUCTION

I

At an early age she told my informant, Mr Abbey, that she must and would have a husband. . . . [and] it was not long before she found a husband, nor did she go far for him—a helper in her father's livery stables appeared sufficiently desirable in her eyes to make her forget the disparity of their circumstances, and it was not long before Thomas Keats had the honour to be united to his master's daughter.

John Taylor, Keats's publisher, had this information from Richard Abbey who had been guardian of the Keats children, and passed it on to Richard Woodhouse, an inveterate collector of anything to do with the poet. The lady was Frances Jennings, of the Swan and Hoop Livery Stables, Moorfields, who on 31 October 1795 became the mother of John Keats. She was "a singular character, and from her he may be supposed to derive whatever was peculiar in his mind and disposition". His father, however,

> did not possess or display any great accomplishments. Elevated perhaps in his notions by the sudden rise of his fortunes. . . . he kept a remarkably fine horse for his own riding . . . One Sunday night in April 1804 he was riding home when his horse leaped upon the pavement opposite the Methodist Chapel in City Road, and falling with him against the iron railings so dreadfully crushed him that he died as they were carrying him home.

It was the first in a long series of misfortunes that stretched through the life of Keats. In two months his mother had married again, and the Keats children lived with their grandmother, Mrs Alice Jennings, at Ponders End. Keats was at Enfield School, when in 1810 his mother died suddenly, and the boy "gave way to such impassioned and prolonged grief (hiding himself in a nook under the master's desk) as awakened the liveliest pity in all who saw him"—or so said a schoolfellow decades later. This was the second blow.

A year later Keats left school and became apprenticed to a surgeon in Edmonton, where grandmother Jennings had moved. In common with all schoolboys Keats was required to practise verse-writing, and Leigh Hunt later lamented that he himself "had not the luck to possess such a guide in poetry as Keats had in excellent Charles Cowden Clarke", to whom Keats wrote his earliest surviving prose letter, on 9 October 1816. By this time Keats had already written a good deal of verse, had gone through his ten months' training at Guy's Hospital, and was qualified by examination to practise as a physician and surgeon. His interest in medicine and surgery went no further, and he turned to writing, and by the time C. & J. Ollier published his *Poems* in March 1817 he had already met Leigh Hunt, Haydon, Reynolds, Severn, Horace Smith and Shelley. Three months later, on a visit alone to Hastings, he met the mysterious Isabella Jones, who was always "an enigma" to him.

Keats had by this time already begun *Endymion*. He continued writing the poem during a visit to Bailey at Magdalen Hall, Oxford, in September. Next month *Blackwood's Edinburgh Magazine* published "a flaming attack upon Hunt", and associated Keats's name with his as one of "the Cockney School of Poetry". Keats had "never read anything so virulent", but coldly said of the author that he did "not relish his abuse" and would "infallibly call him to an account if he be a human being and appears in squares and theatres".

In November Keats visited Burford Bridge and finished the first draft of *Endymion*. In December he met Wordsworth, and on 28 December there was "the immortal dinner" with Haydon, Wordsworth, Lamb and others. By January 1818 the first part of *Endymion* was with Taylor and Hessey, his new publishers, and he had seen "a good deal" of Wordsworth. It is clear that the attack by the reviewers hardly put Keats out of his stride.

Much more disturbing was the state of health of his younger brother, Tom, who was consumptive. On 4 March 1818 Keats set

INTRODUCTION

off to join Tom in Teignmouth "on the night of the storm on the *outside* of the coach". It was hoped that Tom's health would improve by a stay in Devonshire with the Jeffreys—"steady quiet Marian, and laughing thoughtless Sarah", as George Keats described the girls. But the visit was marred by wretched weather, Tom's illness worsened, and on 17 May Tom was back in Hampstead having been very ill "and lost much blood" on the way. He wrote to Marian Jeffrey telling how very soon "John will have set out on his Northern Expedition, George on his Western, and I shall be preparing for mine to the South. John's will take four months at the end of which time he expects to have achieved two thousand miles mostly on foot. George embarks for America. I shall go by vessel to some port in the Adriatic, or down the Rhine. . ."

Keats together with Charles Brown accompanied George and his wife Georgiana to Liverpool on 22 and 23 June. Keats and Brown went on to the Lake District, and George and Georgiana sailed for America. Tom Keats was dying, and his own hopes for his journey south were vain. It seems strange to us that Keats should leave his brother in such a desperate illness; but the doctors probably failed to recognize its seriousness, as they failed later in the case of Keats himself. The tour with Brown taxed Keats's strength, and he returned alone with a sore throat, reaching Well Walk, Hampstead, on 18 August, to find Tom had been "worse than ever". Keats nursed his brother assiduously from now till his death in December and wrecked his own chances of escaping the disease. Upon Tom's death Keats went to live with Brown at Wentworth Place.

Meanwhile *Endymion* had been published in May, and the reviewers continued their attacks. In August *Blackwood's Edinburgh Magazine*, "a work", wrote Woodhouse, "as infamous in character as the man who bears its name", delivered its fourth "Cockney School" tirade, and in September J. W. Croker's "most unjust and illiberal criticism upon *Endymion*" appeared in the *Quarterly Review*. Reynolds defended the poem in the *Examiner*. Keats had now written "Isabella", and, equally important, had met Fanny Brawne. On Christmas Day Keats dined with Mrs Brawne and Fanny looked back on this as the happiest day of her life.

Brown had gone to Chichester a few days before Christmas, and a persistent sore throat prevented Keats's following him till mid-January. At Chichester he wrote "The Eve of St Agnes", and by early February 1819 was back at Wentworth Place, again with a sore throat. In April Keats sent Woodhouse the manuscript of "Hyperion", and decided not to finish the poem. The decision was fruitful in another way, for the next month he wrote the great Odes on a Grecian Urn, a Nightingale, Melancholy and Indolence. About this time Keats toyed with the idea of living in Devonshire, and wrote to Sarah Jeffrey to "enquire in the villages round Teignmouth if there is any lodging commodious for its cheapness". On the other hand, he thought he might go "voyaging to and from India for a few years". He did neither, but instead went to stay in Shanklin, Isle of Wight, accompanied by Rice. From Shanklin, on 1 July, he sent the first letter we know of to Fanny Brawne, who after this dominated his life.

Towards the end of July, a few days before Rice left on the 25th, Brown joined Keats in Shanklin. They moved to Winchester on 12 August. In Shanklin Keats had begun writing *Otho* and "Lamia", both of which he finished in Winchester. Here also he began "The Fall of Hyperion", and revised "The Eve of St Agnes". He visited London on business from 11–14 September, during which time he saw Woodhouse, Hessey, the Wylies, Rice and Fanny Keats, but returned to Winchester without visiting Hampstead and Fanny Brawne. In Winchester on 16 September, Keats wrote "To Autumn", and gave up writing "The Fall of Hyperion" about the same time. He returned to London with Brown early in October, and visited Fanny Brawne on 10 October. For a few days Keats took up lodgings at 25 College Street, Westminster, but he was soon back in Hampstead with Brown. During these months despite pressure from his friends Keats maintained his determination not to publish what he had written.

As Christmas approached he was still "rather unwell". George Keats came back to London in January 1820, and on 3 February, a few days after George sailed again for America, Keats's consumption declared itself in a severe haemorrhage. He had returned to

INTRODUCTION

Hampstead from London late at night by coach, and Brown described how

> at eleven o'clock he came into the house in a state that looked like fierce intoxication. Such a state in him, I knew, was impossible; it therefore was the more fearful. I asked hurriedly, 'What is the matter?—you are fevered?' 'Yes, yes,' he answered, 'I was on the outside of the coach this bitter day till I was severely chilled—but now I don't feel it. Fevered—of course, a little.' He mildly and instantly yielded, a property in his nature towards any friend, to my request that he should go to bed. I followed with the best immediate remedy in my power. I entered his chamber as he leapt into bed. On entering the cold sheets, before his head was on the pillow, he slightly coughed, and I heard him say, 'That is blood from my mouth.' I went towards him; he was examining a single drop of blood upon the sheet. 'Bring me the candle, Brown, and let me see this blood.' After regarding it steadfastly, he looked up in my face, with a calmness of countenance that I can never forget, and said, 'I know the colour of that blood: it is arterial blood. I cannot be deceived in that colour; that drop of blood is my death-warrant—I must die.' I ran for a surgeon. My friend was bled, and at five in the morning I left him after he had been, some time, in a quiet sleep.
>
> His surgeon and physician both unhesitatingly declared that his lungs were uninjured. This satisfied me but not him.

The apparently strange part of this account is Keats's "state that looked like fierce intoxication" when he arrived home. Sir William Hale-White suggests the probability that the bleeding started on the night-coach, when the taste of blood in his mouth would throw Keats into a state of excited anxiety.

The doctors remained sanguine, failed utterly to recognize the consumption, and treated Keats with the customary doses of mercury, by starving him, and by keeping him in a closed room. In spite of the haemorrhage, he was bled frequently. On 10 March Brown wrote to Taylor that "Keats is so well as to be out of danger. . . . we are now assured there is no pulmonary affection, no organic defect whatever—

the disease is on his *mind*". This seems to us beyond belief; but Keats had noted earlier: "In disease, medical men guess. If they cannot ascertain a disease they call it nervous". During early March Keats had "a palpitation at the heart". But he had taken a walk in the garden and by the middle of April had been to town more than once. By early May he had considered and given up the idea of accompanying Brown once more to Scotland. Brown now let Wentworth Place, and Keats moved to Kentish Town, and from there on 23 June he went to live with Leigh Hunt. During this month the violent attacks of blood-spitting returned, and a visitor to the Hunts told how she "was much pained by the sight of poor Keats, under sentence of death from Dr Lamb. He never spoke and looks emaciated." The physicians had changed their views. Keats had been ordered to Italy. Severn was seeing him frequently, and said "his appearance is shocking and now reminds me of poor Tom".

In early July Taylor and Hessey published *Lamia, Isabella, The Eve of St Agnes and other Poems*. This book of poems, among the greatest ever published, was to bring Keats immortality. Ironically he was too ill to take much comfort from it.

On 13 August Keats wrote to his sister to tell her that he had left the Hunts' house after "an accident of an unpleasant nature" over his mail. Fortunately Mrs Brawne, who had taken over the Dilkes' half of Wentworth Place, looked after him: the relief to Keats during his last few weeks in England must have been immense. Exactly a month later Severn decided to go with him to Italy. On 17 September, having made over the copyright of his books to the publishers, he went aboard the *Maria Crowther* with Severn. For a brief time at the beginning of the voyage Keats was "quite the 'special fellow' of olden time", backing Severn up before the ladies with his "golden jokes". But the voyage soon became an exhausting nightmare, ending in ten days' quarantine in Naples.

After a week in Naples, Keats and Severn left for Rome, which they reached on 15 November. On 30 November, "leading a posthumous existence", Keats wrote his last known letter. His life dragged on till 23 February 1821, and he was buried in the Protestant Cemetery, Rome.

INTRODUCTION

2

In the past much pathos has been read into Keats's poems from the terrifying suffering, mental and physical, he went through between February 1820 and February 1821, from his early death, and from his forlorn love for Fanny Brawne. But Keats wrote hardly any verse after 1819, and his circumstances in 1820 and 1821 can be of no critical consequence for his poetry which had already been written. With the letters it is a different matter, and this year is the tragic climax to the story they reveal. They also bring vividly to life for us the Keats of pre-1820, a man quite different from the maudlin wraith evoked by comments on his pathetic death. In the letters the ultimate year speaks for itself, and needs no tragic emphasis from us.

Letters written in the past have a strange fascination. They expose personalities in a way no other medium can. The quickness of consideration, the juxtaposition of triviality and profundity, the sympathy, in its real sense, for the correspondent, all lend an immediacy to the writing that eludes the recollections of autobiography. The presence in letters of personal references now insignificant, obscure or lost, only adds to their savour.

Keats's letters are not only the best commentary on his poetry, they are the perfect antidote to a century that made a sentimental mockery of Keats's life, personality and writing. Keats was clearly no shrinking violet. He was companionable and could be intensely practical. He did not batten on his friends either emotionally or financially. He would openly ask for a loan if he needed it, and lend to a friend in need without feeling self-warmed by his own generosity. He addressed even intimate friends like Reynolds, Brown and Rice with habitual reserve, and, though he addressed Fanny Brawne by her Christian name, even here he never signed himself "John". Clearly, as Fanny remarked, he was "the last person to exert himself to gain people's friendship". Yet he knew what friendship meant, and in a memorable phrase almost defined it: "The sure way, Bailey, is first to know a man's faults and then be passive. If after that he insensibly draws you towards him then you have no power to break the link." This gift for friendship is an outstanding feature of the letters, and gets rid of the romantic fiction of the withdrawn, rejected poet, misunderstood by society and scorned by the critics. The strength of Keats's personality grows as the months pass, and when he watched his looking-glass demonstrate the coming of death during the last year of his life, he still spared the feelings of Fanny Brawne and his sister.

The letters also tell us a great deal about Keats's method of work, the long periods of indolence, contemplation or brooding, and then hectic activity; and all the time, an unremitting determination to write poetry, a determination qualified by a sense of humour. Keats was self-critical, rarely self-important, and it is this that enabled him to keep in proportion the attacks of the reviewers. Writing to America of the tragedy *Otho* in September 1819 he said: "At Covent Garden there is a great chance of it being damned. Were it to succeed even there it would lift me out of the mire. I mean the mire of a bad reputation which is continually rising against me. My name with the literary fashionables is vulgar. I am a weaver boy to them. A tragedy would lift me out of this mess. And a mess it is as far as it regards our pockets. . . ." Keats disliked the abuse; he was hardly appalled by it, and that he was destroyed by it is a literary myth.

In 1826 *Blackwood's* printed an "Apologia" in which it extolled Wordsworth, typically, as "by birth, education, character and independence, precisely the man best fitted to hold in any country an office of trust and responsibility". *Blackwood's* was, as it said, basically a political magazine, "Tory through thick and thin", "honouring and venerating the churches established under divine Providence in these islands", and "believing that a kingly government, checked and balanced by a proud aristocracy, and a due mixture of a popular representation, is the only one fit for these kingdoms". So Wordsworth had become politically acceptable, and as political assumptions moulded critical assessment, Wordsworth's poetry was acceptable. By the same token, Keats's radical views and his association with Leigh Hunt had made an attack on him by *Blackwood's* inevitable, and in August 1818 in its fourth article on "The Cockney School of Poetry", the magazine rounded on Keats, and "the calm, settled, imperturbable drivelling of *Endymion*". Keats, in his sonnet "Great spirits now on earth are sojourning" had dared to set Hunt, "the meanest, the filthiest, and the most vulgar of Cockney poetasters", alongside Wordsworth. "Mr Hunt", wrote *Blackwood's*, "is a small poet, but he is a clever man. Mr Keats is a still smaller poet, and he is only a boy of pretty abilities, which he has done everything in his power to spoil". There was, of course, plenty of material in *Poems* (1817) and *Endymion* for the reviewers to quote to drive home their attacks.

In April 1818 the *Quarterly Review* had flayed *Endymion* even more fiercely: "This author is a copyist of Mr Hunt; but he is more unintelligible, almost as rugged, twice as diffuse, and ten times more tiresome and absurd than his prototype." The reviewer fastened on Keats's disastrous Preface to the poem, and down came the chastisement:

> Mr Keats, however, deprecates criticism on this 'immature and feverish work' in terms which are themselves sufficiently feverish; we confess that we should have abstained from inflicting upon him any of the tortures of the 'fierce hell' of criticism, which terrify his imagination, if he had not begged to be spared in order that he might write more ... and if, finally, he had not told us that he is of an age and temper which imperiously require mental discipline.

The reviewer could understandably not resist quoting Keats's ingenuous admission in the Preface:

> The two first books, and indeed the two last, I feel sensible are not of such completion as to warrant their passing the press.

Thus, as the previewer was quick to point out, "the two first books are, even in his own judgment, unfit to appear, and the two last are, it seems, in the same condition—and as two and two make four, and as that is the whole number of books, we have a clear and, we believe, very just estimate of the entire work".

Less smartly, but more reasonably, the *Quarterly* went on to expose the poem's faults, quoting them one after another: "turtles *passion* their voices", the "*honey-feel* of bliss", a lady's locks "*gordian'd* up", "the wine *out-sparkled*", "night *up-took*", a lady "whispers *pantingly* and close", "*ripply* cove", "*hushing* signs".

By August 1820, Jeffrey in the *Edinburgh Review* told a different story, writing of *Endymion* and the 1820 *Poems*, and set Keats alongside Ben Johnson, Milton and Shakespeare.

Keats was not the only victim of the reviewers. In 1815 the *Edinburgh Review* called Wordsworth's *The White Doe of Rylstone* "the very worst poem we ever saw imprinted in a quarto volume", in which the poet "appears in a state of low and maudlin imbecility". And, indeed, it has been shown that the journals which attacked Keats, powerful as they were, "were outnumbered seven or eight to one by periodicals that were either friendly or tolerant". It is clear from the letters that the criticism and abuse only strengthened Keats's friends in their allegiance to him; and that he was not, as Byron put it and so many later agreed, "snuffed out by an article". In October 1818 Keats thanking Hessey for sending him a copy of such an article, commented:

> Praise or blame has but a momentary effect on the man whose love of beauty in the abstract makes him a severe critic of his own works. My own domestic criticism has given me pain without comparison beyond what Blackwood or the Quarterly could possibly inflict, and also when I feel I am right, no external praise can give me such a glow as my own solitary reperception and ratification of what is fine. J. S. is perfectly right in regard to the slip-shod *Endymion*. That it is so is no fault of mine. No!—though it may sound a little paradoxical. It is as good as I had power to make it—by myself. Had I been nervous about its being a perfect piece, and with that view asked advice, and trembled over every page, it would not have been written; for it is not in my nature to fumble. I will write independently. I have written independently *without judgment*—I may write independently, and *with judgment* hereafter. The genius of poetry must work out its own salvation in a man: it cannot be matured by law and precept, but by sensation and watchfulness in itself. That which is creative must create itself. In *Endymion*, I leaped headlong into the sea, and thereby have become better acquainted with the soundings, the quicksands and the rocks, than if I had stayed upon the green shore and piped a silly pipe, and took tea and comfortable advice. I was never afraid of failure; for I would sooner fail than not be among the greatest.

INTRODUCTION

Time and again in correspondence Keats returned to the discussion of the nature of poetry, genius, truth and beauty. Even in 1816, in the early, mannered letter to C. C. Clarke he is thinking for himself. Keats says that he will be gratified to meet "men who in their admiration of poetry do not jumble together Shakespeare and Darwin".

Now Erasmus Darwin used the principle of association (John Locke first used the phrase "the association of ideas") initiated by David Hartley in his *Observations on Man* (1749) to explain the workings of the imagination, upon which he expounded in *The Loves of Plants* (1789). By 1815 this aesthetic theory was "now universally accepted", Coleridge, Wordsworth and Leigh Hunt all more or less subscribed to it, and Hunt's verse was heavy with it. And of course Keats's own early verse was deeply influenced by Hunt. Keats's scepticism, before he met Hunt, about contemporary critical dogma, shows a touch of independence that could have seemed the perverse arrogance of youth to his established new friends; and the observation in this early letter is reinforced by the fact that (Severn said in 1845) Mark Akenside, who had versified and philosophized on the principle of association in *The Pleasures of the Imagination*, was "a poet he so hated that he would not look in him". So it is perhaps not strange that Keats outgrew Hunt's influence, and that the early remark is only a foretaste of later observations.

From the letters we see clearly that Keats would agree with Hazlitt: "In proportion as men may command the immediate and vulgar applause of others, they become indifferent to that which is remote and difficult of attainment". He knew Hazlitt and respected his views. But if, as has been said, he echoed Hazlitt's critical opinions in the letters, the echo has always a memorable ring that the original lacks. Keats said, "The imagination may be compared to Adam's dream—he awoke and found it truth". Alongside this we may set the famous remarks "That if poetry comes not as naturally as the leaves to a tree it had better not come at all", and that "men of genius . . . have not any individuality, and determined character". Hazlitt had written that "it is indeed one characteristic mark of the highest class of excellence to appear to come naturally from the mind of the author, without consciousness or effort", and that Shakespeare "seemed scarcely to have an individual existence of his own, but to borrow that of others at will".

What Keats read he transformed, so that even if the opinions are not original to him, we refer them to him; it was Keats who wrote of Shakespeare's "Negative Capability", and observed so tellingly on Wordsworth's "egotistical sublime".

Keats himself sought "a life of sensations rather than of thoughts", where sensation was related to a creative frame of mind, and perception was heightened in proportion as circumstantial existence and "consequitive reasoning" were in abeyance. Almost all his great poetry was generated in this frame of mind, which he describes so often and so attentively.

Of course, Keats was not saying that a poem must be written as an effusion, in a state of half-dream, and then left unaltered; and we have only to look at the many changes he made in poems such as "Autumn" and "The Eve of St Agnes" to see how he strove for perfection. But the alterations are all aimed at heightening the poem's impact, on enlivening and illuminating perception, rather than on clarifying a narrative or philosophical argument.

So the letters are important, indeed indispensable, towards an understanding of the poetry. True, the poems speak for themselves and stand alone (as do the letters); but the letters inform the poetry, and the reader of the letters is strategically placed under Keats's own guidance to appreciate the poetry in depth.

The value of these letters goes far beyond commentary on the poetry. Beside this, and beside the profound comments on life, personalities and criticism, the letters have a quality that marks them as the greatest ever written. This quality lies not only in the range of mood and observation, but in the tragic completeness of the theme they expound. It is fortuitous that Keats happened to die young, and to know that he was dying. But this remains a fact, however fortuitous, and it makes the letters tragic. Through them we see a man of supreme sensitivity facing the inevitable end of things, and the impact is profound. In 1820 the tone of the letters changes, and the contrast with the earlier years moves us to more than pity. The end is tragic in its release.

In February 1820 Keats wrote to Fanny Brawne that he feared he

INTRODUCTION

would leave "no immortal work" behind him should he die. In 1829 Fanny wrote to Charles Brown that she feared "the kindest act would be to let him rest for ever in the obscurity to which unhappy circumstances have condemned him. Will the writings that remain of his rescue him from it?" Time has not only confirmed the greatness of the poetry, but has asserted the immortality of the letters he wrote to her and others near him.

SUGGESTIONS FOR FURTHER READING

BATES, W. J., *John Keats*. Harvard University Press: O.U.P. (London, 1963).
EDGCUMBE, F., (ed.), *The Letters of Fanny Brawne to Fanny Keats*. O.U.P. (London, 1936).
FORD, N. B., *The Prefigurative Imagination of John Keats*. Stanford University Press: O.U.P. (London, 1951).
FORMAN, M. B. (ed.), *The Letters of John Keats*. O.U.P. (London, 4th ed. 1952).
GITTINGS, ROBERT, *John Keats: The Living Year*. Heinemann (London, 1954).
HEWLETT, DOROTHY, *A Life of John Keats*. Hurst and Blackett (London, 2nd ed. 1949).
HALE-WHITE, SIR WILLIAM, *Keats as Doctor and Patient*. O.U.P. (London, 1938).
ROLLINS, HYDER E., (ed.), *The Keats Circle*. Harvard University Press: O.U.P., 2 vols. (London, 1948).
ROLLINS, HYDER E., (ed.), *The Letters of John Keats*. O.U.P., 2 vols. (London, 1958).
ROLLINS, HYDER E., (ed.), *More Letters and Poems of the Keats Circle*. Harvard University Press: O.U.P. (London, 1955).
TRILLING, L., *The Opposing Self*. Secker and Warburg (London, 1952).
WAIN, JOHN, (ed.), *Contemporary Reviews of Romantic Poetry*. Harrap (London, 1953).
WARD, AILEEN, *John Keats; the Making of a Poet*. Secker and Warburg (London, 1963).

BIOGRAPHICAL NOTES

RICHARD ABBEY

RICHARD ABBEY was a City tea merchant of considerable substance, and guardian of the Keats children after 1810. Fanny Keats lived with the Abbeys until she was 21, except for four years at school, while her brothers soon moved out to lodgings. It was Fanny's unhappiness with her guardian and Mrs Abbey, who was illiterate when she married in 1786, that drew from Keats such delicate understanding.

As John Taylor remarked "never were there two people more opposite than the poet and this good man". This "good man" was prominent in public affairs in Walthamstow and London, sitting on many committees. It was 1827 before he saw fit "to come into the fashion" and wear trousers instead of "white cotton stockings and breeches and half boots", because "for a long time there had been no other man on the Exchange in that dress and he was become so conspicuous for it". A few weeks after Keats's death he replied to a note from John Taylor denying any responsibility for expenses incurred by Keats's journey to Italy, saying, "he having withdrawn himself from my control and acted contrary to my advice, I cannot interfere in his affairs".

Abbey was scornful of John's imagination and opposed his intentions. Yet by accepted standards Abbey's attitude was "correct", even commonplace. He tried to put Keats into some line of business. He was strict with Fanny, tight with money, and kept her away from her brother's influence. To George Keats who showed more signs of being a commercial worthy, Abbey was more helpful. George's "unlimited confidence in Mr Abbey" was the cause of much coldness between Fanny and him, and was not disturbed till 1826 when he was prepared to acknowledge Abbey's "probable dishonesty". To Fanny, he appeared always a tyrannical guardian and later "that consummate villain, Abbey". In the circumstances, John's tender letters to his younger sister are remarkable in their maturity, temperance and complete absence of personal animosity towards Abbey. Keats had more judgment than to make Fanny's unhappiness more bitter by fostering her dislike.

Even George remarked on Mrs Abbey's "unfeeling and ignorant gabble", and Fanny Brawne noticed that she was "more disagreeable" when Fanny Keats had visitors. Keats thought it worth comment to Fanny in June 1819 that on one visit "They really surprised me with super civility—how did Mrs A. manage it?"

BENJAMIN BAILEY

BAILEY, four years older than Keats, was a close friend of Rice and Reynolds, through whom he met Keats early in 1817. Keats stayed with Bailey in his rooms at Magdalen Hall (now Hertford College) Oxford in September 1817, and wrote there the third book of *Endymion*. Keats saw little of Bailey after this. In February 1819 Keats wrote to George and Georgiana Keats of Bailey's broken engagement to Mariane Reynolds, though how one makes "impatient love" (as he said Bailey did to Mariane) "with the bible and Jeremy Taylor under his arm", Keats does not explain. After his Oxford visit, Keats wrote Bailey some stimulating letters, and clearly had found his conversation congenial. However it was August 1819 before Keats overcame the awkwardness of sending his formal congratulations (four months late) to the Revd. B. Bailey on his marriage to the daughter of the Bishop of Brechin.

Bailey's estrangement from Mariane broke up his friendship with Reynolds and Rice. Bailey defended Keats against the reviewers, and always wrote of him in letters to John Taylor with real, if stylized and self-conscious, affection.

Bailey clearly had more than one side to his nature. He wrote verse without distinction, and his pompous gravity comes through his letter to Taylor of February 1821, when he heard of Keats's final illness:

> I am deeply affected with your communication respecting poor Keats. "The flower in ripened bloom unmatched, must fall the earliest prey." Still there is this consolation—in the dispensation of a

kind Providence—that his sanguine temper would have been rendered miserable by the excitements produced by successive disappointments. And I fear he is not possessed with philosophic nor religious resignation enough to have borne the slow ascent up the ladder of literary fame. Poor fellow, my heart bleeds for him; but human sorrow is very unavailing. Pray be so good as apprize me of any material change in him.

Bailey wrote a letter of pious solace to Taylor on 26 March 1821, to say that he was "very much shocked at seeing poor Keats's death in the newspaper". At once he became very guarded and self-interested. He asked Taylor to make sure that his letters to Keats "may be destroyed or returned to me", unless "before he went abroad poor Keats took the precaution of burning his letters". At the end of April 1821, having read again in the papers, of the intention (not fulfilled) "to publish the Literary Remains of our poor young friend, with an account of his life", Bailey wrote to Taylor saying that he had no objection—"that the conversation I have related to you between Lockhart and myself should be stated *anonymously*". (It was J. G. Lockhart who wrote the abusive article on Keats and the Cockney School of Poetry in the *Blackwood's Edinburgh Magazine*, and Bailey had taken Keats's part.) Bailey also expressed the hope that the *Life* would "come out as soon as, with a careful selection of all the interesting particulars of so short a life, it can appear. If it be not intended to be kept secret", he pointedly went on to ask, "I am naturally curious who will write it. Will Reynolds?"

By 1824 Bailey's prudence had hardened even further, and he wrote to Taylor that he "had much rather that my facts, relative to Lockhart, were not made use of", since it "might involve me in an unpleasant state of literary hostility for no adequate end". Nevertheless he went on, "my opinion of the treatment of this poor young man, and my dislike of that publication, have never varied".

It is difficult to see the man reflected here attracting Keats for long, even without the jilting of Mariane Reynolds. Against it all, however, Keats expressed his gratitude (albeit to Mariane Reynolds *before* the broken engagement) for having known "so real a fellow as Bailey".

BIOGRAPHICAL NOTES

Bailey migrated to Ceylon in 1831, and was so out of touch that when Richard Monckton Milnes (Lord Houghton) published his *Life, Letters, and Literary Remains of John Keats* in 1848 he wrote pathetically of Bailey: "Brothers they were in affection and in thought —brothers in destiny. Mr Bailey died soon after Keats". Bailey hastily wrote denying his death, and sustained the denial till 1853.

FANNY BRAWNE

MRS SAMUEL BRAWNE, a widow, had three children, Frances (universally and now immortally known as Fanny), Samuel and Margaret. She was a close friend of the Dilkes, and in the summer of 1818 rented Brown's half of Wentworth Place while the latter was in the north with Keats. In the autumn of that year Keats and Fanny Brawne met through the Dilkes. Fanny was just eighteen. From Wentworth Place the Brawnes moved to Elm Cottage, but by April 1819 were back at Wentworth Place, this time in the half of the house that belonged to the Dilkes, who had moved to Westminster. So the Brawnes were Keats's next door neighbours from October 1819 till May 1820, and for some weeks in August and September 1820 he lived with them, and was nursed by Mrs Brawne. On 13 September Keats left Wentworth Place for Fleet Street "to be ready to go by the vessel". He wrote nothing to Fanny after that except the heart-rending farewell in his letter to her mother at the end of October, and he could not bear to read her letters.

In late September and October 1818, though he said he "never was in love", Keats was impressed "in a worldly way" by Jane Cox, a cousin of the Reynolds sisters, who had "a rich eastern look". "When she comes into the room", he wrote to the George Keatses, "she makes an impression the same as the beauty of a leopardess." At the same time there was his acquaintance with Mrs Isabella Jones, "the Hastings lady". Though Keats mentions both these women to George and Georgiana with interest in late October 1818, there is no mention of Fanny Brawne till mid-December. Then this: "Mrs Brawne who took Brown's house for last Summer still resides in Hampstead—she is a very nice woman—and her daughter senior is I think beautiful and elegant, graceful, silly, fashionable and strange. We have a little tiff now and then and she behaves a little better, or I must have sheered off." On 18 December, in the same letter, is the second mention of Fanny:

> Shall I give you Miss Brawne? She is about my height, with a fine style of countenance of the lengthened sort—she wants sentiment in every feature—she manages to make her hair look well—her nostrils are fine—though a little painful—her mouth is bad and good —her profile is better than her full-face which indeed is not full but pale and thin without showing any bone. Her shape is very graceful and so are her movements—her arms are good, her hands badish, her feet tolerable. She is not seventeen [in fact she was eighteen in August], but she is ignorant—monstrous in her behaviour, flying out in all directions, calling people such names, that I was forced lately to make use of the term *Minx*—this is not I think from any innate vice but from a penchant she has for acting stylishly. I am however tired of such style and shall decline any more of it.

On 24 January 1819 Brown and Keats wrote a joint letter to the Dilkes in which Keats asked to be remembered to "Elm Cottage— not forgetting Millament". Six months later, however, he recollected "the very first week I knew you I wrote myself your vassal".

The desperate love of Keats for Fanny Brawne during his last illness can be followed through his letters. On 18 September 1820, a few hours before he sailed for Gravesend in the *Maria Crowther*, Fanny Brawne had already at his wish written introducing herself to his sister as "a great friend of Mrs Dilke's who I believe you like". Fanny Brawne kept up the correspondence, and did her best to break the news of the extent of Keats's illness. "Oh my dear, he is very ill", she wrote on 1 February 1821, and told how Severn reported that Keats had "given up wishing to live. . . . If I should lose him I lose everything". On 27 March, she wrote "had he returned I should have been his wife and he would have lived with us. All, all now in vain—could we have foreseen—but he did foresee and every one thought it was only his habit of looking for the worst". These regrets may hint at something in her lively manner that wounded the jealous imagination of the dying poet. She was vivacious and young, and Keats hardly knew her except when he was desperately ill, bound to the necessity of concealing from her the death to which he knew he was committed. By then he was frustrated, desolate and ultimately alone. Through her correspondence with Fanny Keats, Fanny Brawne grows in stature and shows herself worthy of the poet whose letters have immortalized her.

"It's better for me that I should not forget him", she wrote, and it was twelve years before she married Louis Lindo (later Lindon). For the most time the family lived abroad, but returned to London in 1859 where Fanny died on 4 December 1865. By that time Keats was famous, while her name remained unknown to all but a few till 1878, and then she was generally vilified as shallow and vain. That their friends in the main disapproved of Fanny is clear from what Keats wrote. Fanny herself wrote of George to Fanny Keats, "He is no favourite of mine and he never liked me", and yet she was prepared to add, "but I must say I think he is more blamed than he should be". Mrs Brawne could "not prevent" the engagement, the Dilkes thought it "a bad thing for them", to Severn she appeared "cold and conventional" (though later he changed his mind), Brown flirted and found fault with her, and Reynolds expressed his gratification to Taylor that Keats had left England "so comfortably, so cheerfully, so sensibly", and added, "absence from the poor idle thing of woman-kind, to whom he has so unaccountably attached himself, will not be an ill thing".

When the letters from Keats to Fanny were first published in 1878 her reputation was hounded by the critics. Her vindication did not come till 1936, when her letters to Fanny Keats were printed, and she could speak for herself. "All his friends have forgotten him", she wrote in May 1821, "they have got over the first shock, and that with them is all. They think I have done the same, which I do not wonder at, for I have taken care never to trouble them with any feelings of mine, but I can tell you who next to me (I must say *next* to me) loved him best, that I have not got over it and never shall". In 1847 Fanny Brawne (by then Mrs Lindon) wrote an anonymous "kind communication" on Keats for Thomas Medwin's *Life* of Shelley, in which she wrote of his last months: "his anger seemed rather to turn on himself than on others, and in moments of greatest irritation, it was only by a sort of savage despondency that he sometimes grieved and wounded his friends". Twenty-six years after the suffering it describes, that is a remarkably vivid and perceptive recollection, hardly the phrasing of a "poor idle thing", "not in the least fitted", as his niece observed, "to have been the companion of John Keats".

CHARLES BROWN

BROWN was born on 14 April 1787. By the age of eighteen he was a merchant in St Petersburg. The firm went bankrupt and in 1810 Brown was back in London down and out, until his brother James, of the East India Company, made him his London agent. When James died in 1815, Charles came into his fortune "which allowed him to live a life of literary leisure", and two years later he met Keats.

For two years Brown was the closest of Keats's friends, and their movements may be followed through the Letters where Brown's name recurs frequently. In the Summer of 1818 Brown and Keats were on their famous tour of the Lake District and Scotland, and after Tom Keats's death on 1 December, John went to live with Brown at Wentworth Place, Hampstead. They spent some time during the summer of 1819 in the Isle of Wight and Winchester. In October Keats left Brown and took lodgings at College Street, Westminster "for the purpose of being in the reach of books", though doubtless there were other reasons too. But in a few days he was back with Brown at Wentworth Place, "induced to it by the habit I have acquired of this room I am new in and also from the pleasure of being free from paying any petty attentions to a diminutive housekeeping". Keats was writing to his sister, and added, "Mr Brown has been my great friend for some time—without him I should have been in, perhaps, personal distress. As I know you love me though I do not deserve it, I am sure you will take pleasure in being a friend to Mr Brown even before you know him." Keats had expressed this wish once before, but in 1826 Brown had still not met Fanny Keats—"for which her guardian is answerable". But Abbey had his reasons for keeping Brown off.

Brown was present on the "bitter day" 3 February 1820, when Keats recognized a haemorrhage as his "death-warrant", it was Brown who ran for the surgeon, looked after Keats till May, and settled the doctors' bills.

At the same time life with Brown was a business arrangement, as George Keats made clear to Dilke in 1830: "I cannot swear that John paid half the expenses of the house-keeping with Brown throughout, but I can that it was understood between them that he should". Moreover many years later Sir Charles W. Dilke wrote that Brown "certainly never spent money on Keats", and that he "was a scrupulously honest man, but by no means a noble one". Brown had Keats to live with him "to eke out his small income". So in May 1820, ill or not, Keats had to move into lodgings while Brown rented his house, and set off again for the north. He failed Keats in his hope that he would accompany him to Italy, and they never met again. Keats's death clearly shocked him.

It is difficult to judge Brown's apparent callousness to Keats at the end. For a while in 1820 Keats's health seemingly improved, and the doctors had "declared his lungs to be uninjured". Even as late as 21 December 1820 Brown was writing to Keats in a tone perhaps too jocular to be simply a cover for anxiety over a dying friend. On the other hand he was anxious after Keats's death to cover up the fact that he had been asked to go to Italy, and in December made lame financial excuses for not following Keats. He said that he had intended to join Keats in Rome "very early in the spring and not return, should he prefer to live there".

In late 1819 besides Keats and Brown, Abigail Donaghue, "a handsome woman of the peasant class", lived at Wentworth Place in an ill-defined capacity as house-keeper to Brown. Some time in August–September 1819 Brown and Abby (as she was called) went through a form of marriage "performed by a Catholic priest, and therefore not legal", as their son Carlino Brown explained; "but as she was a bigoted Catholic, and Irish, she was satisfied with the blessing of the priest, and cared not for the illegality". Neither, clearly, did Brown, and his attitude to Abby was crude and cynical. Carlino was born in July 1820 while Brown was away and his house was rented. After that Abby was back at Wentworth Place. The affair was common knowledge among many of Brown's friends, and Keats was concerned that Brown "with his indecencies" should be living near Fanny Brawne.

After Keats's death, Brown called himself "Keats's literary executor", and divided the poet's books among some of his friends—excluding George Keats and Haydon, and including Isabella Jones. Brown went to Italy in 1822, stayed there twelve years, and seriously considered writing a biography of Keats. In 1841 he passed his Keats manuscript over to Milnes, migrated to New Zealand, and died the next year. His tombstone now bears the inscription "The Friend of Keats".

Brown was a talented writer, a radical and a free-thinker. He was coarse-grained, brilliant, wayward, callous, self-centred, generous, business-like to the point of meanness, and clearly irresistible to Keats, which somehow redeems his faults. Further, against everything else is the simple and overwhelming fact that it was in Brown's house that Keats wrote much of his greatest poetry. And Keats's letters to Brown are unguarded and immediate. It was to Brown that Keats felt he could pour out his terrors and wretchedness at the end of his life. And these late letters to Brown are the climax, not only of his friendship and his physical agony, but of his tragic love for Fanny Brawne as well. Such phrases as Keats's bewildered question, "My dear Brown, what am I to do?" which the context charges with pathos and despair express a feeling that no other friend drew from Keats.

CHARLES COWDEN CLARKE

CLARKE was born on 15 December 1787, the son of the master of the school the Keats brothers attended at Enfield. Keats's first extant letter (apart from verse letters) is addressed to Clarke, but the correspondence ended, as far as we know, in March 1817. By February 1819 Keats was sending regards to Clarke by a mutual friend "with the assurance of my constant idea of him—not withstanding our long separation and my antipathy—indolentissimum to letter writing".

Clarke encouraged Keats in his early attempts at versifying, and introduced him to Leigh Hunt. But in 1817 he moved away from London, and it was 1823 before, on meeting Woodhouse, he heard how Keats left for Italy. Clarke lived till 1877, and was a literary figure of consequence in his day, and a life-long friend to Keats's reputation.

death. Haslam would clearly have accompanied Keats to Italy if family commitments had not held him back, and it was he who within a week of the sailing induced Severn to go. He did much towards the arrangements for the journey, and almost certainly gave £50 to Taylor for Keats's use. With Taylor and Woodhouse he accompanied Keats and Severn to Gravesend, and it was he who rushed back to London for the passport Severn had left behind, and sure enough, as Severn wrote, "at six came down my passport—we were not surprised—for we made sure of it since our oak friend Haslam had the getting of it". On 16 September 1820 Haslam and Woodhouse witnessed Keats's assignment of the copyright of his books to Taylor, from which the poet got £200.

On 18 September 1820 Fanny Brawne wrote to Fanny Keats telling her that Haslam would call on her "very soon", and that "his kindness cannot be described.... In Mr Haslam you will see the best person in the world to raise your spirits, he feels so certain your brother will soon recover". "Keats must get himself well again, Severn", Haslam wrote, "if but for us. I, for one, cannot afford to lose him. If I know what it is to love, I truly love John Keats."

Haslam married on 16 October 1819 and, as usual with his friends' love affairs, Keats was intolerant. "He showed me her picture by Severn", he wrote to George in September. "I think she is, though not very cunning, too cunning for him.... His love is very amusing." In November Haslam was "entirely taken up with his sweetheart", and in January 1820 Keats was apparently still holding off meeting Mrs Haslam. He wrote to Georgiana Keats (George was in England): "Haslam is a very good fellow indeed; he has been excessively anxious and kind to me. But is this fair? He has an *inamorata* at Deptford and he has been wanting me for some time past to see her. This is a thing which it is impossible not to shirk. A man is like a magnet, he must have a repelling end."

Haslam quarrelled bitterly with George towards the end of Keats's life and after his death, because of the latter's alleged dishonesty to his brother. Only three letters exist from Keats to Haslam, Haslam having taken such good care of the rest that he could not find them. He died in 1851.

LEIGH HUNT

LEIGH HUNT was born in 1784. Hunt's influence on Keats's early poetry was profound. In 1816 Hunt showed Keats's verse to the critic William Hazlitt, and introduced him to Shelley, Haydon and others. Hunt's admiration of Keats was instant, and during his final illness, 23 June–12 August 1820, Keats lived with the Hunts. It was largely due to Hunt that the "Cockney" label stuck to Keats. In December 1818 Keats described Hunt as

> vain, egotistical and disgusting in matters of taste and in morals. He understands many a beautiful thing, but then, instead of giving other minds credit for the same degree of perception as he himself possesses, he begins an explanation in such a curious manner that our taste and self love is offended continually. Hunt does one harm by making fine things petty and beautiful things hateful.

Hunt published the first biography of Keats in 1828, and George Keats took exception to its patronizing tone.

THE JEFFREYS OF TEIGNMOUTH

MRS MARGARET JEFFREY and her daughters Marian, Sarah and Fanny were "some acquaintances in Devonshire" with whom John and Tom Keats stayed during March and April 1818. Little is known of the Jeffreys, but they were clearly gay company. Most significant was the location of their house, 20 The Strand (now Northumberland Place), of which Sir William Hale-White said, "A more unsuitable lodging for a consumptive cannot be imagined". The house had one window, facing north, and enjoyed little light. Keats was confined to this house during long periods of bad weather with his brother when he was dying of consumption.

FANNY KEATS

FRANCES MARY KEATS was born on 3 June 1803. When her grandmother died she came under the control of Richard Abbey, a guardian "said

BIOGRAPHICAL NOTES

THE DILKES

DILKE was six years older than Keats. In 1815-16 he and Brown built the double house Wentworth Place (now Keats House) in Hampstead, and the Dilkes (Maria probably more than her husband) brought gaiety into Keats's life. Time and again they are affectionately remembered, sometimes repeatedly in one letter, as in that to George and Georgiana in January 1819—"with Dilke and Brown I am quite thick", "Mrs Dilke went with me to see Fanny last week", "on Sunday I brought from her a present of face-screens and a work bag for Mrs D.", "Dilke and I frequently have some chat about you—I have now and then some doubts but he seems to have a great confidence", "Mrs D. and myself dined at Mrs Brawne's", "Dilke has promised to sit with me this evening, I wish he would come this minute for I want a pinch of snuff very much just now", "I have been dining with Dilke today—he is up to his ears in Walpole's letters", "Mrs Dilke has two cats, a mother and a daughter. . . . Mrs Dilke is knocking on the wall for tea is ready", and (the next morning) "Nothing particular happened yesterday evening, except that when the tray came up Mrs Dilke and I had a battle with celery stalks—she sends her love to you".

The Dilkes took care of Tom, had the brothers in their house frequently and Mrs Dilke brought colour to Fanny Keats's existence. On 3 April 1819 the Dilkes moved to Great Smith Street, Westminster, to be near their son Charles at Westminster School—"that obstinate boy" on whom Dilke doted.

'Tis really lamentable, [Keats wrote to America in September 1819] to what a pitch he carries a sort of parental mania. . . . Brown complained very much in his letter to me of yesterday of the great alteration the disposition of Dilke has undergone. He thinks of nothing but "Political Justice" [i.e. William Godwin's book] and his boy. Now the first political duty a man ought to have a mind to is the happiness of his friends. I wrote Brown a comment on the subject, wherein I explained what I thought of Dilke's character, which resolved itself into this conclusion: that Dilke was a man who cannot feel he has a personal identity unless he has made up his mind about everything. The only means of strengthening one's intellect is to make up one's mind about nothing—to let the mind be a thoroughfare for all thoughts. Not a select party. The genus is not scarce in population. All the stubborn arguers you meet with are of the same brood—they never begin upon a subject they have not pre-resolved on. They want to hammer their nail into you and if you turn the point, still they think you wrong. Dilke will never come to a truth as long as he lives, because he is always trying at it. He is a Godwin-Methodist.

If, as this suggests, Keats and the Dilkes moved apart, especially as they disapproved of the engagement to Fanny Brawne, nevertheless before he left for Italy (so Fanny Brawne wrote to Fanny Keats on 1 February 1821) Keats had expressed a wish for "my Mother and Mrs Dilke to call and see you". And although Keats begged Brown, "for my sake, be her advocate for ever", it was Dilke who gave an eye to Fanny Brawne's financial affairs, and indeed Fanny Keats's too. His sense of justice led him to support George against the attacks of Brown and Haslam, and he even broke with Brown. He bought control of the *Athenaeum* in 1830, and used it to promote interest in Keats. He was a scholar of some standing, and died respected in 1864. Maria Dilke had died in 1850.

His son, the "obstinate boy", became a baronet, and his grandson inherited Dilke's interest in Keats together with his invaluable Keats documents, which are now in the possession of Hampstead Public Library.

WILLIAM HASLAM

HASLAM, who never wavered in his belief in Keats's greatness, was one of his oldest and staunchest friends. "And now I am talking of those to whom you have made me known", Keats wrote to George, "I cannot forbear mentioning Haslam as a most kind and obliging and constant friend. His behaviour to Tom during my absence and since my return has endeared him to me for ever—besides his anxiety about you." In December 1818 Haslam went for the first time with Keats to visit Fanny, and it was Haslam who had to tell her of her brother's to be so much more than strict", and his wife. "Oh my dear", Fanny Brawne wrote in 1821, "what a woman for a girl to be brought up with. The description I have of her manners and conversation has quite shocked me." Abbey successfully kept John at a distance for long periods and, as his letters show, Fanny Keats was seldom far from her brother's thoughts. Fanny Brawne told her in February 1821 that "he has talked of you continually; he did when he was in great danger last spring". At the end of the last letter he wrote, Keats mentions his sister "who walks about my imagination like a ghost".

Forty-eight of the letters Keats wrote to Fanny still exist. Severn, having "well examined them", told Lord Houghton in 1864 that he could not "find any thing suited for publication as they are all addressed to a little girl and constrained in style". These beautiful and delicate letters are now famous.

After Keats's death, Fanny's relationship with George was unhappy. In 1832 he wrote to Dilke that "she never writes but when she requires something of me, she now complains that I have neglected her and treated her with coldness when she was unprotected". It was Dilke who acted as her trustee when she came of age in 1824, and helped to secure her inheritance from Abbey. This money was largely lost by the business efforts of her husband, Valentin Llanos. Fanny lived till 1889, and is buried in Madrid.

GEORGE AND GEORGIANA KEATS

GEORGE KEATS was born on 28 February 1797. He worked for a time in Abbey's counting house, but left in 1816 after a quarrel, and the three brothers lived in Southwark, in Cheapside and then at the house of Bentley the postman, 1 Well Walk, Hampstead. George introduced John to many of his friends. In May 1818 George married Georgiana Wylie, and that summer they sailed for America. His affairs did not prosper at first, and when Tom Keats died he returned to England to claim his share of Tom's estate. The speed with which he had to act gave an impression of callousness, and Brown, Taylor, Haslam and Severn suspected him of taking away a good part of John's share of Tom Keats's estate as well as his own. He wrote in 1833 to Dilke that he could not "forgive Brown for helping to poison John's mind" against him. Fanny Brawne put Fanny Keats "on her guard" about George. She thought him "extravagant and selfish but people in their great zeal make him out much worse than that". Moreover she makes it clear that John's mind was not "poisoned" against his brother: "They tell me that latterly he thought worse of George, but I own I do not believe it". George himself lamented to Dilke twelve years later: "Poor John is gone, and I grieve to say with incorrect impressions of my worthiness". In 1818 Keats said, "George has ever been more than a brother to me, he has been my greatest friend", and later, "George always stood between me and any dealings with the world". Nevertheless, when he was severely pressed with money troubles, he left John dependent on his friends through his final illness. Ultimately George paid all John's debts, and tried hard, but unsuccessfully, to persuade Dilke to interest himself in a biography. But in time they drifted apart, and in 1846 Dilke wrote to Milnes presuming there could "be no doubt that George is dead", not knowing that he had died, a prosperous and influential member of Louisville society, as long ago as Christmas Eve 1841.

Keats was extremely fond both of Georgiana and of Mrs Wylie her mother. He had known Georgiana "some time" when she married George, and always mentioned her with esteem.

TOM KEATS

IN 1825 George remarked that "no one in England understood his [John's] character perfectly but poor Tom and he had not the power to divert his frequent melancholy, and eventually increased his disease most fearfully by the horrors of his own lingering death".

In their effort to care for Tom, his brothers often took him away from London, and it is strange that they should both have left him with Bentley while seriously ill on 22 June 1818. Dilke's urgent message recalling John from Scotland was in the event needless, as he was already on the way home. From his return until Tom died on 1 December 1818, John nursed him selflessly, and broke his own health by doing so. "The last days of poor Tom were of the most distressing nature", Keats wrote to the George Keatses a few weeks later, "but his last moments were not so painful, and his very last was without a pang. I will not enter into any parsonic comments on death, yet the common observations of the commonest people on death are as true as their proverbs. I have scarce a doubt of immortality of some nature or other—neither had Tom."

Keats was utterly devoted to Tom, and never forgot him.

J. H. REYNOLDS AND HIS SISTERS

ACCORDING to Dilke, John Reynolds knew Keats "first and best". Edward Moxen, Milnes's publisher, recognized that Reynolds "was Keats's most intimate friend", and Reynolds himself, on hearing the possibility that his name "should not be mentioned in the Memoir", simply remarked that "it would be playing Hamlet without Laertes".

Reynolds was a year older than Keats. By 1815 he knew Rice and Bailey and had published *Safie, an Eastern Tale*, *The Eden of Imagination* and *An Ode*. By 1816 Bailey and he had written *Poems by Two Friends*, and Reynolds had met Keats at Leigh Hunt's house. Though he continued to write and publish, Reynolds took up the law in 1817 with the help of Rice, and it was the firm of Rice and Reynolds that managed (and it was thought mismanaged) the legal affairs of George and Fanny Keats. By 1833 we learn from Dilke that Reynolds's affairs "have been long desperate", and he finished his life as an assistant clerk to the County Court at Newport, Isle of Wight, "a broken-down, discontented man". He died in 1852, and though he came so near to greatness his books have not survived him. He is remembered, as his gravestone proclaims, as "the friend of Keats".

From the Summer of 1817 to June 1818 Reynolds was an ailing man. In August 1817 Keats noticed "all kinds of distressing symptoms", and in February 1818 told George and Tom "Reynolds has been very ill for some time ... and had leeches applied to the chest ... and he is in the worst place in the world for amendment—among the strife of women's tongues in a hot and parched room". In March George Keats wrote to John at Teignmouth that Reynolds had "a very bad rheumatic fever and suffers constant pain. It is not said that he is dangerously ill, but I cannot help thinking that so many evils acting upon his most irritable disposition . . . must make this illness somewhat dangerous". It was June before Reynolds was "robust".

Though in December 1818 Keats said "John Reynolds is very dull at home", there is no evidence that he noticed his "irritable disposition". Reynolds's gaiety and companionship are mentioned repeatedly. Reynolds was the "playfullest" of wits, who "makes you laugh and not think". Keats and he found much in common. They shared ideas on poetry, and he stimulated Keats to write. When *Poems* (1817) came out he applauded it in the *Champion*. He persuaded Keats against the first disastrous preface to *Endymion*, defended him in print when that poem was cruelly attacked, and countered the unhappy influence of Leigh Hunt—indeed was said to have "poisoned" Keats against him. Certainly four days after Keats had boarded the *Maria Crowther* Reynolds wrote to Taylor to say how well it was that Keats was not only separated from Fanny Brawne, "the poor idle thing of womankind", but also "banished from the vain and heartless eternity of Mr Leigh Hunt's indecent discoursings".

The last letter we possess written by Keats to Reynolds is dated 28 February 1820, and there are indications that their friendship was then under strain, mainly because of the "malice" of all the Reynolds towards Fanny Brawne, who warned Fanny Keats: "never be intimate with the Reynolds". Reynolds had to be told of Keats's departure for Italy by Taylor, and did not see him off, much less consider going with him.

Keats was familiar with the whole Reynolds family. The two sisters, Jane (who married Thomas Hood) and Mariane, he said in October 1818 "are very kind to me—but they have lately displeased me much". In February 1819 they were "very dull", and by January 1820 it was "the Miss Reynolds I am afraid to speak to for fear of some sickly reiteration of phrase or sentiment. When they were at the dance [at the Dilkes] the other night I tried manfully to sit near and talk to them, but to no purpose, and if I had it would have been to no purpose still. My question or observation must have been an old one, and the rejoinder very antique indeed".

Brown said in 1821 that Reynolds "was no dear friend of Keats, nor did Keats think him so". If this were ever true, if it reflects something Keats expressed during the unhappy months of 1820, it certainly was not always true. In 1818 Keats looked to be "bound up" with Reynolds "in the shadows of mind, as we are in our matters of human life", and he was always at ease writing to Reynolds. He did not have to force his wit, yet he could write profoundly and be understood, or gaily and be appreciated. With Reynolds Keats shared "the bread of friendship", and Milnes recognized the Reynolds letters as "by far the best letters in the whole collection I have".

JAMES RICE

JAMES RICE, whose name recurs throughout the letters, was introduced to Keats by Reynolds early in 1817. Keats had "a great deal of pleasant time" with Rice. At one late party Rice "said he cared less about the hour than anyone, and the proof", observed Keats, "is his dancing— he cares not for time, dancing as if he was deaf".

In June 1819 Rice invited Keats to the Isle of Wight where they were both ill and nervous. But they remained firm friends, and in September Keats said of Rice: "I know him better since we have lived a month together in the Isle of Wight. He is the most sensible, and even wise man I know. He has a few John Bull prejudices, but they improve him. His illness is at times alarming. We are great friends, and there is no-one I like to pass a day with better."

Keats constantly referred to the illness which tormented Rice all his life, to his wisdom and his wit. Rice "makes you laugh and think", he said, and the respect he had for Rice's judgment is shown in his account of the jilting of Mariane Reynolds.

When Keats was in great distress in 1820, Rice passed over £10 to Taylor to use on his behalf.

Reporting his death to George Keats in February 1833, Dilke wrote: "Poor Rice, you will be sorry to hear, is dead. He was the best of all who formed the associates of my early life—the best man indeed I ever knew. His life has been a long lingering ever since you knew him, although his good heart and good spirits kept him up." George agreed "he was indeed a noble fellow", and thirteen years later Reynolds recollected that Rice "was in the Law—drew me into that dreary profession—and ultimately took me into partnership. . . . For every quality that marks the sensible companion, the valuable friend, the gentleman and the man, I have known no-one to surpass him".

JOSEPH SEVERN

JOSEPH SEVERN achieved immortality when he allowed Haslam, his life-long friend, to persuade him to accompany Keats to Italy. If Severn had not at the last moment agreed to go, Keats would have travelled alone. With little credit, Reynolds remarked to Taylor, "Severn will much like the voyage, and greatly pleasure Keats, if I mistake not; though he is scarcely the resolute, intelligent or cheerful companion which a long voyage and a sickly frame so anxiously call for". Dr James Clark, who tended Keats in Rome, wrote that "he has a friend with him who seems very attentive to him but between you and I is not the best suited for his companion, but I suppose, poor fellow, he had no choice".

Indeed, he had not. And if some of the motives that moved Severn to accompany Keats were selfish, and if he gained in sentimental esteem in later life, he alone was prepared to commit himself to attending a friend desperately ill. While the others could hardly be blamed for not going, it is ironic to find Severn's motives and personality criticized because he went. Dilke, who was uncompromising in his honesty, "always liked Severn", and remarked in 1848 that no friendship could have been "more severely tried, and no friend found more nobly self-devoted. For that Severn deserves all honour . . . but I did not and cannot see the wonderful sacrifice of going on a journey to Italy." It was in character that Dilke should add that as a matter of *fact;* others were saying such things less generously.

Severn knew well enough Keats's condition before he left, and while he perhaps did not guess in full the horror that was ahead of him, he could have had few illusions about the burden the journey to Italy must be. He needed all his resilience to survive, let alone be nurse, amanuensis, protector, cook, cleaner, friend and messenger for Keats between life and death. The magnitude of Keats's ordeal is expressed in Severn's letters from Italy. Through it he kept his head, and when he felt the strain breaking had the magnanimity to recall "the advantages I have gained by knowing John Keats".

At whatever date Keats and Severn met, Keats was still addressing him "My dear Sir" in November 1816, and Severn was never one of the intimate circle of Keats's friends. In July 1819 Fanny Brawne's admiration for Severn drew a jealous remark from Keats. They visited art galleries and the British Museum together, and in the Summer of 1820 Severn was seeing Keats frequently. Fanny Brawne later spoke familiarly of "Mr Severn who I never imagined it was possible for anything to make unhappy, who I never saw for ten minutes serious"; and yet, strangely, when they left England, Severn "certainly was not aware of Keats's being more than a common acquaintance with this lady", as he told Milnes in 1845.

After Keats's death Severn "remained twenty years without returning to England and during that time the Patrons I most valued came to me as 'the friends of Keats'. These have remained faithful to me and to mine no doubt inspired by the revered name of the poet". "The success of my family. . . . has turned on this", Severn admitted in 1863, when he was back again in Rome as Consul, "where I first came in his dear company in November 1820 and on his account—although on my part so mad a thing as it seemed at the time and was pronounced so by most of my friends; yet it was the best and perhaps the only step to insure my artistic career, which no doubt was watched and blessed by this dear Spirit". Whatever Severn's faults and inadequacies, such modesty and frankness makes criticism churlish. And it is difficult to see how anyone could have done more for Keats on his death-bed. Severn himself died at the age of 86, venerated, even legendary, and is buried beside Keats in Rome.

JOHN TAYLOR AND JAMES AUGUSTUS HESSEY

KEATS's last two books were published by Taylor and Hessey, who were lifelong friends. Taylor figures more often in Keats's affairs than Hessey, affectionately known as "Mistessey", though both helped Keats in many ways. It was through their efforts at raising money that the voyage to Italy was made possible, and Taylor was one of the friends who saw Keats and Severn off. For Taylor (and indeed Hessey) Keats was "a true poet", and they were prepared to rank him with the greatest.

Taylor and Hessey were writing to George Keats by 17 February 1821, pointing out that "the poems do not sell so well as to produce any return of profit. We are still minus £110 by *Endymion* and about £100 by the last poem *Lamia*." They knew Keats was dying, and wanted George to authorize the repayment of contributions made to Keats. They approached Abbey too, less successfully.

Taylor subsequently cherished an unfulfilled ambition to write a biography of Keats, and he and Reynolds quarrelled fiercely over the copies of the Keats-Reynolds letters that he passed to Milnes. Taylor died in 1864, and Hessey six years later.

RICHARD WOODHOUSE

WOODHOUSE was born in 1788. He was legal adviser and reader to Taylor and Hessey. He was at all times convinced of Keats's genius, and prepared to support his conviction with discriminating argument. He saw through Leigh Hunt's faults: "His thoughts have 'leaden eyes which love the ground'—they do not come naturally: they seem as if they were pressed into the service and brought into action before they were drilled. And instead of power and range of expression, he substitutes quaintness and conceit. It is the same in his prose—and both seem a sample of the heroics of the servants' hall."

He brought similar perception to bear on Keats, especially criticizing his diction. Having weighed the evidence, he compared Keats's early work favourably with Shakespeare's; and having admitted "that he has great faults—enough indeed to sink another writer", Woodhouse wrote in October 1818: "And now, while Keats is unknown, unheeded, despised of one of our arch-critics, neglected by the rest—in the teeth of the world and in the face of 'these curious days' I express my conviction that Keats . . . will rank on a level with the best of the last or of the present generation; and after his death will take his place at their head."

BIOGRAPHICAL NOTES

Woodhouse's critical shrewdness led him to make copies of everything relating to Keats that came his way. He applied to friends for assistance, as to Taylor in November 1818, when he sent him two bottles of his own sherry ("perhaps better 'tipple' than you can procure at the short notice elsewhere"), and then asked him to get a copy of a sonnet they had discussed, perhaps through Reynolds, he suggested. "Keats may not be disposed, out of his excessive modesty, to give copies", he wrote, "and I would not wish to make an unpleasant application to him . . . but I should like to add that to my collection of 'Keatsiana' ".

Woodhouse's "collection of Keatsiana" has proved invaluable. It is remarkable that Woodhouse even copied Keats's letters to other friends when he had the chance, and most of the Keats–Reynolds letters we possess are in Woodhouse's transcripts, the originals being lost. When Woodhouse died in 1834 of the disease that had killed Keats, the papers passed by his will to Taylor.

Woodhouse was never as intimate with Keats as other friends, but no one remained more true to him. He helped Keats repeatedly with loans of books and money, saying, "Whatever people regret that they could not do for Shakespeare or Chatterton, because he did not live in their time, that I would embody into a rational principle, and (with due regard to certain expediencies) do for Keats". Soon after Tom died he offered Keats "an introduction to a class of society from which you may possibly derive advantage as well as gratification, if you think proper to avail yourself of it", and did so with a promise to say no more should Keats "decline the overture". Keats was "flattered by making an impression on a set of ladies", but was "unable to afford time for new acquaintances". It made no difference to Woodhouse's "good wishes towards Keats, as well as their complete disinterestedness", which lasted to the end, and when Keats was dead Woodhouse fostered his reputation as unsparingly as he had assisted him when he was dying. As Reynolds wrote in 1846 "he was a good and enthusiastic friend of Keats. *He* meant nothing cringing towards money."

EDITOR'S NOTE

Readers may observe that some of the letters in this selection are fragmentary. This is the result not of editorial omission or suppression but simply of the fact that, while many of the originals of Keats's letters still exist, others have only come down to us in partial transcripts made by his friends.

Punctuation and spelling have, generally speaking, been modernized, but occasionally the original spelling or punctuation has been retained, e.g. in some of the later letters, so as not to impair the intensity of feeling.

The editor acknowledges his debt to the many scholars who have worked on Keats's life and letters, and especially to the late Professor Hyder E. Rollins and his magnificent edition of the poet's letters.

LETTERS

LETTER I

To C. C. Clarke *Wednesday*, 9 *October* 1816

My dear Sir,
   The busy time has just gone by, and I can now devote any time you may mention to the pleasure of seeing Mr Hunt—'twill be an era in my existence—I am anxious too to see the author of the Sonnet to the Sun, for it is no mean gratification to become acquainted with men who in their admiration of poetry do not jumble together Shakespeare and Darwin—I have copied out a sheet or two of verses which I composed some time ago, and find so much to blame in them that the best part will go into the fire—those to G. Mathew I will suffer to meet the eye of Mr H. notwithstanding that the Muse is so frequently mentioned. I here sinned in the face of heaven even while remembering what, I think, Horace says, "never presume to make a god appear but for an action worthy of a god". From a few words of yours when I last saw you, I have no doubt but that you have something in your portfolio which I should by rights see—I will put you in mind of it. Although the Borough is a beastly place in dirt, turnings and windings, yet No. 8 Dean Street is not difficult to find; and if you would run the gauntlet over London Bridge, take the first turning to the left and then the first to the right and moreover knock at my door which is nearly opposite a Meeting, you would do one a charity which as St Paul saith is the father of all the virtues—at all events let me hear from you soon—I say at all events not excepting the gout in your fingers.
                              Yours sincerely,
                                   John Keats

LETTER 2

To J. H. Reynolds   *Monday, 17 March 1817*
19 Lamb's Conduit Street

My dear Reynolds,
  My brothers are anxious that I should go by myself into the country—they have always been extremely fond of me, and now that Haydon has pointed out how necessary it is that I should be alone to improve myself, they give up the temporary pleasure of living with me continually for a great good which I hope will follow. So I shall soon be out of town. You must soon bring all your present troubles to a close, and so must I, but we must, like the fox, prepare for a fresh swarm of flies. Banish money—banish sofas—banish wine—banish music; but right Jack Health, honest Jack Health, true Jack Health—banish Health and banish all the world. I must . . . myself . . . if I come this evening, I shall horribly commit myself elsewhere. So I will send my excuses to them and Mrs Dilke by my brothers.

                                            Your sincere friend,
                                                               John Keats

LETTER 3

To George and Thomas Keats   *Tuesday, 15 April 1817*
Mr G. Keats, No. 1 Well Walk, Hampstead, Middx.

                                                  Tuesday Morn—
My dear Brothers,
  I am safe at Southampton—after having ridden three stages outside and the rest in for it began to be very cold. I did not know the names of any of the towns I passed through. All I can tell you is that sometimes I saw dusty hedges, sometimes ponds—then nothing—then a little wood with trees look you like Launce's Sister "as white as a lily and as small as a wand"—then came houses which died away into a few

TO GEORGE AND THOMAS KEATS

straggling barns, then came hedgetrees aforesaid again. As the lamplight crept along the following things were discovered: "long heath, brown furze"—hurdles here and there half a mile—park palings when the windows of a house were always discovered by reflection—one nymph of fountain—*N.B. Stone*—lopped trees—cow ruminating—ditto donkey—man and woman going gingerly along—William seeing his sisters over the heath—John waiting with a lantern for his mistress—barber's pole—doctor's shop. However after having had my fill of these I popped my head out just as it began to dawn—*N.B. this Tuesday morn saw the sun rise*—of which I shall say nothing at present. I felt rather lonely this morning at breakfast so I went and unboxed a Shakespeare—"Here's my comfort". I went immediately after breakfast to the Southampton Water where I enquired for the boat to the Isle of Wight as I intend seeing that place before I settle—it will go at 3, so shall I after having taken a chop. I know nothing of this place but that it is long—tolerably broad—has bye streets—two or three churches—a very respectable old gate with two lions to guard it. The men and women do not materially differ from those I have been in the habit of seeing. I forgot to say that from dawn till half past six I went through a most delightful country—some open down but for the most part thickly wooded. What surprised me most was an immense quantity of blooming furze on each side the road cutting a most rural dash. The Southampton water when I saw it just now was no better than a low water, water which did no more than answer my expectations—it will have mended its manners by 3. From the wharf are seen the shores on each side stretching to the Isle of Wight. You, Haydon, Reynolds, etc., have been pushing each other out of my brain by turns. I have conned over every head in Haydon's picture—you must warn them not to be afraid should my ghost visit them on Wednesday. Tell Haydon to kiss his hand at Betty over the way for me, yea and to spy at her for me. I hope one of you will be competent to take part in a trio while I am away—you need only aggravate your voices a little, and mind not to speak cues and all—when you have said rum-ti-ti you must not be rum any more or else another will take up the ti-ti alone and then he might be taken, God shield us, for little better than a titmouse. By the by, talking of titmouse, remember me particularly to all my friends. Give my love to the Miss Reynoldses and to Fanny who I hope you will soon see. Write to me soon about them all—and you George particularly, how you get on with Wilkinson's plan. What could I have done without my plaid? I don't feel inclined to write any more at present for I feel rather muzzy. You must be content with this facsimile of the rough plan of Aunt Dinah's counterpane.

Your most affectionate brother,
John Keats

Reynolds shall hear from me soon.

LETTER 4

To J. H. Reynolds   *Thursday–Friday, 17–18 April* 1817
Mr J. H. Reynolds, 19 *Lamb's Conduit Str. London*

Carisbrooke, April 17th

My dear Reynolds,

Ever since I wrote to my brothers from Southampton I have been in a taking, and at this moment I am about to become settled, for I have unpacked my books, put them into a snug corner, pinned up Haydon, Mary Queen of Scots, and Milton with his daughters in a row. In the passage I found a head of Shakespeare which I had not before seen. It is most likely the same that George spoke so well of; for I like it extremely. Well—this head I have hung over my books, just above the three in a row, having first discarded a French Ambassador—now this alone is a good morning's work.

Yesterday I went to Shanklin, which occasioned a great debate in my mind whether I should live there or at Carisbrooke. Shanklin is a most beautiful place—sloping wood and meadow ground reaches round the Chine, which is a cleft between the cliffs of the depth of nearly 300 feet at least. This cleft is filled with trees and bushes in the narrow part; and as it widens becomes bare, if it were not for primroses on one side, which spread to the very verge of the sea, and some fishermen's huts on the other, perched midway in the balustrades of beautiful green hedges along their steps down to the sands. But the sea, Jack, the sea—the little waterfall—then the white cliff—then St Catherine's Hill—"the sheep in the meadows, the cows in the corn". Then, why are you at Carisbrooke? say you—because, in the first place, I should be at twice the expense, and three times the inconvenience—next that from here I can see your continent—from a little hill close by, the whole north angle of the Isle of Wight, with the water between us. In the third place, I see Carisbrooke Castle from my window, and have found several delightful wood-alleys, and copses, and quick freshes. As for primroses—the island ought to be called Primrose Island: that is, if the nation of cowslips agree thereto, of which there are diverse clans just beginning to lift up their heads and if and how the rain holds whereby, that is, birds'-eyes abate. Another reason of my fixing is that I am more in reach of the places around me—I intend to walk over the island east, west, north, south. I have not seen many specimens of ruins—I don't think however I shall ever see one to surpass Carisbrooke Castle. The trench is o'ergrown with the smoothest turf, and the walls with ivy—the keep within side is one bower of ivy—a colony of jackdaws have been there many years. I daresay I have seen many a descendant of some old cawer who peeped through the bars at Charles the First, when he was there in confinement. On the road from Cowes to Newport I saw some extensive barracks which disgusted me extremely with government for placing such a nest of debauchery in so beautiful a place—I asked a man on the coach about this—and he said that the people had been spoiled. In the room where I slept at Newport I found this on the window "O Isle spoilt by the Mil*a*tary!" I must in honesty however confess that I did not feel very sorry at the idea of the women being a little profligate. The wind is in a sulky fit, and I feel that it would be no bad thing to be the favourite of some fairy who would give one the power of seeing how our friends got on, at a distance. I should like, of all loves, a sketch of you and Tom and George in ink which Haydon will do if you tell him how I want them. From want of regular rest, I have been rather *narvus*—and the passage in *Lear*—"Do you not hear the sea?"—has haunted me intensely.

ON THE SEA

It keeps eternal whisperings around
Desolate shores, and with its mighty swell
Gluts twice ten thousand caverns; till the spell
Of Hecate leaves them their old shadowy sound.
Often 'tis in such gentle temper found
That scarcely will the very smallest shell
Be moved for days from whence it sometime fell
When last the winds of heaven were unbound.
O ye who have your eyeballs vext and tired
Feast them upon the wideness of the sea.
O ye whose ears are dinned with uproar rude
Or fed too much with cloying melody—
Sit ye near some old cavern's mouth and brood
Until ye start as if the sea nymphs quired—

April 18

Will you have the goodness to do this? Borrow a botanical dictionary—turn to the words laurel and prunus, show the explanations to your sisters and Mrs Dilke and without more ado let them send me the cups, basket and books they trifled and put off while I was in town—ask them what they can say for themselves—ask Mrs Dilke wherefore she does so distress me. Let me know how Jane has her health—the weather is unfavourable for her. Tell George and Tom to write. I'll tell you what—on the 23rd was Shakespeare born—now if I should receive a letter from you and another from my brothers on that day 'twould be a parlous good thing. Whenever you write say a word or two on some passage in Shakespeare that may have come rather new to you; which must be continually happening, notwithstanding that we read the same play forty times—for instance, the following, from *The Tempest*, never struck me so forcibly as at present:

> Urchins
> *Shall, for that vast of Night that they may work,*
>   All exercise on thee

How can I help bringing to your mind the line:

TO J. H. REYNOLDS
In the dark backward and abysm of time

I find that I cannot exist without poetry—without eternal poetry—half the day will not do—the whole of it—I began with a little, but habit has made me a Leviathan—I had become all in a tremble from not having written anything of late—the sonnet overleaf did me some good. I slept better last night for it—this morning, however, I am nearly as bad again—Just now I opened Spenser, and the first lines I saw were these:

> The noble heart that harbours virtuous thought,
> And is with child of glorious great intent,
> Can never rest, until it forth have brought
> Th' eternal brood of glory excellent.

Let me know particularly about Haydon; ask him to write to me about Hunt, if it be only ten lines—I hope all is well—I shall forthwith begin my *Endymion*, which I hope I shall have got some way into by the time you come, when we will read our verses in a delightful place I have set my heart upon near the Castle. Give my love to your sisters severally—to George and Tom. Remember me to Rice, Mr and Mrs Dilke and all we know.

Your sincere friend,
John Keats

Direct J. Keats, Mrs Cook's, New Village, Carisbrooke.

LETTER 5

To Fanny Keats *Wednesday,* 10 *September* 1817
Miss Keats, Miss Caley's School, Walthamstow, Essex

Oxford Septr. 10th

My dear Fanny,
 Let us now begin a regular question and answer—a little pro and con; letting it interfere as a pleasant method of my coming at your

favourite little wants and enjoyments, that I may meet them in a way befitting a brother.

 We have been so little together since you have been able to reflect on things that I know not whether you prefer *The History of King Pepin* to Bunyan's *Pilgrim's Progress*—or Cinderella and her glass slipper to Moore's Almanack. However in a few letters I hope I shall be able to come at that and adapt my scribblings to your pleasure. You must tell me about all you read if it be only six pages in a week—and this transmitted to me every now and then will procure you full sheets of writing from me pretty frequently. This I feel as a necessity, for we ought to become intimately acquainted, in order that I may not only as you grow up love you as my only sister, but confide in you as my dearest friend. When I saw you last I told you of my intention of going to Oxford and 'tis now a week since I disembarked from his whipship's coach the Defiance in this place. I am living in Magdalen Hall on a visit to a young man with whom I have not been long acquainted, but whom I like very much—we lead very industrious lives, he in general studies and I in proceeding at a pretty good rate with a poem which I hope you will see early in the next year. Perhaps you might like to know what I am writing about. I will tell you.

 Many years ago there was a young handsome shepherd who fed his flocks on a mountain's side called Latmos—he was a very contemplative sort of a person and lived solitary among the trees and plains little thinking that such a beautiful creature as the moon was growing mad in love with him—however so it was; and when he was asleep on the grass, she used to come down from heaven and admire him excessively for a long time; and at last could not refrain from carrying him away in her arms to the top of that high mountain Latmos while he was a-dreaming—but I daresay you have read this and all the other beautiful tales which have come down from the ancient times of that beautiful Greece. If you have not, let me know and I will tell you more at large of others quite as delightful.

 This Oxford I have no doubt is the finest city in the world—it is full of old Gothic buildings—spires—towers—quadrangles, cloisters, groves, etc, and is surrounded with more clear streams than ever I saw together. I take a walk by the side of one of them every evening and thank God, we have not had a drop of rain these many days. I had a long and interesting letter from George, cross lines by a short one from Tom yesterday dated Paris. They both send their loves to you. Like most Englishmen they feel a mighty preference for everything English —the French meadows, the trees, the people, the towns, the churches, the books, the everything—although they may be in themselves good, yet when put in comparison with our green island they all vanish like swallows in October. They have seen cathedrals, manuscripts, fountains, pictures, tragedy, comedy—with other things you may by chance meet with in this country such as washerwomen, lamplighters, turnpikemen, fish kettles, dancing masters, kettle drums, sentry boxes, rocking horses, etc, and now they have taken them over a set of boxing gloves. I have written to George and requested him, as you wish I should, to write to you. I have been writing very hard lately even till an utter incapacity came on, and I feel it now about my head: so you must not mind a little out of the way sayings—though bye the bye were my brain as clear as a bell I think I should have a little propensity thereto. I shall stop here till I have finished the 3rd book of my story, which I hope will be accomplished in at most three weeks from to-day—about which time you shall see me. How do you like Miss Taylor's *Essays in Rhyme*—I just looked into the book and it appeared to me suitable to you—especially since I remember your liking for those pleasant little things the *Original Poems*—the essays are the more mature production of the same hand. While I was speaking about France it occurred to me to speak a few words on their language—it is perhaps the poorest one ever spoken since the jabbering in the Tower of Babel, and when you come to know that the real use and greatness of a tongue is to be referred to its literature, you will be astonished to find how very inferior it is to our native speech—I wish the Italian would supersede French in every school throughout the country for that is full of real poetry and romance of a kind more fitted for the pleasure of ladies than perhaps our own. It seems that the only end to be gained in acquiring French is the immense accomplishment of speaking it—it is none at all—a most lamentable mistake indeed. Italian indeed would sound most musically from lips which had begun to pronounce it as early as French is crammed down our mouths, as if we were young jackdaws at the mercy of an overfeeding schoolboy.

Now Fanny you must write soon—and write all you think about, never mind what—only let me have a good deal of your writing. You need not do it all at once—be two or three or four days about it, and let it be a diary of your little life. You will preserve all my letters and I will secure yours, and thus in the course of time we shall each of us have a good bundle which, hereafter, when things may have strangely altered and God knows what happened, we may read over together and look with pleasure on times past that now are to come. Give my respects to the ladies—and so my dear Fanny I am ever

                        Your most affectionate brother,
                                       John

If you direct—Post Office Oxford—your letter will be brought to me.

LETTER 6

To Benjamin Bailey   *28–30 October 1817*
Mr B. Bailey, Magdalen Hall, Oxford

My dear Bailey,

So you have got a curacy! Good, but I suppose you will be obliged to stop among your Oxford favourites during term time—never mind. When do you preach your first sermon? Tell me, for I shall propose to the two Rs to hear it, so don't look into any of the old corner oaken pews, for fear of being put out by us. Poor Johnny Martin can't be there. He is ill I suspect—but that's neither here nor there—all I can say I wish him as well through it as I am like to be. For this fortnight I have been confined at Hampstead. Saturday evening was my first day in town, when I went to Rice's as we intend to do every Saturday till we know not when. Rice had some business at Highgate yesterday, so he came over to me, and I detained him for the first time of I hope 24,860 times. We hit upon an old Gent we had known some few years ago and had a veray pleausante daye. In this world there is no quiet, nothing but teasing and snubbing and vexation. My brother Tom looked very unwell yesterday and I am for shipping him off to Lisbon—perhaps I ship there with him. I have not seen Mrs Reynolds since I left you wherefore my conscience smites me—I think of seeing her tomorrow: have you any message? I hope Gleig came soon after I left.

I don't suppose I've written as many lines as you have read volumes or at least chapters since I saw you. However, I am in a fair way now to come to a conclusion in at least three weeks when I assure you I shall be glad to dismount for a month or two although I'll keep as tight a rein as possible till then nor suffer myself to sleep. I will copy for you the opening of the 4 Book—in which you will see from the manner I had not an opportunity of mentioning any poets, for fear of spoiling the effect of the passage by particularizing them!

> Muse of my Native Land! Loftiest Muse!
> O first born of the mountains, by the hues
> Of heaven on the spiritual air begot—
> Long didst thou sit alone in northern grot
> While yet our England was a wolfish den;
> Before our forests heard the talk of men;
> Before the first of druids was a child.
> Long didst thou sit amid our regions wild
> Wrapt in a deep, prophetic solitude.
> There came a hebrew voice of solemn mood
> Yet wast thou patient: then sang forth the Nine,
> Apollo's garland; yet didst thou divine
> Such homebred glory, that they cried in vain
> "Come hither Sister of the Island". Plain
> Spake fair Ausonia, and once more she spake
> A higher summons—still didst thou betake
> Thee to thy darling hopes. O thou hast won
> A full accomplishment—the thing is done,
> Which undone these our latter days had risen
> On barren souls. O Muse thou knowst what prison

> Of flesh and bone curbs and confines and frets
> Our spirit's wings: despondency besets
> Our pillows and the fresh tomorrow morn
> Seems to give forth its light in very scorn
> Of our dull uninspired snail-paced lives.
> Long have I said "how happy he who shrives
> To thee"—but then I thought on poets gone
> And could not pray—nor can I now—so on
> I move to the end in humbleness of heart.

Thus far had I written when I received your last which made me at the sight of the direction caper for despair—but for one thing I am glad that I have been neglectful—and that is, therefrom I have received a proof of your utmost kindness which at this present I feel very much, and I wish I had a heart always open to such sensations. But there is no altering a man's nature and mine must be radically wrong for it will lie dormant a whole month. This leads me to suppose that there are no men thoroughly wicked, so as never to be self spiritualized into a kind of sublime misery—but alas! 'tis but for an hour. He is the only man "who has kept watch on man's mortality" who has philanthropy enough to overcome the disposition to an indolent enjoyment of intellect—who is brave enough to volunteer for uncomfortable hours. You remember in Hazlitt's essay on commonplace people, he says they read the *Edinburgh* and *Quarterly* and think as they do. Now with respect to Wordsworth's "Gypsies" I think he is right and yet I think Hazlitt is righter and yet I think Wordsworth is rightest. Wordsworth had not been idle, he had not been without his task—nor had they Gypsies—they in the visible world had been as picturesque an object as he in the invisible. The smoke of their fire—their attitudes—their voices were all in harmony with the evenings. It is a bold thing to say and I would not say it in print, but it seems to me that if Wordsworth had thought a little deeper at that moment he would not have written the poem at all. I should judge it to have been written in one of the most comfortable moods of his life—it is a kind of sketchy intellectual landscape—not a search after truth; nor is it fair to attack him on such a subject, for it is with the critic as with the poet. Had Hazlitt thought

TO BENJAMIN BAILEY

a little deeper and been in a good temper he would have never spied an imaginary fault there. The Sunday before last I asked Haydon to dine with me, when I thought of settling all matters with him in regard to Crips and let you know about it. Now although I engaged him a fortnight before, he sent illness as an excuse—he never will come. I have not been well enough to stand the chance of a wet night, and so have not seen him nor been able to expurgatorize those masks for you. But I will not speak. Your speakers are never doers. Then Reynolds—every time I see him and mention you he puts his hand to his head and looks like a son of Niobe's—but he'll write soon. Rome you know was not built in a day—I shall be able, by a little perseverance to read your letters off-hand. I am afraid your health will suffer from over-study before your examination. I think you might regulate the thing according to your own pleasure—and I would too. They were talking of your being up at Christmas—will it be before you have passed? There is nothing my dear Bailey I should rejoice at more than to see you comfortable with a little Peona wife—an affectionate wife I have a sort of confidence would do you a great happiness. May that be one of the many blessings I wish you. Let me be but the one tenth of one to you, and I shall think it great. My brother George's kindest wishes to you. My dear Bailey, I am

Your affectionate friend,
John Keats

P.S.—I should not like to be pages in your way when in a tolerable hungry mood you have no mercy. Your teeth are the Rock Tarpeian down which you capsize epic poems like mad—I would not for 40 shillings be Coleridge's *Lays* in your way. I hope you will soon get through this abominable writing in the Schools—and be able to keep the terms with more comfort in the hope of retiring to a comfortable and quiet home out of the way of all Hopkinses and black beetles. When you are settled I will come and take a peep at your church—your house—try whether I shall have grown too lusty for my chair—by the fireside—and take a peep at my cardinal's bower. A question is the best beacon towards a little speculation. You ask me after my health and spirits—this question ratifies in my mind what I have said above—health and spirits can only belong unalloyed to the selfish man. The man who thinks much of his fellows can never be in spirits—when I am not suffering for vicious beastliness I am the greater part of the week in spirits.

You must forgive although I have only written 300 lines—they would have been five but I have been obliged to go to town. Yesterday I called at Lamb's Street. Jane looked very flush when I first went in but was much better before I left.

LETTER 7

To Benjamin Bailey   *Monday, 3 November* 1817
Mr B. Bailey, Magdalen Hall, Oxford

                                              Monday—Hampstead

My dear Bailey,

Before I received your letter I had heard of your disappointment—an unlooked-for piece of villainy. I am glad to hear there was an hindrance to your speaking your mind to the Bishop, for all may go straight yet as to being ordained. But the disgust consequent cannot pass away in a hurry—it must be shocking to find in a sacred profession such barefaced oppression and impertinence. The Stations and Grandeurs of the world have taken it into their heads that they cannot commit themselves towards an inferior in rank—but is not the impertinence from one above to one below more wretchedly mean than from the low to the high? There is something so nauseous in self-willed yawning impudence in the shape of conscience—it sinks the Bishop of Lincoln into a smashed frog putrefying: that a rebel against common decency should escape the pillory! That a mitre should cover a man guilty of the most coxcombical, tyrannical and indolent impertinence! I repeat this word for the offence appears to me most especially *impertinent*, and a very serious return would be the rod—yet doth he sit in his Palace. Such is this world, and we live (you

TO BENJAMIN BAILEY

have surely) in a continual struggle against the suffocation of accidents—we must bear (and my spleen is mad at the thought thereof) the proud man's contumely. O for a recourse somewhat human independent of the great consolations of religion and undepraved sensations—of the beautiful—the poetical in all things. O for a remedy against such wrongs within the pale of the world! Should not those things be pure enjoyment, should they stand the chance of being contaminated by being called in as antagonists to bishops? Would not earthly things do? By heavens my dear Bailey, I know you have a spice of what I mean—you can set me and have set it in all the rubs that may befall me. You have, I know, a sort of pride which would kick the devil on the jawbone and make him drunk with the kick. There is nothing so balmy to a soul embittered as yours must be, as pride. When we look at the heavens we cannot be proud—but shall sticks and stones be impertinent and say it does not become us to kick them? At this moment I take your hand—let us walk up yon mountain of common sense. Now if our pride be vainglorious such a support would fail, yet you feel firm footing—now look beneath at that parcel of knaves and fools. Many a mitre is moving among them. I cannot express how I despise the man who would wrong or be impertinent to you. The thought that we are mortal makes us groan.

I will speak of something else or my spleen will get higher and higher—and I am not a bearer of the two edged sword. I hope you will receive an answer from Haydon soon—if not, pride! pride! pride! I have received no more subscription—but shall soon have a full health, liberty and leisure to give a good part of my time to him—I will certainly be in time for him. We have promised him one year, let that have elapsed and then do as we think proper. If I did not know how impossible it is, I should say, "do not at this time of disappointments disturb yourself about others".

There has been a flaming attack upon Hunt in the *Edinburgh Magazine*. I never read anything so virulent—accusing him of the greatest crimes depreciating his wife, his poetry, his habits, his company, his conversation. These Philippics are to come out in Numbers called "The Cockney School of Poetry". There has been but one number published—that on Hunt to which they have prefixed a motto from one Cornelius Webb, Poetaster, who unfortunately was of our party occasionally at Hampstead and took it into his head to write the following—something about—"we'll talk on Wordsworth, Byron, a theme we never tire on," and so forth till he comes to Hunt and Keats. In the motto they have put Hunt and Keats in large letters—I have no doubt that the second number was intended for me, but have hopes of its non-appearance from the following advertisement in last Sunday's *Examiner*. "To Z. The writer of the article signed Z. in Blackwood's *Edinburgh Magazine* for October 1817 is invited to send his address to the printer of the *Examiner*, in order that justice may be executed on the proper person". I don't mind the thing much—but if he should go to such lengths with me as he has done with Hunt I must infallibly call him to an account—if he be a human being and appears in squares and theatres where we might possibly meet. I don't relish his abuse.

Yesterday Rice and I were at Reynolds'—John was to be articled tomorrow. I suppose by this time it is done. Jane was much better. At one time or other I will do you a pleasure and the poets a little justice—but it ought to be in a poem of greater moment than *Endymion*. I will do it some day. I have seen two letters of a little story Reynolds is writing. I wish he would keep at it. Here is the song I enclosed to Jane if you can make it out in this cross-wise writing.

> O Sorrow!
> Why dost borrow
> The natural hue of health from vermeil lips?
> To give maiden blushes
> To the white rose bushes
> Or is't thy dewy hand the daisy tips?
>
> O Sorrow
> Why dost borrow
> The lustrous passion from an orbed eye?
> To give the glow worm light?
> Or on a moonless night
> To tinge on syren shores the salt sea-spry?

TO BENJAMIN BAILEY

    O Sorrow
    Why dost borrow
The tender ditties from a mourning tongue?
      To give at evening pale
      Unto the nightingale
That thou mayest listen the cold dews among?

    O Sorrow
    Why dost borrow
Heart's lightness from the merriment of May?
      A lover would not tread
      A cowslip on the head
Though he should dance from eve till peep of day;
      Nor any drooping flower
      Held sacred to thy bower
Wherever he may sport himself and play.

    To Sorrow
    I bade good morrow
And thought to leave her far away behind
      But cheerly, cheerly,
      She loves me dearly—
She is to me so constant, and so kind—
      I would deceive her
      And so leave her
But ah! she is too constant and too kind.

O that I had Orpheus' lute—and was able to charm away all your griefs and cares—but all my power is a mite—amid all your troubles I shall ever be

                Your sincere and affectionate friend,
                              John Keats

My brothers' remembrances to you.
Give my respects to Gleig and Whitehead.

LETTER 8

To Benjamin Bailey   *Saturday, 22 November* 1817
Mr B. Bailey, Magdalen Hall, Oxford—

My dear Bailey,
    I will get over the first part of this (*un*said) letter as soon as possible for it relates to the affair of poor Crips. To a man of your nature such a letter as Haydon's must have been extremely cutting. What occasions the greater part of the world's quarrels? Simply this, two minds meet and do not understand each other time enough to prevent any shock or surprise at the conduct of either party. As soon as I had known Haydon three days I had got enough of his character not to have been surprised at such a letter as he has hurt you with. Nor when I knew it, was it a principle with me to drop his acquaintance although with you it would have been an imperious feeling. I wish you knew all that I think about genius and the heart—and yet I think you are thoroughly acquainted with my innermost breast in that respect, or you could not have known me even thus long and still hold me worthy to be your dear friend. In passing however I must say of one thing that has pressed upon me lately and increased my humility and capability of submission and that is this truth: men of genius are great as certain ethereal chemicals operating on the mass of neutral intellect—but they have not any individuality, and determined character. I would call the top and head of those who have a proper self men of power.
    But I am running my head into a subject which I am certain I could not do justice to under five years study and 3 vols octavo, and moreover long to be talking about the imagination—so my dear Bailey do not think of this unpleasant affair if possible—do not—I defy any harm to come of it—I defy. I'll write to Crips this week and request him to tell me all his goings on from time to time by letter wherever I may be. It will all go on well, so don't, because you have suddenly discovered a coldness in Haydon, suffer yourself to be teased. Do not my

dear fellow. O I wish I was as certain of the end of all your troubles as that of your momentary start about the authenticity of the imagination. I am certain of nothing but of the holiness of the heart's affections and the truth of imagination. What the imagination seizes as beauty must be truth, whether it existed before or not, for I have the same idea of all our passions as of love: they are all in their sublime, creative of essential beauty. In a word, you may know my favourite speculation by my first book and the little song I sent in my last—which is a representation from the fancy of the probable mode of operating in these matters. The imagination may be compared to Adam's dream—he awoke and found it truth. I am the more zealous in this affair, because I have never yet been able to perceive how anything can be known for truth by consequitive reasoning—and yet it must be. Can it be that even the greatest philosopher ever arrived at his goal without putting aside numerous objections. However it may be, O for a life of sensations rather than of thoughts! It is "a Vision in the form of Youth", a shadow of reality to come—and this consideration has further convinced me for it has come as auxiliary to another favourite speculation of mine, that we shall enjoy ourselves hereafter by having what we called happiness on earth repeated in a finer tone and so repeated. And yet such a fate can only befall those who delight in sensation rather than hunger as you do after truth. Adam's dream will do here and seems to be a conviction that imagination and its empyreal reflection is the same as human life and its spiritual repetition. But as I was saying—the simple imaginative mind may have its rewards in the repetition of its own silent working coming continually on the spirit with a fine suddenness. To compare great things with small—have you never by being surprised with an old melody—in a delicious place, by a delicious voice—felt over again your very speculations and surmises at the time it first operated on your soul—do you not remember forming to yourself the singer's face more beautiful than it was possible and yet with the elevation of the moment you did not think so—even then you were mounted on the wings of imagination so high—that the prototype must be hereafter—that delicious face you will see.

What a time! I am continually running away from the subject, sure this cannot be exactly the case with a complex mind—one that is imaginative and at the same time careful of its fruits—who would exist partly on sensation, partly on thought—to whom it is necessary that years should bring the philosophic mind—such an one I consider yours and therefore it is necessary to your eternal happiness that you not only drink this old Wine of Heaven, which I shall call the redigestion of our most ethereal musings on earth, but also increase in knowledge and know all things. I am glad to hear you are in a fair way for Easter—you will soon get through your unpleasant reading and then!—but the world is full of troubles and I have not much reason to think myself pestered with many—I think Jane or Mariane has a better opinion of me than I deserve—for really and truly I do not think my brother's illness connected with mine—you know more of the real cause than they do nor have I any chance of being racked as you have been. You perhaps at one time thought there was such a thing as worldly happiness to be arrived at, at certain periods of time marked out. You have of necessity from your disposition been thus led away. I scarcely remember counting upon any happiness. I look not for it if it be not in the present hour—nothing startles me beyond the moment. The setting sun will always set me to rights—or if a sparrow come before my window I take part in its existence and pick about the gravel. The first thing that strikes me on hearing a misfortune having befallen another is this. "Well, it cannot be helped—he will have the pleasure of trying the resources of his spirit." And I beg now my dear Bailey that hereafter should you observe anything cold in me not to put it to the account of heartlessness but abstraction, for I assure you I sometimes feel not the influence of a passion or affection during a whole week—and so long this sometimes continues I begin to suspect myself and the genuineness of my feelings at other times, thinking them a few barren tragedy-tears. My brother Tom is much improved —he is going to Devonshire, whither I shall follow him. At present I am just arrived at Dorking to change the scene, change the air and give me a spur to wind up my poem, of which there are wanting 500 lines. I should have been here a day sooner but the Reynoldses persuaded me to stop in town to meet your friend Christie. There were Rice and Martin—we talked about ghosts. I will have some talk with

Taylor and let you know—when please God I come down at Christmas. I will find that *Examiner* if possible. My best regards to Gleig. My brothers, to you—and Mrs Bentley's.

Your affectionate friend,
John Keats

P.S. I want to say much more to you—a few hints will set me going. Direct Burford Bridge near Dorking.

LETTER 9

To George and Thomas Keats (?) *Sunday, 21 December* 1817
Messrs Keats, Teignmouth, Devonshire

Hampstead, Sunday

My dear Brothers,

I must crave your pardon for not having written ere this.... I saw Kean return to the public in *Richard III*, and finely he did it, and at the request of Reynolds I went to criticize his Luke in *Riches*. The critique is in to-day's *Champion*, which I send you with the *Examiner*, in which you will find very proper lamentation on the obsoletion of Christmas gambols and pastimes: but it was mixed up with so much egotism of that drivelling nature that pleasure is entirely lost. Hone the publisher's trial you must find very amusing, and, as Englishmen, very encouraging—his *Not Guilty* is a thing which not to have been would have dulled still more Liberty's Emblazoning—Lord Ellenborough has been paid in his own coin. Wooler and Hone have done us an essential service. I have had two very pleasant evenings with Dilke, yesterday and to-day, and am at this moment just come from him, and feel in the humour to go on with this, begun in the morning, and from which he came to fetch me. I spent Friday evening with Wells, and went next morning to see "Death on the Pale Horse". It is a wonderful picture, when West's age is considered; but there is nothing to be intense upon; no women one feels mad to kiss, no face swelling into reality. The excellence of every art is its intensity, capable of making all disagreeables evaporate, from their being in close relationship with beauty and truth. Examine *King Lear* and you will find this exemplified throughout; but in this picture we have unpleasantness without any momentous depth of speculation excited, in which to bury its repulsiveness. The picture is larger than "Christ Rejected".

I dined with Haydon the Sunday after you left, and had a very pleasant day. I dined too (for I have been out too much lately) with Horace Smith, and met his two brothers, with Hill and Kingston, and one Du Bois. They only served to convince me how superior humour is to wit in respect to enjoyment. These men say things which make one start, without making one feel. They are all alike. Their manners are alike. They all know fashionables; they have a mannerism in their very eating and drinking, in their mere handling a decanter. They talked of Kean and his low company—would I were with that company instead of yours, said I to myself! I know such like acquaintance will never do for me, and yet I am going to Reynolds on Wednesday . . . Brown and Dilke walked with me and back from the Christmas pantomime. I had not a dispute but a disquisition with Dilke on various subjects; several things dove-tailed in my mind, and at once it struck me what quality went to form a man of achievement, especially in literature, and which Shakespeare possessed so enormously—I mean *Negative Capability*, that is, when a man is capable of being in uncertainties, mysteries, doubts, without any irritable reaching after fact and reason. Coleridge, for instance, would let go by a fine isolated verisimilitude caught from the penetralium of mystery, from being incapable of remaining content with half knowledge. This pursued through volumes would perhaps take us no further than this, that with a great poet the sense of beauty overcomes every other consideration, or rather obliterates all consideration.

Shelley's poem is out, and there are words about its being objected to as much as "Queen Mab" was. Poor Shelley, I think he has his quota of good qualities, in sooth la!

Write soon to your most sincere friend and affectionate brother

John

LETTER 10

To George and Thomas Keats 13, 19 *January* 1818
Messrs Keats, Teignmouth, Devonshire

Hampstead, Tuesday

My dear Brothers,
 I am certain I think, of having a letter tomorrow morning, for I expected one so much this morning, having been in town two days, at the end of which my expectations began to get up a little. I found two on the table, one from Bailey and one from Haydon. I am quite perplexed in a world of doubts and fancies—there is nothing stable in the world. Uproar's your only music—I don't mean to include Bailey in this and so I dismiss him from this with all the opprobrium he deserves—that is in so many words, he is one of the noblest men alive at the present day. In a note to Haydon about a week ago (which I wrote with a full sense of what he had done, and how he had never manifested any little mean drawback in his value of me) I said if there were three things superior in the modern world, they were "The Excursion", Haydon's pictures, and Hazlitt's depth of taste. So I do believe—not thus speaking with any poor vanity—that works of genius were the first things in this world. No! for that sort of probity and disinterestedness which such men as Bailey possess, does hold and grasp the tip-top of any spiritual honours that can be paid to anything in this world. And moreover having this feeling at this present come over me in its full force, I sat down to write to you with a grateful heart, in that I had not a brother who did not feel and credit me for a deeper feeling and devotion for his uprightness than for any marks of genius however splendid.
 I was speaking about doubts and fancies—I mean there has been a quarrel of a severe nature between Haydon and Reynolds, and another ("the Devil rides upon a fiddle stick") between Hunt and Haydon. The first grew from the Sunday on which Haydon invited some friends to meet Wordsworth. Reynolds never went, and never sent any notice about it. This offended Haydon more than it ought to have done—he wrote a very sharp and high note to Reynolds and then

another in palliation—but which Reynolds feels as an aggravation of the first. Considering all things, Haydon's frequent neglect of his appointments etc, his notes were bad enough to put Reynolds on the right side of the question, but then Reynolds has no powers of sufferance, no idea of having the thing against him; so he answered Haydon in one of the most cutting letters I ever read, exposing to himself all his own weaknesses and going on to an excess which, whether it is just or no, is what I would fain have unsaid. The fact is they are both in the right and both in the wrong.

The quarrel with Hunt I understand thus far. Mrs H. was in the habit of borrowing silver of Haydon—the last time she did so, Haydon asked her to return it at a certain time—she did not—Haydon sent for it—Hunt went to expostulate on the indelicacy, etc—they got to words and parted forever. All I hope is at some time to bring them all together again. Lawk! Molly, there's been such doings. Yesterday evening I made an appointment with Wells to go to a private theatre and, it being in the neighbourhood of Drury Lane, and thinking we might be fatigued with sitting the whole evening in one dirty hole, I got the Drury Lane ticket and therewith we divided the evening with a spice of *Richard III*.

Good Lord! I began this letter nearly a week ago, what have I been doing since! I have been—I mean not been—sending last Sunday's paper to you, I believe because it was not near me—for I cannot find it and my conscience presses heavy on me for not sending it. You would have had one last Thursday, but I was called away, and have been about somewhere ever since. Where? What? Well I rejoice almost that I have not heard from you because no news is good news. I cannot for the world recollect why I was called away, all I know is that there has been a dance at Dilke's, and another at the London Coffee House, to both of which I went. But I must tell you in another letter the circumstances thereof—for though a week should have passed since I wrote on the other side it quite appals me—I can only write in scraps and patches. Brown is returned from Hampstead—Haydon has returned an answer in the same style—they are all dreadfully irritated against each other. On Sunday I saw Hunt and dined with Haydon, met Hazlitt and Bewick there, and took Haslam with me—forgot to speak about

TO J. H. REYNOLDS

Crips though I broke my engagement to Haslam's on purpose. Mem.—Haslam came to meet me, found me at breakfast, had the goodness to go with me my way. I have just finished the revision of my first book, and shall take it to Taylor's to-morrow—intend to persevere. Do not let me see many days pass without hearing from you.

Your most affectionate brother,
John

LETTER 11

To J. H. Reynolds   *Tuesday, 3 February* 1818

Hampstead, Tuesday

My dear Reynolds,

I thank you for your dish of filberts. Would I could get a basket of them by way of dessert every day for the sum of two pence. Would we were a sort of ethereal pigs, and turned loose to feed upon spiritual mast and acorns, which would be merely being a squirrel and feeding upon filberts. For what is a squirrel but an airy pig, or a filbert but a sort of archangelical acorn? About the nuts being worth cracking, all I can say is that where there are a throng of delightful images ready drawn simplicity is the only thing. The first is the best on account of the first line, and the "arrow—foiled of its antlered food", and moreover (and this is the only word or two I find fault with, the more because I have had so much reason to shun it as a quicksand) the last has "tender and true". We must cut this, and not be rattlesnaked into any more of the like. It may be said that we ought to read our contemporaries, that Wordsworth, etc, should have their due from us. But, for the sake of a few fine imaginative or domestic passages, are we to be bullied into a certain philosophy engendered in the whims of an egotist? Every man has his speculations, but every man does not brood and peacock over them till he makes a false coinage and deceives himself. Many a man can travel to the very bourne of heaven, and yet want confidence to put down his half-seeing. Sancho will invent a journey heavenward as well as anybody. We hate poetry that has a palpable design upon us—and if we do not agree, seems to put its hand in its breeches pocket. Poetry should be great and unobtrusive, a thing which enters into one's soul, and does not startle it or amaze it with itself, but with its subject—how beautiful are the retired flowers! How would they lose their beauty were they to throng into the highway crying out, "admire me I am a violet! dote on me I am a primrose!" Modern poets differ from the Elizabethans in this. Each of the moderns like an Elector of Hanover governs his petty state, and knows how many straws are swept daily from the causeways in all his dominions and has a continual itching that all the housewives should have their coppers well scoured. The ancients were emperors of vast provinces, they had only heard of the remote ones and scarcely cared to visit them. I will cut all this—I will have no more of Wordsworth or Hunt in particular. Why should we be of the tribe of Manasseh, when we can wander with Esau? Why should we kick against the pricks, when we can walk on roses? Why should we be owls, when we can be eagles? Why be teased with "nice eyed wagtails", when we have in sight "the cherub Contemplation?" Why with Wordsworth's "Matthew with a bough of wilding in his hand" when we can have Jacques "under an oak, etc"? The secret of the bough of wilding will run through your head faster than I can write it—Old Matthew spoke to him some years ago on some nothing, and because he happens in an evening walk to imagine the figure of the old man he must stamp it down in black and white, and it is henceforth sacred. I don't mean to deny Wordsworth's grandeur and Hunt's merit, but I mean to say we need not be teased with grandeur and merit when we can have them uncontaminated and unobtrusive. Let us have the old poets, and Robin Hood. Your letter and its sonnets gave me more pleasure than will the 4th Book of *Childe Harold* and the whole of anybody's life and opinions. In return for your dish of filberts, I have gathered a few catkins. I hope they'll look pretty.

To J.H.R. In answer to his Robin Hood Sonnets.

TO J. H. REYNOLDS

No! those days are gone away
And their hours are old and grey,
And their minutes buried all
Under the down-trodden pall
Of the leaves of many years.
Many times have Winter's shears,
Frozen North and chilling East,
Sounded tempests to the feast
Of the forest's whispering fleeces,
Since men paid no rent and leases.
  No, the bugle sounds no more,
And the twanging bow no more;
Silent is the ivory shrill
Past the heath and up the hill:
There is no mid forest laugh,
Where lone Echo gives the half
To some wight amaz'd to hear
Jesting, deep in forest drear.
  On the fairest time of June
You may go with Sun or Moon,
Or the seven stars to light you,
Or the polar ray to right you;
But you never may behold
Little John or Robin bold;
Never one of all the clan
Thrumming on an empty can
Some old hunting ditty, while
He doth his green way beguile
To fair Hostess Merriment
Down beside the pasture Trent,
For he left the merry tale,
Messenger to spicy ale.
  Gone the merry morris din,
Gone the song of Gamelyn,
Gone the tough-belted outlaw
Idling in the 'grene shawe':

>All are gone away and past!
>And if Robin *should be* cast
>Sudden from his turfed grave;
>And if Marian *should* have
>Once again her forest days;
>She would weep, and he would craze:
>He would swear, for all his oaks,
>Fallen beneath the dock-yard strokes,
>Have rotted on the briny seas:
>She would weep that her wild bees
>Sang not to her—'Strange that honey
>Can't be got without hard money'.
>
> So it is: yet let us sing,
>Honour to the old bow-string,
>Honour to the bugle horn,
>Honour to the woods unshorn,
>Honour to the Lincoln green,
>Honour to the archer keen,
>Honour to tight little John,
>And the horse he rode upon;
>Honour to bold Robin Hood
>Sleeping in the underwood,
>Honour to maid Marian,
>And to all the Sherwood-clan—
>Though their days have hurried by
>Let us two a burden try.

I hope you will like them—they are at least written in the Spirit of Outlawry. Here are the Mermaid lines.

>Souls of poets dead and gone,
>What Elysium have ye known,
>Happy field, or mossy cavern,
>Fairer than the Mermaid Tavern?
> Have ye tippled drink more fine
>Than mine Host's Canary wine?
>Or are fruits of Paradise

TO J. H. REYNOLDS

Sweeter than those dainty pies
Of venison. O generous food
Dress'd as though bold Robin Hood
Would with his Maid Marian
Sup, and booze from horn and can.
   I have heard that on a day
Mine host's sign-board flew away,
Nobody knew whither, till
An astrologer's old quill
To a sheepskin gave the story;
Says he saw you in your glory
Underneath a new old sign
Sipping beverage divine,
And pledging with contented smack
The Mermaid in the zodiac.
   Souls of Poets dead and gone,
Are the winds a sweeter home,
Richer is uncellar'd cavern
Than the merry Mermaid Tavern?

I will call on you at 4 to-morrow and we will trudge together for it is not the thing to be a stranger in the Land of Harpsicols. I hope also to bring you my 2nd book. In the hope that these scribblings will be some amusement for you this evening—I remain copying on the hill,
        Your sincere friend and co-scribbler,
                          John Keats

LETTER 12

To J. H. Reynolds   *Thursday, 19 February* 1818
Mr John Reynolds, Little Britain, Christ's Hospital

My dear Reynolds,
    I had an idea that a man might pass a very pleasant life in this manner —let him on a certain day read a certain page of full poesy or distilled prose, and let him wander with it, and muse upon it, and reflect from it, and bring home to it, and prophesy upon it, and dream upon it, until it becomes stale—but when will it do so? Never. When man has arrived at a certain ripeness in intellect any one grand and spiritual passage serves him as a starting-post towards all "the two-and-thirty palaces". How happy is such a voyage of conception, what delicious diligent indolence! A doze upon a sofa does not hinder it, and a nap upon clover engenders ethereal finger-pointings—the prattle of a child gives it wings, and the converse of middle-age a strength to beat them —a strain of music conducts to "an odd angle of the isle", and when the leaves whisper it puts a "girdle round the earth". Nor will this sparing touch of noble books be any irreverence to their writers, for perhaps the honours paid by man to man are trifles in comparison to the benefit done by great works to the "spirit and pulse of good" by their mere passive existence. Memory should not be called knowledge. Many have original minds who do not think it—they are led away by custom. Now it appears to me that almost any man may, like the spider, spin from his own inwards his own airy citadel—the points of leaves and twigs on which the spider begins her work are few, and she fills the air with a beautiful circuiting. Man should be content with as few points to tip with the fine web of his soul, and weave a tapestry empyrean full of symbols for his spiritual eye, of softness for his spiritual touch, of space for his wandering, of distinctness for his luxury. But the minds of mortals are so different and bent on such diverse journeys that it may at first appear impossible for any common taste and fellowship to exist between two or three under these suppositions. It is however quite the contrary. Minds would leave each other in contrary direc-

tions, traverse each other in numberless points, and at last greet each other at the journey's end. An old man and a child would talk together and the old man be led on his path and the child left thinking. Man should not dispute or assert but whisper results to his neighbour and thus by every germ of spirit sucking the sap from mould ethereal every human might become great, and humanity instead of being a wide heath of furze and briars with here and there a remote oak or pine, would become a grand democracy of forest trees! It has been an old comparison for our urging on—the beehive; however, it seems to me that we should rather be the flower than the bee—for it is a false notion that more is gained by receiving than giving—no, the receiver and the giver are equal in their benefits. The flower, I doubt not, receives a fair guerdon from the bee—its leaves blush deeper in the next spring— and who shall say between man and woman which is the most delighted? Now it is more noble to sit like Jove than to fly like Mercury— let us not therefore go hurrying about and collecting honey-bee like, buzzing here and there impatiently from a knowledge of what is to be arrived at; but let us open our leaves like a flower and be passive and receptive—budding patiently under the eye of Apollo and taking hints from every noble insect that favours us with a visit. Sap will be given us for meat and dew for drink. I was led into these thoughts, my dear Reynolds, by the beauty of the morning operating on a sense of idleness—I have not read any books—the morning said I was right— I had no idea but of the morning, and the thrush said I was right, seeming to say,

> O thou whose face hath felt the Winter's wind,
> Whose eye has seen the snow-clouds hung in mist
> And the black elm-tops 'mong the freezing stars,
> To thee the Spring will be a harvest-time.
> O thou, whose only book has been the light
> Of supreme darkness which thou feddest on
> Night after night when Phoebus was away,
> To thee the Spring shall be a triple morn.
> O fret not after knowledge—I have none,
> And yet my song comes native with the warmth.

> O fret not after knowledge—I have none,
> And yet the evening listens. He who saddens
> At thought of idleness cannot be idle
> And he's awake who thinks himself asleep.

Now I am sensible all this is a mere sophistication (however it may neighbour to any truths) to excuse my own indolence, so I will not deceive myself that man should be equal with Jove—but think himself very well off as a sort of scullion-Mercury, or even a humble bee. It is no matter whether I am right or wrong, either one way or another, if there is sufficient to lift a little time from your shoulders.

Your affectionate friend,
John Keats

LETTER 13

To John Taylor   *Friday, 27 February* 1818
J. Taylor Esq, New Bond Street

Hampstead, 27 Feby—

My dear Taylor,

   Your alteration strikes me as being a great improvement—the page looks much better. And now I will attend to the punctuations you speak of—the comma should be at *soberly*, and in the other passage the comma should follow *quiet*. I am extremely indebted to you for this attention and also for your after admonitions. It is a sorry thing for me that any one should have to overcome prejudices in reading my verses—that affects me more than any hyper-criticism on any particular passage. In *Endymion* I have most likely but moved into the go-cart from the leading strings. In poetry I have a few axioms, and you will see how far I am from their centre. First, I think poetry should surprise by a fine excess and not by singularity—it should strike the reader as a wording of his own highest thoughts, and appear almost a remembrance. Second, its touches of beauty should never be half way, thereby making the reader breathless instead of content: the rise, the progress, the setting of imagery should like the sun come natural to him—shine over him and set soberly although in magnificence leaving him in the luxury of twilight—but it is easier to think what poetry should be than to write it, and this leads me on to another axiom. That if poetry comes not as naturally as the leaves to a tree it had better not come at all. However it may be with me I cannot help looking into new countries with "O for a muse of fire to ascend!" If *Endymion* serves me as a pioneer perhaps I ought to be content. I have great reason to be content, for I thank God I can read and perhaps understand Shakespeare to his depths, and I have I am sure many friends, who, if I fail, will attribute any change in my life and temper to humbleness rather than to pride—to a cowering under the wings of great poets rather than to a bitterness that I am not appreciated. I am anxious to get *Endymion* printed that I may forget it and proceed. I have copied the third book and have begun the fourth. On running my eye over the proofs—I saw one mistake I will notice it presently and also any others if there be any. There should be no comma in the "raft branch down sweeping from a tall ash top". I have besides made one or two alterations and also altered the 13th line page 32 to make sense of it as you will see. I will take care the printer shall not trip up my heels. There should be no dash after Dryope in this line, "Dryope's lone lulling of her child". Remember me to Percy Street.

Your sincere and obliged friend,
John Keats

P.S. You shall have a short *Preface* in good time.

LETTER 14

To Benjamin Bailey *Friday, 13 March* 1818
Mr B. Bailey, Magdalen Hall, Oxford

Teignmouth, Friday

My dear Bailey,

When a poor devil is drowning, it is said he comes thrice to the surface, ere he makes his final sink—if however, even at the third rise, he can manage to catch hold of a piece of weed or rock, he stands a fair chance, as I hope I do now, of being saved. I have sunk twice in our correspondence, have risen twice and been too idle, or something worse, to extricate myself. I have sunk the third time and just now risen again at this two of the clock p.m. and saved myself from utter perdition by beginning this, all drenched as I am and fresh from the water, and I would rather endure the present inconvenience of a wet jacket than you should keep a laced one in store for me. Why did I not stop at Oxford in my way? How can you ask such a question? Why did I not promise to do so? Did I not in a letter to you make a promise to do so? Then how can you be so unreasonable as to ask me why I did not? This is the thing—for I have been rubbing up my invention, trying several sleights—I first polished a cold, felt it in my fingers, tried it on the table, but could not pocket it. I tried chilblains, rheumatism, gout, tight boots, nothing of that sort would do, so this is, as I was going to say, the thing—I had a letter from Tom saying how much better he had got, and thinking he had better stop—I went down to prevent his coming up. Will not this do? Turn it which way you like—it is selvaged all round. I have used it these three last days to keep out the abominable Devonshire weather—by the by you may say what you will of Devonshire: the truth is, it is a splashy, rainy, misty snowy, foggy, haily floody, muddy, slipshod county—the hills are very beautiful, when you get a sight of 'em—the primroses are out, but then you are in—the cliffs are of a fine deep colour, but then the clouds are continually vieing with them—the women like your London people in a sort of negative way, because the native men are the poorest creatures in England—because Government never have thought it worth while to send a recruiting party among them. When I think of Wordsworth's sonnet "Vanguard of Liberty! Ye Men of Kent!" the degenerated race about me are *pulvis ipecac. simplex*—a strong dose. Were I a corsair I'd make a descent on the south coast of Devon, if I did not run the chance of having cowardice imputed to me. As for the men they'd run away into the Methodist meeting houses, and the women would be glad of it. Had England been a large Devonshire we should not have won the Battle of Waterloo. There are knotted oaks, there are lusty rivulets, there are meadows such as are not, there are valleys of feminine climate but there are no thews and sinews—Moore's Almanack is here a curiosity—arms neck and shoulders may at least be seen there, and the ladies read it as some out of the way romance. Such a quelling power have these thoughts over me that I fancy the very air of a deteriorating quality—I fancy the flowers, all precocious, have an Acrasian spell about them—I feel able to beat off the Devonshire waves like soap froth. I think it well for the honour of Britain that Julius Caesar did not first land in this county. A Devonshirer standing on his native hills is not a distinct object—he does not show against the light—a wolf or two would dispossess him. I like, I love England. I like its strong men. Give me a long brown plain, for my money, so I may meet with some of Edmond Ironside's descendants. Give me a barren mould so I may meet with some shadowing of Alfred in the shape of a gipsy, a huntsman or a shepherd. Scenery is fine—but human nature is finer. The sward is richer for the tread of a real, nervous, English foot—the eagle's nest is finer for the mountaineer has looked into it—Are these facts or prejudices? Whatever they are, for them I shall never be able to relish entirely any Devonshire scenery. Homer is very fine, Achilles is fine, Diomed is fine, Shakespeare is fine, Hamlet is fine, Lear is fine, but dwindled Englishmen are not fine—where too the women are so passable, and have such English names, such as Ophelia, Cordelia, etc—that they should have such paramours or rather imparamours! As for them I cannot, in thought, help wishing as did the cruel emperor that they had but one head and I might cut it off to deliver them from any horrible courtesy they may do their undeserving countrymen. I wonder I meet with no born monsters. O Devonshire, last night I thought the moon had dwindled in heaven.

I have never had your sermon from Wordsworth but Mrs Dilke lent it me. You know my ideas about religion. I do not think myself more in the right than other people, and that nothing in this world is proveable. I wish I could enter into all your feelings on the subject merely for one short 10 minutes and give you a page or two to your liking. I am sometimes so very sceptical as to think poetry itself a mere Jack-a-lantern to amuse whoever may chance to be struck with its brilliance. As tradesmen say, everything is worth what it will fetch, so probably every mental pursuit takes its reality and worth from the ardour of the pursuer—being in itself a nothing. Ethereal things may at least be thus real, divided under three heads—things real—things semi-real—and nothings. Things real, such as existences of sun, moon and stars and passages of Shakespeare. Things semi-real, such as love, the clouds, etc, which require a greeting of the spirit to make them wholly exist. And nothings which are made great and dignified by an ardent pursuit—which by the by stamps the Burgundy mark on the bottles of our minds, in so much as they are able to "consecrate whate'er they look upon". I have written a sonnet here of a somewhat collateral nature—so don't imagine it an *à propos des bottes*.

>   Four seasons fill the measure of the year;
>   Four seasons are there in the mind of man.
>   He hath his lusty Spring when fancy clear
>   Takes in all beauty with an easy span:
>   He hath his Summer, when luxuriously
>   He chews the honied cud of fair Spring thoughts,
>   Till, in his soul dissolved they come to be
>   Part of himself. He hath his Autumn ports
>   And havens of repose, when his tired wings
>   Are folded up, and he content to look
>   On mists in idleness; to let fair things
>   Pass by unheeded as a threshold brook.
>   He hath his Winter too of pale misfeature
>   Or else he would forget his mortal nature.

TO J. H. REYNOLDS

Aye this may be carried—but what am I talking of—it is an old maxim of mine and of course must be well known that every point of thought is the centre of an intellectual world—the two uppermost thoughts in a man's mind are the two poles of his world; he revolves on them and everything is southward or northward to him through their means. We take but three steps from feathers to iron. Now my dear fellow I must once for all tell you I have not one idea of the truth of any of my speculations—I shall never be a reasoner because I care not to be in the right, when retired from bickering and in a proper philosophical temper. So you must not stare if in any future letter I endeavour to prove that Apollo as he had cat gut strings to his lyre used a cat's paw as a pecten—and further from said pecten's reiterated and continual teasing came the term henpecked. My brother Tom desires to be remembered to you—he has just this moment had a spitting of blood, poor fellow. Remember me to Gleig and Whitehead.

Your affectionate friend,
John Keats

LETTER 15

To J. H. Reynolds *Saturday*, 14 *March* 1818
Mr John H. Reynolds, Little Britain, Christ's Hospital, London

Teignmouth, Saturday

Dear Reynolds,

I escaped being blown over and blown under and trees and houses being toppled on me. I have since hearing of Brown's accident had an aversion to a dose of parapet, and being also a lover of antiquities I would sooner have a harmless piece of herculaneum sent me quietly as a present than ever so modern a chimney pot tumbled on to my head. Being agog to see some Devonshire, I would have taken a walk the first day, but the rain would not let me; and the second, but the rain would not let me; and the third, but the rain forbade it—ditto 4—ditto 5—ditto. So I made up my mind to stop indoors, and catch a sight flying between the showers, and behold I saw a pretty valley, pretty cliffs, pretty brooks, pretty meadows, pretty trees, both standing as they were created and blown down as they are uncreated. The green is beautiful, as they say, and pity it is that it is amphibious—*mais*! but alas! the flowers here wait as naturally for the rain twice a day as the mussels do for the tide, so we look upon a brook in these parts as you look upon a dash in your country—there must be something to support this, aye fog, hail, snow, rain, mist blanketing up three parts of the year. This Devonshire is like Lydia Languish, very entertaining when at smiles, but cursedly subject to sympathetic moisture. You have the sensation of walking under one great lamplighter: and you can't go on the other side of the ladder to keep your frock clean, and cosset your superstition. Buy a girdle—put a pebble in your mouth—loosen your braces—for I am going among scenery whence I intend to tip you the Damosel Radcliffe. I'll cavern you, and grotto you, and waterfall you, and wood you, and water you, and immense-rock you, and tremendous-sound you, and solitude you. I'll make a lodgment on your glacis by a row of pines, and storm your covered way with bramble bushes. I'll have at you with hip and haw smallshot, and cannonade you with shingles. I'll be witty upon salt fish, and impede your cavalry with clotted cream. But ah coward! To talk at this rate to a sick man, or I hope to one that was sick—for I hope by this you stand on your right foot. If you are not—that's all. I intend to cut all sick people if they do not make up their minds to cut sickness—a fellow to whom I have a complete aversion, and who strange to say is harboured and countenanced in several houses where I visit. He is sitting now quite impudent between me and Tom, he insults me at poor Jem Rice's, and you have seated him before now between us at the theatre, where I thought he looked with a longing eye at poor Kean. I shall say, once for all, to my friends generally and severally, cut that fellow, or I cut you.

I went to the theatre here the other night which I forgot to tell George, and got insulted, which I ought to remember to forget to

TO J. H. REYNOLDS

tell anybody, for I did not fight, and as yet have had no redress—"Lie thou there, sweetheart!" I wrote to Bailey yesterday, obliged to speak in a high way, and a damme who's afraid—for I had owed him a letter so long; however, he shall see I will be better in future. Is he in town yet? I have directed to Oxford as the better chance. I have copied my fourth Book, and shall write the preface soon. I wish it was all done, for I want to forget it and make my mind free for something new. Atkins the coachman, Bartlet the surgeon, Simmons the barber, and the girls over at the bonnet shop, say we shall now have a month of seasonable weather—warm, witty, and full of invention. Write to me and tell me you are well or thereabouts, or by the holy Beaucoeur—which I suppose is the Virgin Mary, or the repented Magdalen (beautiful name, that Magdalen), I'll take to my wings and fly away to anywhere but old or Nova Scotia. I wish I had a little innocent bit of metaphysic in my head, to criss-cross this letter; but you know a favourite tune is hardest to be remembered when one wants it most and you, I know, have long ere this taken it for granted that I never have any speculations without associating you in them, where they are of a pleasant nature, and you know enough of me to tell the places where I haunt most, so that if you think for five minutes after having read this you will find it a long letter, and see written in the air above you,

Your most affectionate friend,
John Keats

Remember me to all. Tom's remembrances to you.

LETTER 16

To J. H. Reynolds *Thursday, 9 April* 1818
J. H. Reynolds Esq, Little Britain, Christ's Hospital, London

Thursday Morning

My dear Reynolds,
 Since you all agree that the thing is bad, it must be so—though I am not aware there is anything like Hunt in it (and if there is, it is my natural way, and I have something in common with Hunt); look it over again and examine into the motives, the seeds from which any one sentence sprung—I have not the slightest feel of humility towards the public, or to anything in existence, but the eternal Being, the principle of beauty, and the memory of great men. When I am writing for myself for the mere sake of the moment's enjoyment, perhaps nature has its course with me. But a preface is written to the public, a thing I cannot help looking upon as an enemy, and which I cannot address without feelings of hostility. If I write a preface in a supple or subdued style, it will not be in character with me as a public speaker. I would be subdued before my friends, and thank them for subduing me, but among multitudes of men I have no feel of stooping, I hate the idea of humility to them.
 I never wrote one single line of poetry with the least shadow of public thought.
 Forgive me for vexing you and making a Trojan horse of such a trifle, both with respect to the matter in question, and myself—but it eases me to tell you. I could not live without the love of my friends. I would jump down Etna for any great public good, but I hate a mawkish popularity. I cannot be subdued before them. My glory would be to daunt and dazzle the thousand jabberers about pictures and books—I see swarms of porcupines with their quills erect "like lime-twigs set to catch my winged book" and I would fright them away with a torch. You will say my preface is not much of a torch. It would have been too insulting "to begin from Jove" and I could not set a golden head upon a thing of clay—if there is any fault in the preface it is not affectation, but an undersong of disrespect to the

TO J. H. REYNOLDS

public. If I write another preface, it must be done without a thought of those people—I will think about it. If it should not reach you in four or five days tell Taylor to publish it without a preface, and let the dedication simply stand "inscribed to the memory of Thomas Chatterton".

I had resolved last night to write to you this morning—I wish it had been about something else, something to greet you towards the close of your long illness. I have had one or two intimations of your going to Hampstead for a space, and I regret to see your confounded rheumatism keeps you in Little Britain where I am sure the air is too confined. Devonshire continues rainy. As the drops beat against the window, they give me the same sensation as a quart of cold water offered to revive a half-drowned devil. No feel of the clouds dropping fatness, but as if the roots of the earth were rotten cold and drenched. I have not been able to go to Kents Cave at Babbacombe. However on one very beautiful day I had a fine clamber over the rocks all along as far as that place. I shall be in town in about ten days. We go by way of Bath on purpose to call on Bailey. I hope soon to be writing to you about the things of the north, purposing to wayfare all over those parts. I have settled my accoutrements in my own mind and will go to gorge wonders. However we'll have some days together before I set out.

I have many reasons for going wonder-ways: to make my winter chair free from spleen—to enlarge my vision—to escape disquisitions on poetry and Kingston criticism—to promote digestion and economize shoe-leather—I'll have leather buttons and belt; and if Brown holds his mind, over the hills we go. If my books will help me to it, thus will I take all Europe in turn, and see the kingdoms of the earth and the glory of them. Tom is getting better, he hopes you may meet him at the top o' the hill. My love to your nurses. I am ever

Your affectionate friend,
John Keats

LETTER 17

To J. H. Reynolds Sunday, 3 May 1818
Mr John H. Reynolds, Little Britain, Christ's Hospital, London

Teignmouth, May 3rd

My dear Reynolds,

What I complain of is that I have been in so an uneasy a state of mind as not to be fit to write to an invalid. I cannot write to any length under a disguised feeling. I should have loaded you with an addition of gloom, which I am sure you do not want. I am now, thank God, in a humour to give you a good groat's worth—for Tom, after a night without a wink of sleep, and overburdened with fever, has got up after a refreshing day sleep and is better than he has been for a long time; and you I trust have been again round the common without any effect but refreshment. As to the matter I hope I can say with Sir Andrew "I have matter enough in my head" in your favour. And now, in the second place—for I reckon that I have finished my *Imprimis*—I am glad you blow up the weather—all through your letter, there is a leaning towards a climate-curse, and you know what a delicate satisfaction there is in having a vexation anathematized: one would think there has been growing up for these last four thousand years, a grandchild scion of the old forbidden tree, and that some modern Eve had just violated it; and that there was come with double charge "Notus and Afer, black with thunderous clouds from Sierraleona".

I shall breathe worsted stockings sooner than I thought for—Tom wants to be in town. We will have some such days upon the heath like that of last summer—and why not with the same book? Or what say you to a black-letter Chaucer printed in 1596? Aye I've got one, huzza! I shall have it bounden gothique—a nice sombre binding—it will go a little way to unmodernize. And also I see no reason, because I have been away this last month, why I should not have a peep at your Spenserian—notwithstanding you speak of your office, in my thought a little too early, for I do not see why a mind like yours is not capable of harbouring and digesting the whole mystery of law

TO J. H. REYNOLDS

as easily as Parson Hugh does pippins—which did not hinder him from his poetic canary. Were I to study physic or rather medicine again, I feel it would not make the least difference in my poetry; when the mind is in its infancy a bias is in reality a bias, but when we have acquired more strength, a bias becomes no bias. Every department of knowledge we see excellent and calculated towards a great whole. I am so convinced of this, that I am glad at not having given away my medical books, which I shall again look over to keep alive the little I know thitherwards; and moreover intend through you and Rice to become a sort of pip-civilian. An extensive knowledge is needful to thinking people—it takes away the heat and fever, and helps, by widening speculation, to ease the burden of the mystery—a thing I begin to understand a little, and which weighed upon you in the most gloomy and true sentence in your letter. The difference of high sensations with and without knowledge appears to me this—in the latter case we are falling continually ten thousand fathoms deep and being blown up again without wings and with all the horror of a bare-shouldered creature—in the former case, our shoulders are fledged, and we go through the same air and space without fear. This is running one's rigs on the score of abstracted benefit—when we come to human life and the affections it is impossible to know how a parallel of breast and head can be drawn (you will forgive me for thus privately treading out of my depth, and take it for treading as schoolboys tread the water) —it is impossible to know how far knowledge will console us for the death of a friend and the ill "that flesh is heir to". With respect to the affections and poetry you must know by a sympathy my thoughts that way; and I dare say these few lines will be but a ratification. I wrote them on May-day, and intend to finish the ode all in good time.

> Mother of Hermes! and still youthful Maia!
>   May I sing to thee
> As thou wast hymned on the shores of Baiae?
>   Or may I woo thee
> In earlier Sicilian? or thy smiles
> Seek as they once were sought, in Grecian isles,

> By bards who died content in pleasant sward,
> Leaving great verse unto a little clan?
> O give me their old vigour, and unheard,
> Save of the quiet primrose, and the span
>   Of heaven and few ears,
> Rounded by thee my song should die away
>   Content as theirs,
> Rich in the simple worship of a day.

You may be anxious to know for fact to what sentence in your letter I allude. You say "I fear there is little chance of anything else in this life". You seem by that to have been going through with a more painful and acute zest the same labyrinth that I have—I have come to the same conclusion thus far. My branchings out therefrom have been numerous: one of them is the consideration of Wordsworth's genius and as a help—in the manner of gold being the meridian line of worldly wealth—how he differs from Milton. And here I have nothing but surmises from an uncertainty whether Milton's apparently less anxiety for humanity proceeds from his seeing further or no than Wordsworth: and whether Wordsworth has in truth epic passion, and martyrs himself to the human heart, the main region of his song. In regard to his genius alone, we find what he says true as far as we have experienced and we can judge no further but by larger experience, for axioms in philosophy are not axioms until they are proved upon our pulses. We read fine things but never feel them to the full until we have gone the same steps as the author. I know this is not plain; you will know exactly my meaning when I say, that now I shall relish Hamlet more than I ever have done—or, better—you are sensible no man can set down venery as a bestial or joyless thing until he is sick of it and therefore all philosophizing on it would be mere wording. Until we are sick, we understand not—in fine, as Byron says, "Knowledge is Sorrow", and I go on to say that "Sorrow is Wisdom"—and further for aught we can know for certainty, "Wisdom is folly!" So you see how I have run away from Wordsworth, and Milton, and shall still run away from what was in my head, to observe, that some kind of letters are good squares, others handsome ovals, and others—some orbicular, others spheroid. And why should there not be another species with two rough edges like a rat-trap? I hope you will find all my long letters of that species, and all will be well; for by merely touching the spring delicately and ethereally, the rough-edged will fly immediately into a proper compactness, and thus you may make a good wholesome loaf, with your own leaven in it, of my fragments. If you cannot find this said rat-trap sufficiently tractable—alas for me, it being an impossibility in grain for my ink to stain otherwise: if I scribble long letters I must play my vagaries. I must be too heavy, or too light, for whole pages— I must be quaint and free of tropes and figures—I must play my draughts as I please, and for my advantage and your erudition, crown a white with a black, or a black with a white, and move into black or white, far and near as I please—I must go from Hazlitt to Patmore, and make Wordsworth and Colman play at leap-frog—or keep one of them down a whole half-holiday at fly the garter—"from Gray to Gay, from Little to Shakespeare". Also, as a long cause requires two or more sittings of the court, so a long letter will require two or more sittings of the breech, wherefore I shall resume after dinner.

Have you not seen a gull, an auk, a sea mew, or anything to bring this line to a proper length, and also fill up this clear part; that like the gull I may *dip*—I hope, not out of sight—and also, like a gull, I hope to be lucky in a good sized fish. This crossing a letter is not without its association, for chequer work leads us naturally to a milkmaid, a milkmaid to Hogarth, Hogarth to Shakespeare, Shakespeare to Hazlitt, Hazlitt to Shakespeare and thus by merely pulling an apron string we set a pretty peal of chimes at work. Let them chime on while, with your patience, I will return to Wordsworth—whether or no he has an extended vision or a circumscribed grandeur—whether he is an eagle in his nest, or on the wing. And to be more explicit and to show you how tall I stand by the giant, I will put down a simile of human life as far as I now perceive it; that is, to the point to which I say we both arrived at—well—I compare human life to a large mansion of many apartments, two of which I can only describe, the doors of the rest being as yet shut upon me. The first we step into we call the infant or thoughtless chamber, in which we remain as long as we do not think. We remain there a long while and, notwithstanding the doors of the second chamber remain wide open, showing a bright appearance, we care not to hasten to it, but are at length imperceptibly impelled by the awakening of this thinking principle within us. We no sooner get into the second chamber, which I shall call the chamber of maiden-thought, than we become intoxicated with the light and the atmosphere, we see nothing but pleasant wonders, and think of delaying there for ever in delight. However, among the effects this breathing is father of is that tremendous one of sharpening one's vision into the heart and nature of man—of convincing one's nerves that the world is full of misery and heartbreak, pain, sickness and oppression, whereby this chamber of maiden thought becomes gradually darkened and at the same time on all sides of it many doors are set open—but all dark—all leading to dark passages. We see not the balance of good and evil. We are in a mist. *We* are now in that state—we feel the "burden of the Mystery"; to this point was Wordsworth come, as far as I can conceive, when he wrote "Tintern Abbey" and it seems to me that his genius is explorative of those dark passages. Now if we live, and go on thinking, we too shall explore them. He is a genius and superior to us, in so far as he can, more than we, make discoveries, and shed a light in them. Here I must think Wordsworth is deeper than Milton, though I think it has depended more upon the general and gregarious advance of intellect, than individual greatness of mind. From the *Paradise Lost* and the other works of Milton, I hope it is not too presuming, even between ourselves to say, his philosophy, human and divine, may be tolerably understood by one not much advanced in years. In his time Englishmen were just emancipated from a great superstition, and men had got hold of certain points and resting places in reasoning which were too newly born to be doubted, and too much opposed by the mass of Europe not to be thought ethereal and authentically divine. Who could gainsay his ideas on virtue, vice, and chastity in *Comus*, just at the time of the dismissal of cod-pieces and a hundred other disgraces? Who would not rest satisfied with his hintings at good and evil in the *Paradise Lost*, when just free from the inquisition and burning in Smithfield? The Reformation produced such immediate and great benefits, that Protestantism was considered under the immediate eye of heaven, and its own remaining dogmas and superstitions, then, as it were, regenerated, constituted those resting places and seeming sure points of reasoning. From that I have mentioned, Milton, whatever he may have thought in the sequel, appears to have been content with these by his writings. He did not think into the human heart, as Wordsworth has done. Yet Milton as a philosopher had sure as great powers as Wordsworth. What is then to be inferred? O many things. It proves there is really a grand march of intellect. It proves that a mighty providence subdues the mightiest minds to the service of the time being, whether it be in human knowledge or religion—I have often pitied a tutor who has to hear "*Nom^e: Musa*" so often dinned into his ears—I hope you may not have the same pain in this scribbling. I may have read these things before, but I never had even a thus dim perception of them; and moreover I like to say my lesson to one who will endure my tediousness for my own sake. After all there is certainly something real in the world. Moore's present to Hazlitt is real—I like that Moore, and am glad I saw him at the theatre just before I left town. Tom has spit a leetle blood this afternoon, and that is rather a damper—but I know—the truth is there is something real in the world. Your third chamber of life shall be a lucky and a gentle one, stored with the wine of love and the bread of friendship. When you see George, if he should not have received a letter from me, tell him he will find one at home most likely. Tell Bailey I hope soon to see him. Remember me to all. The leaves have been out here, for mony a day—I have written to George for the first stanzas of my "Isabel"—I shall have them soon and will copy the whole out for you.

Your affectionate friend,
John Keats

LETTER 18

To Benjamin Bailey *Wednesday, 10 June 1818*
Mr B. Bailey, Magdalen Hall, Oxford

London—

My dear Bailey,

I have been very much gratified and very much hurt by your letters in the Oxford paper: because independent of that unlawful and mortal feeling of pleasure at praise, there is a glory in enthusiasm; and because the world is malignant enough to chuckle at the most honourable simplicity. Yes, on my soul, my dear Bailey, you are too simple for the world—and that idea makes me sick of it. How is it that by extreme opposites we have as it were got discontented nerves. You have all your life (I think so) believed everybody—I have suspected everybody —and although you have been so deceived you make a simple appeal. The world has something else to do, and I am glad of it. Were it in my choice I would reject a Petrarchal coronation—on account of my dying day, and because women have cancers. I should not by rights speak in this tone to you, for it is an incendiary spirit that would do so. Yet I am not old enough or magnanimous enough to annihilate self, and it would perhaps be paying you an ill compliment. I was in hopes some little time back to be able to relieve your dullness by my spirits, to point out things in the world worth your enjoyment, and now I am never alone without rejoicing that there is such a thing as death— without placing my ultimate in the glory of dying for a great human purpose. Perhaps if my affairs were in a different state I should not have written the above—you shall judge. I have two brothers, one is driven by the "burden of society" to America; the other, with an exquisite love of life, is in a lingering state. My love for my brothers from the early loss of our parents and even for earlier misfortunes has grown into an affection "passing the love of women". I have been ill tempered with them, I have vexed them, but the thought of them has always stifled the impression that any woman might otherwise have made upon me. I have a sister too—and may not follow them, either to America or to

TO BENJAMIN BAILEY

the grave. Life must be undergone, and I certainly derive a consolation from the thought of writing one or two more poems before it ceases. I have heard some hints of your retiring to Scotland—I should like to know your feeling on it—it seems rather remote. Perhaps Gleig will have a duty near you. I am not certain whether I shall be able to go my journey on account of my brother Tom and a little indisposition of my own—If I do not you shall see me soon—if not, on my return; or I'll quarter myself upon you in Scotland next winter. I had known my sister-in-law some time before she was my sister and was very fond of her. I like her better and better. She is the most disinterested woman I ever knew—that is to say she goes beyond degree in it. To see an entirely disinterested girl quite happy is the most pleasant and extraordinary thing in the world—it depends upon a thousand circumstances—on my word 'tis extraordinary. Women must want imagination and they may thank God for it, and so may we that a delicate being can feel happy without any sense of crime. It puzzles me and I have no sort of logic to comfort me—I shall think it over. I am not at home and your letter being there I cannot look it over to answer any particular—only I must say I felt that passage of Dante—if I take any book with me it shall be those minute volumes of Cary for they will go into the aptest corner. Reynolds is getting I may say robust—his illness has been of service to him—like everyone just recovered he is high-spirited. I hear also good accounts of Rice. With respect to domestic literature—the Edinburgh Magazine in another blow up against Hunt calls me "the amiable Mister Keats" and I have more than a laurel from the Quarterly Reviewers for they have *smothered* me in "Foliage". I want to read you my "Pot of Basil"; if you go to Scotland I should much like to read it there to you among the snows of next winter. My brothers' remembrances to you.

Your affectionate friend,
John Keats

LETTER 19

To Thomas Keats *Thursday–Saturday, 25–27 June* 1818

Here beginneth my journal, this Thursday, the 25th day of June, Anno Domini 1818. This morning we arose at 4, and set off in a Scotch mist; put up once under a tree, and in fine, have walked wet and dry to this place, called in the vulgar tongue Endmoor, 17 miles; we have not been incommoded by our knapsacks; they serve capitally, and we shall go on very well.

June 26—I merely put *pro forma*, for there is no such thing as time and space, which by the way came forcibly upon me on seeing for the first hour the lake and mountains of Winander—I cannot describe them—they surpass my expectation—beautiful water—shores and islands green to the marge—mountains all round up to the clouds. We set out from Endmoor this morning, breakfasted at Kendal with a soldier who had been in all the wars for the last seventeen years—then we have walked to Bowness to dinner—said Bowness situated on the lake where we have just dined, and I am writing at this present. I took an oar to one of the islands to take up some trout for our dinner, which they keep in porous boxes. I enquired of the waiter for Wordsworth—he said he knew him, and that he had been here a few days ago, canvassing for the Lowthers. What think you of that—Wordsworth versus Brougham!! Sad—sad—sad—and yet the family has been his friend always. What can we say? We are now about seven miles from Rydal, and expect to see him tomorrow. You shall hear all about our visit.

There are many disfigurements to this lake—not in the way of land or water. No; the two views we have had of it are of the most noble tenderness—they can never fade away—they make one forget the divisions of life—age, youth, poverty and riches—and refine one's sensual vision into a sort of north star which can never cease to be open lidded and steadfast over the wonders of the great Power. The disfigurement I mean is the miasma of London. I do suppose it contaminated with bucks and soldiers, and women of fashion—and hat-band ignorance. The border inhabitants are quite out of keeping with the romance about them, from a continual intercourse with London rank and fashion. But why should I grumble? They let me have a prime glass of soda water—O they are as good as their neighbours. But Lord Wordsworth, instead of being in retirement, has himself and his house full in the thick of fashionable visitors quite convenient to be pointed at all the summer long. When we had gone about half this morning, we began to get among the hills and to see the mountains grow up before us—the other half brought us to Winandermere, 14 miles to dinner. The weather is capital for the views, but is now rather misty, and we are in doubt whether to walk to Ambleside to tea—it is five miles along the borders of the lake. Loughrigg will swell up before us all the way—I have an amazing partiality for mountains in the clouds. There is nothing in Devon like this, and Brown says there is nothing in Wales to be compared to it. I must tell you, that in going through Cheshire and Lancashire, I saw the Welsh mountains at a distance. We have passed the two castles, Lancaster and Kendal.

27th—We walked here to Ambleside yesterday along the border of Winandermere all beautiful with wooded shores and islands—our road was a winding lane, wooded on each side, and green overhead, full of foxgloves—every now and then a glimpse of the lake, and all the while Kirkstone and other large hills nestled together in a sort of grey black mist. Ambleside is at the northern extremity of the lake. We arose this morning at six, because we call it a day of rest, having to call on Wordsworth who lives only two miles hence. Before breakfast we went to see the Ambleside waterfall. The morning beautiful—the walk early among the hills. We, I may say fortunately, missed the direct path, and after wandering a little, found it out by the noise—for, mark you, it is buried in trees, in the bottom of the valley—the stream itself is interesting throughout with "mazy error over pendant shades". Milton meant a smooth river—this is buffetting all the way on a rocky bed ever various—but the waterfall itself, which I came suddenly upon, gave me a pleasant twinge. First we stood a little below the head about half way down the first fall, buried deep in trees, and saw it streaming down two more descents to the depth of near fifty feet—then we went on a jut of rock nearly level with the second fall-head, where the first fall was above us, and the third below our feet still. At the same time we saw that the water was divided by a sort of cataract island on whose other side burst out a glorious stream—then the thunder and the freshness. At the same time the different falls have as different characters, the first darting down the slate-rock like an arrow, the second spreading out like a fan, the third dashed into a mist, and the one on the other side of the rock a sort of mixture of all these. We afterwards moved away a space, and saw nearly the whole more mild, streaming silverly through the trees. What astonishes me more than anything is the tone, the colouring, the slate, the stone, the moss, the rock-weed; or, if I may so say, the intellect, the countenance of such places. The space, the magnitude of mountains and waterfalls are well imagined before one sees them; but this countenance or intellectual tone must surpass every imagination and defy any remembrance. I shall learn poetry here and shall henceforth write more than ever, for the abstract endeavour of being able to add a mite to that mass of beauty which is harvested from these grand materials, by the finest spirits, and put into ethereal existence for the relish of one's fellows. I cannot think with Hazlitt that these scenes make man appear little. I never forgot my stature so completely—I live in the eye; and my imagination, surpassed, is at rest. We shall see another waterfall near Rydal to which we shall proceed after having put these letters in the post office. I long to be at Carlisle, as I expect there a letter from George and one from you. Let any of my friends see my letters—they may not be interested in descriptions—descriptions are bad at all times—I did not intend to give you any; but how can I help it? I am anxious you should taste a little of our pleasure; it may not be an unpleasant thing, as you have not the fatigue. I am well in health. Direct henceforth to Port Patrick till the 12th July. Content that probably three or four pair of eyes whose owners I am rather partial to will run over these lines I remain; and moreover that I am

Your affectionate brother,
John

LETTER 20

To Fanny Keats   Thursday–Saturday, 2–5 July 1818
Miss F. M. Keats, Richd. Abbey's Esq, Walthamstow, Middx.

                              Dumfries, July 2nd
My dear Fanny,
   I intended to have written to you from Kirkcudbright the town I shall be in tomorrow—but I will write now because my knapsack has worn my coat in the seams, my coat has gone to the tailors and I have but one coat to my back in these parts. I must tell you how I went to Liverpool with George and our new sister and the gentleman my fellow traveller through the summer and autumn. We had a tolerable journey to Liverpool, which I left the next morning before George was up for Lancaster. Then we set off from Lancaster on foot with our knapsacks on, and have walked a little zig-zag through the mountains and lakes of Cumberland and Westmorland. We came from Carlisle yesterday to this place. We are employed in going up mountains, looking at strange towns, prying into old ruins, and eating very hearty breakfasts. Here we are full in the midst of broad Scotch— "How is it a' wi yoursel?"—the girls are walking about bare-footed and in the worst cottages the smoke finds its way out of the door. I shall come home full of news for you and, for fear I should choke you by too great a dose at once, I must make you used to it by a letter or two. We have been taken for travelling jewellers, razor sellers and spectacle vendors because friend Brown wears a pair. The first place we stopped at with our knapsacks contained one Richard Bradshaw, a notorious tippler. He stood in the shape of a 3 and balanced himself as well as he could saying with his nose right in Mr Brown's face "Do-yo-u-sell spec-ta-cles?" Mr Abbey says we are Don Quixotes— tell him we are more generally taken for pedlars. All I hope is that we may not be taken for excisemen in this whisky country. We are generally up about 5 walking before breakfast and we complete our 20 miles before dinner. Yesterday we visited Burns's tomb and this morning the fine ruins of Lincluden. I had done thus far when my

coat came back fortified at all points, so as we lose no time we set forth again through Galloway—all very pleasant and pretty with no fatigue when one is used to it. We are in the midst of Meg Merrilies' country of whom I suppose you have heard:

> Old Meg she was a gipsy
>   And lived upon the moors,
> Her bed it was the brown heath turf
>   And her house was out of doors.
>
> Her apples were swart blackberries
>   Her currants pods o' broom
> Her wine was dew o' the wild white rose
>   Her book a churchyard tomb.
>
> Her brothers were the craggy hills
>   Her sisters larchen trees—
> Alone with her great family
>   She lived as she did please.
>
> No breakfast has she many a morn
>   No dinner many a noon,
> And 'stead of supper she would stare
>   Full hard against the moon.
>
> But every morn of woodbine fresh
>   She made her garlanding
> And every night the dark glen yew
>   She wove and she would sing.
>
> And with her fingers old and brown
>   She plaited mats o' rushes
> And gave them to the cottagers
>   She met among the bushes.
>
> Old Meg was brave as Margaret Queen
>   And tall as Amazon:
> An old red blanket cloak she wore;
>   A chip hat had she on.
> God rest her aged bones somewhere—
>   She died full long agone!

TO FANNY KEATS

If you like these sort of ballads I will now and then scribble one for you—if I send any to Tom I'll tell him to send them to you. I have so many interruptions that I cannot manage to fill a letter in one day. Since I scribbled we have walked through a beautiful country to Kirkcudbright, at which place I will write you a song about myself:

>There was a naughty boy
>   A naughty boy was he
>He would not stop at home
>   He could not quiet be—
>   He took
>   In his knapsack
>   A book
>   Full of vowels
>   And a shirt
>   With some towels—
>   A slight cap
>   For night cap—
>   A hair brush
>   Comb ditto
>   New stockings
>   For old ones
>   Would split O!
>   This knapsack
>   Tight at's back
>   He rivetted close
>   And followed his nose
>   To the north
>   To the north
>   And followed his nose
>   To the north.
>
>There was a naughty boy
>   And a naughty boy was he
>For nothing would he do
>   But scribble poetry—

  He took
  An inkstand
  In his hand
  And a pen
  Big as ten
  In the other
  And away
  In a pother
  He ran
  To the mountains
  And fountains
  And ghostes
  And postes
  And witches
  And ditches
  And wrote
  In his coat
  When the weather
  Was cool
  Fear of gout—
  And without
  When the weather
  Was warm—
  Och the charm
  When we choose
 To follow one's nose
  To the north
  To the north
To follow one's nose to the north!

There was a naughty boy
 And a naughty boy was he
He kept little fishes
 In washing tubs three
  In spite
  Of the might

TO FANNY KEATS

    Of the maid
    Nor afraid
    Of his Granny-good—
    He often would
    Hurly burly
    Get up early
    And go
    By hook or crook
    To the brook
    And bring home
    Miller's thumb
    Tittle bat
    Not over fat
    Minnows small
    As the stall
    Of a glove
    Not above
    The size
    Of a nice
    Little baby's
    Little finger—
    O he made
    'Twas his trade
Of fish a pretty kettle
  A kettle—A kettle
Of fish a pretty kettle
  A kettle!

There was a naughty boy
  And a naughty boy was he
He ran away to Scotland
  The people for to see—
    There he found
    That the ground
    Was as hard,
    That a yard

>   Was as long,
>   That a song
>   Was as merry,
>   That a cherry
>   Was as red—
>   That lead
>   Was as weighty
>   That fourscore
>   Was as eighty
>   That a door
>   Was as wooden
>   As in England—
>   So he stood in
>   His shoes
>   And he wondered
>   He stood in his
>   Shoes and he wondered.

My dear Fanny I am ashamed of writing you such stuff, nor would I if it were not for being tired after my day's walking, and ready to tumble into bed so fatigued that when I am asleep you might sew my nose to my great toe and trundle me round the town like a hoop without waking me. Then I get so hungry—a ham goes but a very little way and fowls are like larks to me. A batch of bread I make no more ado with than a sheet of parliament; and I can eat a bull's head as easily as I used to do bull's eyes—I take a whole string of pork sausages down as easily as a pen'orth of lady's fingers. Oh dear I must soon be contented with an acre or two of oaten cake, a hogshead of milk and a clothes basket of eggs morning noon and night when I get among the Highlanders. Before we see them we shall pass into Ireland and have a chat with the Paddies, and look at the Giant's Causeway which you must have heard of—I have not time to tell you particularly for I have to send a journal to Tom of whom you shall hear all particulars or from me when I return. Since I began this we have walked sixty miles to Newton Stewart at which place I put in this letter—to-night we sleep at Glenluce—tomorrow at Portpatrick and the next day we shall cross in the passage boat to Ireland. I hope Miss Abbey has quite recovered. Present my respects to her and to Mr and Mrs Abbey— God bless you.

Your affectionate brother,
John

Do write me a letter directed to *Inverness*, Scotland.

LETTER 21

To Thomas Keats   *Friday–Thursday, 3–9 July* 1818
Mr Thos. Keats, Well Walk, Hampstead, Middx

Auchencairn, July 3rd

My dear Tom,

    I have not been able to keep up my journal completely on account of other letters to George and one which I am writing to Fanny from which I have turned to lose no time whilst Brown is copying a song about Meg Merrilies which I have just written for her. We are now in Meg Merrilies' country and have this morning passed through some parts exactly suited to her. Kirkcudbright County is very beautiful, very wild with craggy hills somewhat in the Westmorland fashion. We have come down from Dumfries to the sea coast part of it. The song I mention you would have from Dilke: but perhaps you would like it here:

> Old Meg she was a gipsy
>   And lived upon the moors;
> Her bed it was the brown heath turf,
>   And her house was out of doors.
> Her apples were swart blackberries,
>   Her currants pods o' broom,
> Her wine was dew o' the wild white rose,
>   Her book a churchyard tomb.

> Her brothers were the craggy hills,
>   Her sisters larchen trees—
> Alone with her great family
>   She lived as she did please.
> No breakfast had she many a morn,
>   No dinner many a noon;
> And 'stead of supper she would stare
>   Full hard against the moon.
> But every morn, of woodbine fresh
>   She made her garlanding;
> And every night the dark glen yew
>   She wove and she would sing.
> And with her fingers old and brown
>   She plaited mats o' rushes,
> And gave them to the cottagers
>   She met among the bushes.
> Old Meg was brave as Margaret Queen
>   And tall as Amazon:
> An old red blanket cloak she wore
>   A chip hat had she on—
> God rest her aged bones somewhere
>   She died full long agone!

Now I will return to Fanny. It rains. I may have time to go on here presently.

July 5—You see I have missed a day from Fanny's letter. Yesterday was passed in Kirkcudbright—the country is very rich, very fine—and with a little of Devon. I am now writing at Newton Stewart six miles into Wigtown. Our landlady of yesterday said very few southrens passed these ways. The children jabber away as in a foreign language—the barefooted girls look very much in keeping—I mean with the scenery about them. Brown praises their cleanliness and appearance of comfort—the neatness of their cottages, etc. It may be—they are very squat among trees and fern and heaths and broom, on levels, slopes and heights. They are very pleasant because they are very primitive, but I wish they were as snug as those up the Devonshire valleys. We are lodged and entertained in great varieties—we dined yesterday on dirty bacon, dirtier eggs and dirtiest potatoes with a slice of salmon. We breakfast this morning in a nice carpeted room with sofa, hair-bottomed chairs and green-baized mahogany. A spring by the road side is always welcome—we drink water for dinner diluted with a gill of whisky.

July 7th—Yesterday morning we set out from Glenluce going some distance round to see some ruins—they were scarcely worth the while. We went on towards Stranraer in a burning sun and had gone about six miles when the mail overtook us—we got up—were at Portpatrick in a jiffy, and I am writing now in little Ireland. The dialect on the neighbouring shores of Scotland and Ireland is much the same, yet I can perceive a great difference in the nations from the chambermaid at this nate inn kept by Mr Kelly. She is fair, kind and ready to laugh, because she is out of the horrible dominion of the Scotch kirk. A Scotch girl stands in terrible awe of the Elders—poor little Susannas. They will scarcely laugh—they are greatly to be pitied and the kirk is greatly to be damned. These kirkmen have done Scotland good (query?), they have made men, women, old men, young men, old women, young women, boys, girls and infants all careful—so that they are formed into regular phalanges of savers and gainers—such a thrifty army cannot fail to enrich their country and give it a greater appearance of comfort than that of their poor Irish neighbours. These kirkmen have done Scotland harm—they have banished puns and laughing and kissing (except in cases where the very danger and crime must make it very fine and gustful). I shall make a full stop at kissing for after that there should be a better paren*t*-thesis: and go on to remind you of the fate of Burns. Poor unfortunate fellow—his disposition was southern—how sad it is when a luxurious imagination is obliged in self defence to deaden its delicacy in vulgarity, and riot in things attainable that it may not have leisure to go mad after things which are not. No man in such matters will be content with the experience of others. It is true that out of suffrance there is no greatness, no dignity; that in the most abstracted pleasure there is no lasting happiness: yet who would not like to discover over again that Cleopatra was a gipsy, Helen a rogue and Ruth a deep one? I have not sufficient reasoning faculty to settle the doctrine of thrift—as it is consistent with the dignity of human society—with the happiness of cottagers. All I can do is by plump contrasts. Were the fingers made to squeeze a guinea or a white hand? Were the lips made to hold a pen or a kiss? And yet in cities man is shut out from his fellows if he is poor, the cottager must be dirty and very wretched if she be not thrifty. The present state of society demands this and this convinces me that the world is very young and in a very ignorant state. We live in a barbarous age. I would sooner be a wild deer than a girl under the dominion of the kirk, and I would sooner be a wild hog than be the occasion of a poor creature's penance before those execrable elders. It is not so far to the Giant's Causeway as we supposed—we thought it 70, and hear it is only 48 miles—so we shall leave one of our knapsacks here at Donaghadee, take our immediate wants and be back in a week, when we shall proceed to the county of Ayr. In the Packet yesterday we heard some ballads from two old men—one was a romance which seemed very poor—then there was the Battle of the Boyne—then Robin Huid as as they call him—"Before the King you shall go, go, go, before the King you shall go". There were no letters for me at Portpatrick so I am behindhand with you, I daresay, in news from George. Direct to Glasgow till the 17th of this month.

9th—We stopped very little in Ireland and that you may not have leisure to marvel at our speedy return to Portpatrick I will tell you that it is as dear living in Ireland as at the Hummums—thrice the expense of Scotland—it would have cost us £15 before our return. Moreover we found those 48 miles to be Irish ones which reach to 70 English. So having walked to Belfast one day and back to Donaghadee the next we left Ireland with a fair breeze. We slept last night at Portpatrick where I was gratified by a letter from you. On our walk in Ireland we had too much opportunity to see the worse than nakedness, the rags, dirt and misery of the poor common Irish. A Scotch cottage, though in that sometimes the smoke has no exit but at the door, is a palace to an Irish one. We could observe that impetuosity in man, boy and woman. We had the pleasure of finding our way through a peat-bog—three miles long at least—dreary, black, dank, flat and spongy: here and there were poor dirty creatures and a few strong men cutting or carting peat. We heard on passing into Belfast through a most wretched suburb that most disgusting of all noises worse than the bagpipe, the laugh of a monkey, the chatter of women *solus*, the scream of a macaw —I mean the sound of the shuttle. What a tremendous difficulty is the improvement of the condition of such people. I cannot conceive how a mind "with child" of philanthropy could grasp at possibility—with me it is absolute despair. At a miserable house of entertainment half way between Donaghadee and Belfast were two men sitting at whiskey—one a labourer and the other I took to be a drunken weaver. The labourer took me for a Frenchman and the other hinted at bounty money saying he was ready to take it. On calling for the letters at Portpatrick the man snapped out "what regiment?" On our return from Belfast we met a sedan—the Duchess of Dunghill. It is no laughing matter though. Imagine the worst dog kennel you ever saw placed upon two poles from a mouldy fencing. In such a wretched thing sat a squalid old woman squat like an ape half starved from a scarcity of biscuit in its passage from Madagascar to the Cape, with a pipe in her mouth and looking out with a round-eyed skinny lidded inanity— with a sort of horizontal idiotic movement of her head—squat and lean she sat and puffed out the smoke while two ragged tattered girls carried her along. What a thing would be a history of her life and sensations. I shall endeavour when I know more and have thought a little more, to give you my ideas of the difference between the Scotch and Irish. The two Irishmen I mentioned were speaking of their treatment in England when the weaver said "Ah, you were a civil man but I was a drinker". Remember me to all—I intend writing to Haslam, but don't tell him for fear I should delay. We left a notice at Portpatrick that our letters should be thence forwarded to Glasgow. Our quick return from Ireland will occasion our passing Glasgow sooner than we thought—so till further notice you must direct to Inverness.

Your most affectionate brother,
John

Remember me to the Bentleys.

LETTER 22

To J. H. Reynolds Saturday–Monday, 11–13 July 1818
Mr J. H. Reynolds, Little Britain, Christ's Hospital, London

Maybole, July 11

My dear Reynolds,
    I'll not run over the ground we have passed, that would be merely as bad as telling a dream—unless perhaps I do it in the manner of the Laputan printing press—that is I put down mountains, rivers, lakes, dells, glens, rocks, and clouds, with beautiful, enchanting, Gothic, picturesque, fine, delightful, enchanting, grand, sublime—a few blisters, etc—and now you have our journey thus far: where I begin a letter to you because I am approaching Burns's cottage very fast. We have made continual enquiries from the time we saw his tomb at Dumfries—his name of course is known all about. His great reputation among the plodding people is "that he wrote a good *mony* sensible things". One of the pleasantest means of annulling self is approaching such a shrine as the cottage of Burns. We need not think of his misery—that is all gone—bad luck to it. I shall look upon it hereafter with unmixed pleasure as I do upon my Stratford on Avon day with Bailey. I shall fill this sheet for you in the bardie's country, going no further than this till I get into the town of Ayr which will be a 9 miles' walk to tea.
    [*13 July*]. We were talking on different and indifferent things, when on a sudden we turned a corner upon the immediate county of Ayr. The sight was as rich as possible. I had no conception that the native place of Burns was so beautiful. The idea I had was more desolate, his rigs of barley seemed always to me but a few strips of green on a cold hill—O prejudice! It was rich as Devon—I endeavoured to drink in the prospect, that I might spin it out to you as the silkworm makes silk from mulberry leaves—I cannot recollect it. Besides all the beauty, there were the mountains of Arran Isle, black and huge over the sea. We came down upon everything suddenly—there were in our way, the "bonny Doon", with the brig that Tam o' Shanter crossed—

TO J. H. REYNOLDS

Kirk Alloway, Burns's cottage and then the Brigs of Ayr. First we stood upon the bridge across the Doon, surrounded by every phantasy of green in tree, meadow, and hill. The stream of the Doon, as a farmer told us, is covered with trees from head to foot—you know those beautiful heaths so fresh against the weather of a summer's evening—there was one stretching along behind the trees. I wish I knew always the humour my friends would be in at opening a letter of mine, to suit it to them as nearly as possible. I could always find an egg shell for melancholy and as for merriment a witty humour will turn anything to account. My head is sometimes in such a whirl in considering the million likings and antipathies of our moments, that I can get into no settled strain in my letters. My wig! Burns and sentimentality coming across you and Frank Floodgate in the office—O scenery that thou shouldst be crushed between two puns. As for them I venture the rascalliest in the Scotch region—I hope Brown does not put them punctually in his journal. If he does I must sit on the cutty-stool all next winter. We went to kirk Alloway "a Prophet is no Prophet in his own country". We went to the cottage and took some whisky. I wrote a sonnet for the mere sake of writing some lines under the roof—they are so bad I cannot transcribe them. The man at the cottage was a great bore with his anecdotes—I hate the rascal—his life consists in fuz, fuzzy, fuzziest. He drinks glasses five for the quarter and twelve for the hour, he is a mahogany-faced old jackass who knew Burns. He ought to have been kicked for having spoken to him. He calls himself "a curious old bitch", but he is a flat old dog. I should like to employ Caliph Vathek to kick him. O the flummery of a birthplace! Cant! Cant! Cant! It is enough to give a spirit the guts-ache. Many a true word they say is spoken in jest—this may be because his gab hindered my sublimity. The flat dog made me write a flat sonnet. My dear Reynolds, I cannot write about scenery and visitings. Fancy is indeed less than a present palpable reality, but it is greater than remembrance—you would lift your eyes from Homer only to see close before you the real Isle of Tenedos. You would rather read Homer afterwards than remember yourself. One song of Burns's is of more worth to you than all I could think for a whole year in his native country. His misery is a dead weight upon the nimbleness of one's quill. I tried to forget it, to drink toddy without any care, to write a merry sonnet—it won't do—he talked with bitches—he drank with blackguards, he was miserable. We can see horribly clear in the works of such a man his whole life, as if we were God's spies. What were his addresses to Jean in the latter part of his life—I should not speak so to you—yet why not—you are not in the same case—you are in the right path, and you shall not be deceived. I have spoken to you against marriage, but it was general. The prospect in those matters has been to me so blank, that I have not been unwilling to die—I would not now, for I have inducements to life—I must see my little nephews in America, and I must see you marry your lovely wife. My sensations are sometimes deadened for weeks together—but believe me I have more than once yearned for the time of your happiness to come, as much as I could for myself after the lips of Juliet. From the tenor of my occasional rhodomontade in chit-chat, you might have been deceived concerning me in these points—upon my soul, I have been getting more and more close to you every day, ever since I knew you, and now one of the first pleasures I look to is your happy marriage—the more, since I have felt the pleasure of loving a sister-in-law. I did not think it possible to become so much attached in so short a time. Things like these, and they are real, have made me resolve to have a care of my health—you must be as careful. The rain has stopped us to-day at the end of a dozen miles, yet we hope to see Loch Lomond the day after tomorrow. I will piddle out my information, as Rice says, next winter at any time when a substitute is wanted for *vingt-et-un*. We bear the fatigue very well—20 miles a day in general. A cloud came over us in getting up Skiddaw—I hope to be more lucky in Ben Lomond—and more lucky still in Ben Nevis. What I think you would enjoy is poking about ruins, sometimes abbey, sometimes castle. The short stay we made in Ireland has left few remembrances—but an old woman in a dog-kennel sedan with a pipe in her mouth, is what I can never forget —I wish I may be able to give you an idea of her. Remember me to your mother and sisters, and tell your mother how I hope she will pardon me for having a scrap of paper pasted in the book sent to her. I was driven on all sides and had not time to call on Taylor. So Bailey is coming to Cumberland—well, if you'll let me know where at

Inverness, I will call on my return and pass a little time with him—I am glad 'tis not Scotland. Tell my friends I do all I can for them, that is drink their healths in toddy. Perhaps I may have some lines by and by to send you fresh on your own letter—Tom has a few to show you.

Your affectionate friend,
John Keats

LETTER 23

To Mrs James Wylie   *Thursday, 6 August* 1818
Mrs Wylie, Henrietta Street, London

Inverness, 6 August

My dear Madam,

It was a great regret to me that I should leave all my friends, just at the moment when I might have helped to soften away the time for them. I wanted not to leave my brother Tom, but more especially, believe me, I should like to have remained near you, were it but for an atom of consolation after parting with so dear a daughter; my brother George has ever been more than a brother to me, he has been my greatest friend, and I can never forget the sacrifice you have made for his happiness. As I walk along the mountains here I am full of these things, and lie in wait, as it were, for the pleasure of seeing you, immediately on my return to town. I wish above all things, to say a word of comfort to you, but I know not how. It is impossible to prove that black is white. It is impossible to make out, that sorrow is joy, or joy is sorrow.

Tom tells me that you called on Mr Haslam with a newspaper giving an account of a gentleman in a fur cap, falling over a precipice in Kirkcudbrightshire. If it was me, I did it in a dream, or in some magic interval between the first and second cup of tea; which is nothing extraordinary, when we hear that Mahomet, in getting out of bed, upset a jug of water, and whilst it was falling, took a fortnight's trip as it seemed, to Heaven, yet was back in time to save one drop of water being spilt. As for fur caps, I do not remember one beside my own, except at Carlisle—this was a very good fur cap I met in the High Street, and I daresay was the unfortunate one. I daresay that the fates seeing but two fur caps threw the dice which of them should be drowned. The lot fell upon Jonas. I daresay his name was Jonas. All I hope is that the gaunt ladies said not a word about hanging; if they did I shall one day regret that I was not half-drowned in Kirkcudbright. Stop! Let me see!—being half-drowned by falling from a precipice is a very romantic affair—why should I not take it to myself? Keep my secret and I will. How glorious to be introduced in a drawing-room to a lady who reads novels, with—"Mr So-and-So—Miss So-and-So; Miss So-and-So, this is Mr So-and-So who fell off a precipice and was half-drowned". Now I refer it to you whether I should lose so fine an opportunity of making my fortune. No romance lady could resist me, none. Being run under a wagon, side-lamed at a playhouse, apoplectic through brandy, and a thousand other tolerably decent things for badness would be nothing; but being tumbled over a precipice into the sea—oh it would make my fortune, especially if you would contrive to hint, from this bulletin's authority, that I was not upset on my own account, but that I dashed into the waves after Jessie of Dunblane—and pulled her out by the hair. But that, alas! she was dead or she would have made me happy with her hand— however in this you may use your own discretion. But I must leave joking, and seriously aver, that I have been *werry* romantic indeed, among these mountains and lakes. I have got wet through day after day, eaten oat-cake, and drank whisky, walked up to my knees in bog, got a sore throat, gone to see Icolmkill and Staffa, met with wholesome food, just here and there as it happened; went up Ben Nevis and, N.B., came down again. Sometimes when I am rather tired I lean rather languishingly on a rock, and long for some famous beauty to get down from her palfrey in passing, approach me with—her saddle-bags and give me—a dozen or two capital roast-beef sandwiches.

When I come into a large town, you know there is no putting one's knapsack into one's fob; so the people stare. We have been taken for spectacle vendors, razor-sellers, jewellers, travelling linen-drapers, spies, excisemen, and many things else I have no idea of. When I asked for letters at the Post Office, Portpatrick, the man asked what regiment? I have had a peep also at little Ireland. Tell Henry I have not camped quite on the bare earth yet; but nearly as bad, in walking through Mull—for the shepherds' huts you can scarcely breathe in, for the smoke which they seem to endeavour to preserve for smoking on a large scale. Besides riding about 400, we have walked above 600 miles, and may therefore reckon ourselves as set out.

I wish, my dear Madam, that one of the greatest pleasures I shall have on my return, will be seeing you and that I shall ever be,

Yours with the greatest respect and sincerity,

John Keats

LETTER 24

To Fanny Keats *Tuesday, 19 August 1818*
Miss Keats, Miss Tuckey's, Walthamstow

Hampstead, August 18th

My dear Fanny,

I am afraid you will think *me* very negligent in not having answered your letter—I see it is dated June 12—I did not arrive at Inverness till the 8th of this month so I am very much concerned at your being disappointed so long a time. I did not intend to have returned to London so soon but have a bad sore throat from a cold I caught in the island of Mull: therefore I thought it best to get home as soon as possible and went on board the smack from Cromarty. We had a nine days passage and landed at London Bridge yesterday. I shall have a good deal to tell you about Scotland—I would begin here but I have a confounded tooth-ache. Tom has not been getting better since I left London and for the last fortnight has been worse than ever—he has been getting a little better for these two or three days. I shall ask Mr Abbey to let me bring you to Hampstead. If Mr A. should see this letter tell him that he still must if he pleases forward the post bill to Perth as I have empowered my fellow traveller to receive it. I have a few scotch pebbles for you from the Island of Icolmkill—I am afraid they are rather shabby—I did not go near the Mountain of Cairn Gorm. I do not know the name of George's ship—the name of the port he has gone to is Philadelphia whence he will travel to the settlement across the country—I will tell you all about this when I see you—the title of my last book is *Endymion:* you shall have one soon. I would not advise you to play on the flageolet, however I will get you one if you please. I will speak to Mr Abbey on what you say concerning school. I am sorry for your poor canary. You shall have another volume of my first book. My tooth-ache keeps on so that I cannot write with any pleasure—all I can say now is that your letter is a very nice one without any fault and that you will hear from or see in a few days, if his throat will let him,

Your affectionate brother,
John

LETTER 25

To Fanny Keats   *Tuesday, 25 August* 1818
Miss Keats, Miss Tuckey's, Walthamstow

Hampstead, Tuesday

My dear Fanny,

I have just written to Mr Abbey to ask him to let you come and see poor Tom who has lately been much worse. He is better at present, sends his love to you and wishes much to see you—I hope he will shortly—I have not been able to come to Walthamstow on his account as well as a little indisposition of my own. I have asked Mr A. to write me—if he does not mention anything of it to you, I will tell you what reasons he has, though I do not think he will make any objection. Write me what you want with a flageolet and I will get one ready for you by the time you come.

Your affectionate brother,
John

TO J. H. REYNOLDS

LETTER 26

To J. H. Reynolds   *(?) Tuesday, 22 September* 1818

My dear Reynolds,

   Believe me I have rather rejoiced in your happiness than fretted at your silence. Indeed I am grieved on your account that I am not at the same time happy—but I conjure you to think at present of nothing but pleasure—"Gather the rose, etc", gorge the honey of life. I pity you as much that it cannot last for ever, as I do myself now drinking bitters. Give yourself up to it—you cannot help it—and I have a consolation in thinking so. I never was in love—yet the voice and the shape of a woman has haunted me these two days—at such a time when the relief, the feverous relief of poetry seems a much less crime. This morning poetry has conquered—I have relapsed into those abstractions which are my only life. I feel escaped from a new, strange and threatening sorrow, and I am thankful for it. There is an awful warmth about my heart like a load of immortality.

   Poor Tom—that woman—and poetry were ringing changes in my senses. Now I am in comparison happy. I am sensible this will distress you—you must forgive me. Had I known you would have set out so soon I could have sent you "The Pot of Basil" for I had copied it out ready.

   Here is a free translation of a sonnet of Ronsard, which I think will please you—I have the loan of his works—they have great beauties.

> Nature withheld Cassandra in the skies,
>   For more adornment, a full thousand years;
> She took their cream of Beauty's fairest dyes,
>   And shap'd and tinted her above all peers:
> Meanwhile Love kept her dearly with his wings,
>   And underneath their shadow fill'd her eyes
> With such a richness that the cloudy kings
>   Of high Olympus utter'd slavish sighs.
> When from the heavens I saw her first descend,
>   My heart took fire, and only burning pains,

> They were my pleasures—they my life's sad end;
> Love pour'd her beauty into my warm veins . . .

I had not the original by me when I wrote it, and did not recollect the purport of the last lines.

I should have seen Rice ere this—but I am confined by Sawrey's mandate in the house now, and have as yet only gone out in fear of the damp night. You know what an undangerous matter it is. I shall soon be quite recovered. Your offer I shall remember as though it had even now taken place in fact—I think it cannot be. Tom is not up yet—I cannot say he is better. I have not heard from George.

Your affectionate friend,
John Keats

LETTER 27

To J. A. Hessey   *Friday,* 8 *October* 1818
J. A. Hessey Esq, Fleet Street

My dear Hessey,

You are very good in sending me the letter from the Chronicle, and I am very bad in not acknowledging such a kindness sooner—pray forgive me. It has so chanced that I have had that paper every day—I have seen today's. I cannot but feel indebted to those gentlemen who have taken my part. As for the rest, I begin to get a little acquainted with my own strength and weakness. Praise or blame has but a momentary effect on the man whose love of beauty in the abstract makes him a severe critic of his own works. My own domestic criticism has given me pain without comparison beyond what Blackwood or the Quarterly could possibly inflict, and also when I feel I am right, no external praise can give me such a glow as my own solitary re-perception and ratification of what is fine. J.S. is perfectly right in regard to the slip-shod *Endymion*. That it is so is no fault of mine. No!—though it may sound a little paradoxical. It is as good as I had power to make it—by myself. Had I been nervous about its being a perfect piece, and with that view asked advice, and trembled over every page, it would not have been written; for it is not in my nature to fumble. I will write independently. I have written independently *without judgment*. I may write independently, and *with judgment* hereafter. The genius of poetry must work out its own salvation in a man: it cannot be matured by law and precept, but by sensation and watchfulness in itself. That which is creative must create itself. In *Endymion*, I leaped headlong into the sea, and thereby have become better acquainted with the soundings, the quicksands and the rocks, than if I had stayed upon the green shore, and piped a silly pipe, and took tea and comfortable advice. I was never afraid of failure; for I would sooner fail than not be among the greatest. But I am nigh getting into a rant. So, with remembrances to Taylor and Woodhouse, etc, I am

Yours very sincerely,
John Keats

LETTER 28

To Fanny Keats   *Friday,* 16 *October* 1818
Miss Keats, Miss Tuckey's, Walthamstow

Hampstead, Friday Morn

My dear Fanny,

You must condemn me for not being punctual to Thursday, for I really did not know whether it would not affect poor Tom too much to see you. You know how it hurt him to part with you the last time. At all events you shall hear from me; and if Tom keeps pretty well tomorrow I will see Mr Abbey the next day, and endeavour to settle that you shall be with us on Tuesday or Wednesday. I have good news from George. He has landed safely with our sister, they are both in good health, their prospects are good, and they are by this time nighing to their journey's end. You shall hear the particulars soon.

Your affectionate brother,
John

Tom's love to you.

LETTER 29

To Fanny Keats *Monday, 26 October* 1818
Miss Keats, Miss Tuckey's, Walthamstow

My dear Fanny,
　I called on Mr Abbey in the beginning of last week, when he seemed averse to letting you come again from having heard that you had been to other places besides Well Walk. I do not mean to say you did wrongly in speaking of it, for there should rightly be no objection to such things: but you know with what people we are obliged in the course of childhood to associate, whose conduct forces us into duplicity and falsehood to them. To the worst of people we should be openhearted; but it is as well as things are to be prudent in making any communication to anyone, that may throw an impediment in the way of any of the little pleasures you may have. I do not recommend duplicity but prudence with such people. Perhaps I am talking too deeply for you; if you do not now, you will understand what I mean in the course of a few years. I think poor Tom is a little better; he sends his love to you. I shall call on Mr Abbey tomorrow, when I hope to settle when to see you again. Mrs Dilke has been for sometime at Brighton—she is expected home in a day or two. She will be pleased I am sure with your present. I will try for permission for you to remain here all night should Mrs D. return in time.

　　　　　　　　　　　　　　　Your affectionate brother,
　　　　　　　　　　　　　　　　　　　　John

LETTER 30

To Richard Woodhouse   *Tuesday, 27 October 1818*
Richd. Woodhouse Esq, Temple

My dear Woodhouse,

   Your letter gave me a great satisfaction, more on account of its friendliness than any relish of that matter in it which is accounted so acceptable in the "*genus irritabile*". The best answer I can give you is in a clerk-like manner to make some observations on two principal points, which seem to point like indices into the midst of the whole pro and con, about genius, and views and achievements and ambition and *cetera*. First: as to the poetical character itself (I mean that sort of which, if I am anything, I am a member; that sort distinguished from the Wordsworthian or egotistical sublime, which is a thing *per se* and stands alone) it is not itself—it has no self—it is everything and nothing. It has no character—it enjoys light and shade; it lives in gusto, be it foul or fair, high or low, rich or poor, mean or elevated. It has as much delight in conceiving a Iago as an Imogen. What shocks the virtuous philosopher, delights the chameleon poet. It does no harm from its relish of the dark side of things any more than from its taste for the bright one; because they both end in speculation. A poet is the most unpoetical of anything in existence, because he has no identity—he is continually in for, and filling, some other body—the sun, the moon, the sea, and men and women who are creatures of impulse are poetical and have about them an unchangeable attribute—the poet has none; no identity—he is certainly the most unpoetical of all God's creatures. If then he has no self, and if I am a poet, where is the wonder that I should say I would write no more? Might I not at that very instant have been cogitating on the characters of Saturn and Ops? It is a wretched thing to confess, but is a very fact, that not one word I ever utter can be taken for granted as an opinion growing out of my identical nature—how can it, when I have no nature? When I am in a room with people if I ever am free from speculating on creations of my own brain, then not myself goes home to myself, but the identity of every one in the room begins so to press upon me that I am in a very little time annihilated—not only among men; it would be the same in a nursery of children. I know not whether I make myself wholly understood. I hope enough so to let you see that no dependence is to be placed on what I said that day.

In the second place I will speak of my views, and of the life I purpose to myself—I am ambitious of doing the world some good. If I should be spared that may be the work of maturer years—in the interval I will assay to reach to as high a summit in poetry as the nerve bestowed upon me will suffer. The faint conceptions I have of poems to come brings the blood frequently into my forehead. All I hope is that I may not lose all interest in human affairs—that the solitary indifference I feel for applause even from the finest spirits, will not blunt any acuteness of vision I may have. I do not think it will—I feel assured I should write from the mere yearning and fondness I have for the beautiful even if my night's labours should be burnt every morning, and no eye ever shine upon them. But even now I am perhaps not speaking from myself: but from some character in whose soul I now live. I am sure however that this next sentence is from myself. I feel your anxiety, good opinion and friendliness in the highest degree, and am

Yours most sincerely,
John Keats

LETTER 31

To Fanny Keats   30 *November* 1818
Miss Keats, Miss Caley's School, Walthamstow

Tuesday Morn

My dear Fanny,

Poor Tom has been so bad that I have delayed your visit hither—as it would be so painful to you both. I cannot say he is any better this morning—he is in a very dangerous state—I have scarce any hopes of him. Keep up your spirits for me my dear Fanny—repose entirely in

Your affectionate brother,
John

LETTER 32

To John Taylor *Thursday, 24 December* 1818
John Taylor Esq, Taylor & Hessey's, Fleet Street
                                         Wentworth Place
My dear Taylor,
   Can you lend me £30 for a short time?—ten I want for myself—and twenty for a friend, which will be repaid me by the middle of next month. I shall go to Chichester on Wednesday and perhaps stay a fortnight. I am afraid I shall not be able to dine with you before I return. Remember me to Woodhouse.
                                         Yours sincerely,
                                         John Keats

LETTER 33

To Fanny Keats *Saturday, 27 February* 1819
Miss Keats, R^d Abbey's Esq, Walthamstow
                       Wentworth Place, Saturday Morn
My dear Fanny,
   I intended to have not failed to do as you requested, and write you as you say once a fortnight. On looking to your letter I find there is no date; and not knowing how long it is since I received it I do not precisely know how great a sinner I am. I am getting quite well, and Mrs Dilke is getting on pretty well. You must pay no attention to Mrs Abbey's unfeeling and ignorant gabble. You can't stop an old woman's crying more than you can a child's. The old woman is the greatest nuisance because she is too old for the rod. Many people live opposite a blacksmith's till they cannot hear the hammer. I have been in town for two or three days and came back last night. I have been a little concerned at not hearing from George—I continue in daily expectation. Keep on reading and play as much on the music and the grassplot as

you can. I should like to take possession of those grassplots for a month or so; and send Mrs A. to town to count coffee berries instead of currant bunches, for I want you to teach me a few common dancing steps—and I would buy a watch box to practise them in by myself. I think I had better always pay the postage of these letters. I shall send you another book the first time I am in town early enough to book it with one of the morning Walthamstow coaches. You did not say a word about your chilblains. Write me directly and let me know about them—your letter shall be answered like an echo.

Your affectionate brother,
John

LETTER 34

To Fanny Keats   *Saturday, 13 March 1819*
Miss Keats, Rd. Abbey's Esq, Walthamstow

Wentworth Place, March 13th

My dear Fanny,

I have been employed lately in writing to George—I do not send him very short letters—but keep on day after day. There were some young men I think I told you of who were going to the settlement: they have changed their minds, and I am disappointed in my expectations of sending letters by them. I went lately to the only dance I have been to these twelve months or shall go to for twelve months again—it was to our brother-in-law's cousin's. She gave a dance for her birthday and I went for the sake of Mrs Wylie. I am waiting every day to hear from George. I trust there is no harm in the silence: other people are in the same expectation as we are. On looking at your seal I cannot tell whether it is done or not with a Tassie—it seems to me to be paste. As I went through Leicester Square lately I was going to call and buy you some, but not knowing but you might have some I would not run the chance of buying duplicates. Tell me if you have any or if you would like any—and whether you would rather have motto ones like that with which I seal this letter, or heads of great men such as Shakespeare, Milton, etc, or fancy pieces of art, such as Fame, Adonis, etc—those gentry you read of at the end of the English Dictionary. Tell me also if you want any particular book, or pencils, or drawing paper—anything but livestock. Though I will not now be very severe on it, remembering how fond I used to be of goldfinches, tomtits, minnows, mice, ticklebacks, dace, cock salmons and all the whole tribe of the bushes and the brooks: but verily they are better in the trees and the water—though I must confess even now a partiality for a handsome globe of goldfish—then I would have it hold 10 pails of water and be fed continually fresh through a cool pipe with another pipe to let through the floor—well ventilated, they would preserve all their beautiful silver and crimson. Then I would put it before a handsome painted window and shade it all round with myrtles and japonicas. I should like the window to open on to the Lake of Geneva—and there I'd sit and read all day like the picture of somebody reading. The weather now and then begins to feel like spring; and therefore I have begun my walks on the heath again. Mrs Dilke is getting better than she has been as she has at length taken a physician's advice. She ever and anon asks after you and always bids me remember her in my letters to you. She is going to leave Hampstead for the sake of educating their son Charles at the Westminster school. We (Mr Brown and I) shall leave in the beginning of May; I do not know what I shall do or where be all next summer. Mrs Reynolds has had a sick house, but they are all well now. You see what news I can send you I do—we all live one day like the other as well as you do—the only difference is being sick and well—with the variations of single and double knocks; and the story of a dreadful fire in the newspapers. I mentioned Mr Brown's name—yet I do not think I ever said a word about him to you. He is a friend of mine of two years' standing—with whom I walked through Scotland, who has been very kind to me in many things when I most wanted his assistance and with whom I keep house till the first of May—you will know him some day. The name of the young man who came with me is William Haslam.

Ever, your affectionate brother,
John

LETTER 35

To Fanny Keats 1 *May* 1819
Miss Keats, R^d Abbey's Esq, Walthamstow

Wentworth Place, Saturday

My dear Fanny,

If it were but six o'clock in the morning I would set off to see you to-day: if I should do so now I could not stop long enough for a how d'ye do—it is so long a walk through Hornsey and Tottenham—and as for stage coaching it, besides that it is very expensive, it is like going into the boxes by way of the pit. I cannot go out on Sunday, but if on Monday it should promise as fair as to-day I will put on a pair of loose easy palatable boots and *me rendre chez vous*. I continue to increase my letter to George to send it by one of Birkbeck's sons who is going out soon, so if you will let me have a few more lines, they will be in time. I am glad you got on so well with Monsieur le Curé—is he a nice clergyman?—a great deal depends upon a cocked hat and powder—not gunpowder, lord love us, but lady-meal, violet-smooth, dainty-scented, lily-white, feather-soft, wigsby-dressing, coat-collar-spoiling, whisker-reaching, pig-tail loving, swansdown-puffing, parson-sweetening powder—I shall call in passing at the Tottenham nursery and see if I can find some seasonable plants for you. That is the nearest place—or by our la'kin or lady kin, that is by the Virgin Mary's kindred, is there not a twig-manufacturer in Walthamstow? Mr and Mrs Dilke are coming to dine with us to-day—they will enjoy the country after Westminster—O there is nothing like fine weather, and health, and books, and a fine country, and a contented mind, and diligent habit of reading and thinking, and an amulet against the ennui—and, please heaven, a little claret-wine cool out of a cellar a mile deep—with a few or a good many ratafia cakes, a rocky basin to bathe in, a strawberry bed to say your prayers to Flora in, a pad nag to go you ten miles or so; two or three sensible people to chat with; two or three spiteful folks to spar with; two or three odd fishes to laugh at and two or three numskulls to argue with—instead of using dumb-bells on a rainy day:

TO FANNY KEATS

Two or three posies
With two or three simples
Two or three noses
With two or three pimples
Two or three wise men
And two or three ninnies
Two or three purses
And two or three guineas
Two or three raps
At two or three doors
Two or three naps
Of two or three hours—
Two or three cats
And two or three mice
Two or three sprats
At a very great price—
Two or three sandies
And two or three tabbies
Two or three dandies—
And two Mrs—mum!
Two or three smiles
And two or three frowns
Two or three miles
To two or three towns
Two or three pegs
For two or three bonnets
Two or three dove's eggs
To hatch into sonnets

Goodbye, I've an appointment—can't stop—pon word—goodbye—now don't get up—open the door myself—go-o-odbye—see ye Monday

J—K—

LETTER 36

To George and Georgiana Keats   Sunday, 14 February–Monday, 3 May
                                                                 1819

                                         Sunday Morn, Feby 14
My dear Brother and Sister—
   How is it we have not heard from you from the settlement yet? The letters must surely have miscarried. I am in expectation every day. Peachey wrote me a few days ago saying some more acquaintances of his were preparing to set out for Birkbeck, therefore I shall take the opportunity of sending you what I can muster in a sheet or two. I am still at Wentworth Place, indeed I have kept indoors lately, resolved if possible to rid myself of my sore throat. Consequently I have not been to see your mother since my return from Chichester, but my absence from her has been a great weight upon me. I say since my return from Chichester—I believe I told you I was going thither—I was nearly a fortnight at Mr John Snook's and a few days at old Mr Dilke's. Nothing worth speaking of happened at either place. I took down some of the thin paper and wrote on it a little poem called "St Agnes Eve," which you shall have as it is when I have finished the blank part of the rest for you. I went out twice at Chichester to old dowager card parties. I see very little now, and very few persons—being almost tired of men and things. Brown and Dilke are very kind and considerate towards me. The Miss Reynoldses have been stopping next door lately —but all very dull. Miss Brawne and I have every now and then a chat and a tiff. Brown and Dilke are walking round their garden hands in pockets making observations. The literary world I know nothing about—there is a poem from Rogers dead born, and another satire is expected from Byron called "Don Giovanni". Yesterday I went to town for the first time for these three weeks. I met people from all parts and of all sets—Mr Towers, one of the Holts, Mr Domine Williams, Mr Woodhouse, Mrs Hazlitt and son, Mrs Webb, Mrs Septimus Brown. Mr Woodhouse was looking up at a book-window in Newgate

Street and being short-sighted twisted his muscles into so queer a stupe that I stood by in doubt whether it was him or his brother, if he has one, and turning round saw Mrs Hazlitt with that little Nero her son. Woodhouse on his features subsiding proved to be Woodhouse and not his brother.

   I have had a little business with Mr Abbey. From time to time he has behaved to me with a little brusquerie—this hurt me a little especially when I knew him to be the only man in England who dared to say a thing to me I did not approve of without its being resented or at least noticed. So I wrote him about it and have made an alteration in my favour. I expect from this to see more of Fanny, who has been quite shut out from me. I see Cobbett has been attacking the settlement, but I cannot tell what to believe, and shall be all out at elbows till I hear from you. I am invited to Miss Millar's birthday dance on the 19th: I am nearly sure I shall not be able to go—a dance would injure my throat very much. I see very little of Reynolds. Hunt I hear is going on very badly—I mean in money matters. I shall not be surprised to hear of the worst. Haydon too in consequence of his eyes is out at elbows. I live as prudently as it is possible for me to do. I have not seen Haslam lately—I have not seen Richards for this half year—Rice for three months or C.C.C. for God knows when. When I last called in Henrietta Street, Mrs Millar was very unwell, Miss Waldegrave as staid and self possessed as usual. Miss Millar was well. Henry was well. There are two new tragedies, one by the Apostate man, and one by Miss Jane Porter. Next week I am going to stop at Taylor's for a few days when I will see them both and tell you what they are. Mrs and Mr Bentley are well and all the young carrots. I said nothing of consequence passed at Snook's—no more than this, that I like the family very much. Mr and Mrs Snook were very kind—we used to have over a little religion and politics together almost every evening—and sometimes about you. He proposed writing out for me all the best part of his experience in farming to send to you; if I should have an opportunity of talking to him about it I will get all I can at all events, but you may say in your answer to this what value you place upon such information. I have not seen Mr Lewis lately, for I have shrunk from going up the hill. Mr Lewis went a few mornings ago to town with Mrs Brawne: they talked about me, and I heard that Mr L. said a thing I am not at all contented with. Says he "O, he is quite the little poet". Now this is abominable—you might as well say Bonaparte is quite the little soldier. You see what it is to be under six foot and not a lord. There is a long fuzz to-day in the *Examiner* about a young man who delighted a young woman with a Valentine—I think it must be Ollier's. Brown and I are thinking of passing the summer at Brussels; if we do we shall go about the first of May. We, i.e. Brown and I, sit opposite one another all day authorizing (N.B. an *s* instead of a *z* would give a different meaning). He is at present writing a story of an old woman who lived in a forest and to whom the devil or one of his *aide de feus* came one night very late and in disguise. The old dame sets before him pudding after pudding—mess after mess—which he devours and moreover casts his eyes up at a side of bacon hanging over his head and at the same time asks whether her cat is a rabbit. On going he leaves her three pips of Eve's apple—and somehow she, having lived a virgin all her life, begins to repent of it and wishes herself beautiful enough to make all the world and even the other world fall in love with her. So it happens. She sets out from her smoky cottage in magnificent apparel; the first city she enters every one falls in love with her—from the Prince to the blacksmith. A young gentleman on his way to the church to be married leaves his unfortunate bride and follows this nonsuch. A whole regiment of soldiers are smitten at once and follow her. A whole convent of monks in Corpus Christi procession join the soldiers. The Mayor and Corporation follow the same road. Old and young, deaf and dumb—all but the blind are smitten and form an immense concourse of people who—what Brown will do with them I know not. The devil himself falls in love with her, flies away with her to a desert place—in consequence of which she lays an infinite number of eggs. The eggs being hatched from time to time fill the world with many nuisances such as John Knox, George Fox, Johanna Southcott, Gifford.

There have been within a fortnight eight failures of the highest consequence in London. Brown went a few evenings since to Davenport's and on his coming in he talked about bad news in the city with such a face, I began to think of a national bankruptcy. I did not feel much surprised, and was rather disappointed. Carlile, a bookseller on the *Hone* principle has been issuing pamphlets from his shop in Fleet Street called the Deist—he was conveyed to Newgate last Thursday. He intends making his own defence. I was surprised to hear from Taylor the amount of Murray the bookseller's last sale—what think you of £25,000? He sold 4,000 copies of Lord Byron. I am sitting opposite the Shakespeare I brought from the Isle of Wight, and I never look at it but the silk tassels on it give me as much pleasure as the face of the poet itself, except that I do not know how you are going on. In my next packet as this is one by the way, I shall send you "The Pot of Basil", "St Agnes Eve", and if I should have finished it, a little thing called "The Eve of St Mark". You see what fine mother Radcliff names I have—it is not my fault—I did not search for them. I have not gone on with "Hyperion", for to tell the truth I have not been in great cue for writing lately. I must wait for the spring to rouse me up a little. The only time I went out from Bedhampton was to see a chapel consecrated—Brown and I and John Snook the boy, went in a chaise behind a leaden horse Brown drove, but the horse did not mind him. This chapel is built by a Mr Way, a great Jew converter, who in that line has spent one hundred thousand pounds. He maintains a great number of poor Jews. Of course his communion plate was stolen—he spoke to the Clerk about it. The Clerk said he was very sorry, adding "I dare shay your honour its among ush". The chapel is built in Mr Way's park. The consecration was—not amusing—there were numbers of carriages, and his house crammed with clergy. They sanctified the chapel, and it being a wet day consecrated the burial ground through the vestry window. I begin to hate parsons—they did not make me love them that day when I saw them in their proper colours. A parson is a lamb in a drawing room and a lion in a vestry. The notions of society will not permit a parson to give way to his temper in any shape, so he festers in himself—his features get a peculiar, diabolical, self-sufficient, iron stupid expression. He is continually acting. His mind is against every man and every man's mind is against him. He is a hypocrite to the believer and a coward to the unbeliever. He must be either a knave or an idiot. And there is no man so much to be pitied as an idiot parson. The soldier who is cheated into an *esprit de corps* by a red coat, a band and colours for the purpose of nothing, is not half so pitiable as the parson who is led by the nose by the bench of bishops and is smothered in absurdities—a poor necessary subaltern of the church.

Friday Feby. 19—The day before yesterday I went to Romney Street. Your mother was not at home, but I have just written her that I shall see her on Wednesday. I called on Mr Lewis this morning—he is very well—and tells me not to be uneasy about letters, the chances being so arbitrary. He is going on as usual among his favourite democrat papers. We had a chat as usual about Cobbett, and the Westminster electors. Dilke has lately been very much harassed about the manner of educating his son. He at length decided for a public school—and then he did not know what school. He at last has decided for Westminster; and as Charley is to be a day boy, Dilke will remove to Westminster. We lead very quiet lives here—Dilke is at present in Greek histories and antiquities, and talks of nothing but the electors of Westminster and the retreat of the ten-thousand. I never drink now above three glasses of wine, and never any spirits and water. Though by the by the other day Woodhouse took me to his coffee house and ordered a bottle of claret. Now I like claret. Whenever I can have claret I must drink it—'tis the only palate affair that I am at all sensual in. Would it not be a good spec to send you some vine roots—could it be done? I'll enquire—if you could make some wine like claret to drink on summer evenings in an arbour! For really 'tis so fine—it fills the mouth, one's mouth, with a gushing freshness—then goes down cool and feverless. Then you do not feel it quarrelling with your liver—no, it is rather a peace-maker and lies as quiet as it did in the grape. Then it is as fragrant as the queen bee; and the more ethereal part of it mounts into the brain, not assaulting the cerebral apartments like a bully in a bad-house looking for his trull and hurrying from door to door bouncing against the wainscot, but rather walks like Aladdin about his own enchanted palace so gently that you do not feel his step. Other wines of a heavy and spirituous nature transform a man to a Silenus; this makes him a Hermes—and gives a woman the soul and immortality of Ariadne for whom Bacchus always kept a good cellar of claret—and even of that he could never persuade her to take above two cups. I said this same claret is the only palate-passion I have—I forgot game. I must plead guilty to the breast of a partridge, the back of a hare, the backbone of a grouse, the wing and side of a pheasant and a woodcock *passim*.

Talking of game (I wish I could make it) the lady whom I met at Hastings and of whom I said something in my last I think, has lately made me many presents of game, and enabled me to make as many. She made me take home a pheasant the other day which I gave to Mrs Dilke; on which, tomorrow, Rice, Reynolds and the Wentworthians will dine next door. The next I intend for your mother. These moderate sheets of paper are much more pleasant to write upon than those large thin sheets which I hope you by this time have received—though that can't be now I think of it. I have not said in any letter yet a word about my affairs—in a word I am in no despair about them. My poem has not at all succeeded—in the course of a year or so I think I shall try the public again. In a selfish point of view I should suffer my pride and my contempt of public opinion to hold me silent, but for yours and Fanny's sake I will pluck up a spirit and try again. I have no doubt of success in a course of years if I persevere, but it must be patience, for the reviews have enervated and made indolent men's minds—few think for themselves. These reviews too are getting more and more powerful and especially the *Quarterly*. They are like a superstition which the more it prostrates the crowd and the longer it continues the more powerful it becomes just in proportion to their increasing weakness. I was in hopes that when people saw, as they must do now, all the trickery and iniquity of these plagues they would scout them, but no, they are like the spectators at the Westminster cock-pit—they like the battle and do not care who wins or who loses. Brown is going on this morning with the story of his old woman and the devil. He makes but slow progress. The fact is it is a libel on the devil and as that person is Brown's muse, look ye, if he libels his own muse how can he expect to write? Either Brown or his muse must turn tail. Yesterday was Charley Dilke's birthday—Brown and I were invited to tea. During the evening nothing passed worth notice but a little conversation between Mrs Dilke and Mrs Brawne. The subject was the watchman. It was ten o'clock and Mrs Brawne, who lived during the summer in Brown's house and now lives in the road, recognized her old watchman's voice and said that he came as far as her now: "Indeed", said Mrs D, "does he turn the corner?" There have been some letters pass between me and Haslam, but I have not seen him lately. The day before yesterday—which I made a day of business, I called upon him—he was out as usual. Brown has been walking up and down the room a-breeding—now at this moment he is being delivered of a couplet, and I daresay will be as well as can be expected. Gracious—he has twins! I have a long story to tell you about Bailey—I will say first the circumstances as plainly and as well as I can remember and then I will make my comment. You know that Bailey was very much cut up about a little jilt in the country somewhere. I thought he was in a dying state about it when at Oxford with him, little supposing as I have since heard, that he was at that very time making impatient love to Mariane Reynolds—and guess my astonishment at hearing after this that he had been trying at Miss Martin. So matters have been. So matters stood, when he got ordained and went to a curacy near Carlisle where the family of the Gleigs reside. There his susceptible heart was conquered by Miss Gleig, and thereby all his connections in town have been annulled, both male and female. I do not now remember clearly the facts. These however I know. He showed his correspondence with Mariane to Gleig—returned all her letters and asked for his own. He also wrote very abrupt letters to Mrs Reynolds. I do not know any more of the Martin affair than I have written above. No doubt his conduct has been very bad. The great thing to be considered is, whether it is want of delicacy and principle or want of knowledge and polite experience. And again weakness—yes that is it—and the want of a wife. Yes that is it—and then Mariane made great bones of him although her mother and sister have teased her very much about it. Her conduct has been very upright throughout the whole affair. She liked Bailey as a brother—but not as a husband—especially as he used to woo her with the Bible and Jeremy Taylor under his arm—they walked in no grove but Jeremy Taylor's. Mariane's obstinacy is some excuse, but his so quickly taking to Miss Gleig can have no excuse—except that of a ploughman's who wants a wife. The thing which sways me more against him than anything else is Rice's conduct on the occasion; Rice would not make an immature resolve; he was ardent in his friendship for Bailey; he examined the whole for and against minutely; and he has abandoned Bailey entirely. All this I am not supposed by the Reynoldses to have any hint of. It will be a good lesson to the mother and daughters—nothing would serve but Bailey. If you mentioned the word teapot some one of them came out with an *à propos* about Bailey—noble fellow—fine fellow! was always in their mouths. This may teach them that the man who ridicules romance is the most romantic of men—that he who abuses women and slights them loves them the most—that he who talks of roasting a man alive would not do it when it came to the push, and above all that they are very shallow people who take everything literally. A man's life of any worth is a continual allegory, and very few eyes can see the mystery of his life—a life like the scriptures, figurative, which such people can no more make out than they can the Hebrew bible. Lord Byron cuts a figure—but he is not figurative. Shakespeare led a life of allegory: his works are the comments on it.

On Monday we had to dinner Severn and Cawthorn, the bookseller and print-virtuoso; in the evening Severn went home to paint, and we other three went to the play, to see Sheil's new tragedy ycleped *Evadne*. In the morning Severn and I took a turn round the Museum—there is a sphinx there of a giant size, and most voluptuous Egyptian expression. I had not seen it before. The play was bad even in comparison with 1818, the Augustan age of the Drama, *"comme on sait"*, as Voltaire says. The whole was made up of a virtuous young woman, an indignant brother, a suspecting lover, a libertine prince, a gratuitous villain, a street in Naples, a cypress grove, lilies and roses, virtue and vice, a bloody sword, a spangled jacket, one Lady Olivia, one Miss O'Neil alias Evadne, alias Bellamira, alias, alias—Yea, and I say unto you a greater than Elias. There was Abbot, and talking of Abbot his name puts me in mind of a spelling book lesson, descriptive of the whole dramatis personae—Abbot—Abbess—Actor—Actress. The play is a fine amusement, as a friend of mine once said to me: "Do what you will", says he, "a poor gentleman who wants a guinea cannot spend his two shillings better than at the playhouse". The pantomime was excellent, I had seen it before and I enjoyed it again. Your mother and I had some talk about Miss H. Says I, Will Henry have that Miss H, a lath with a bodice? She who has been fine drawn—fit for nothing but to cut up into cribbage pins, to the tune of 15-2; one who is all muslin, all feathers and bone; once in travelling she was made use of as a lynch pin. I hope he will not have her, though it is no uncommon thing to be *smitten with a staff;* though she might be very useful as his walking-stick, his fishing-rod, his tooth-pick, his hat-stick (she runs so much in his head)—let him turn farmer, she would cut into hurdles; let him write poetry, she would be his turnstyle. Her gown is like a flag on a pole; she would do for him if he turn freemason. I hope she will prove a flag of truce. When she sits languishing with her one foot on a stool, and one elbow on the table, and her head inclined, she looks like the sign of the crooked billet, or the frontispiece to Cinderella or a tea-paper wood-cut of Mother Shipton at her studies. She is a make-believe. She is *bona side* a thin young 'oman—but this is mere talk of a fellow creature; yet pardie I would not that Henry have her—*Non volo ut eam possideat, nam,* for, it would be a bam, for it would be a sham.

Don't think I am writing a petition to the Governors of St Luke's—no, that would be in another style. May it please your worships; forasmuch as the undersigned has committed, transferred, given up, made over, consigned, and aberrated himself, to the art and mystery of poetry; forasmuch as he hath cut, rebuffed, affronted, huffed, and shirked, and taken stint, at all other employments, arts, mysteries and occupations, honest, middling, and dishonest; forasmuch as he hath at sundry times and in diverse places told truth unto the men of this generation, and eke to the women, moreover; forasmuch as he hath kept a pair of boots that did not fit, and doth not admire Sheil's play, Leigh Hunt, Tom Moore, Bob Southey, and Mr Rogers; and does admire Wm. Hazlitt; moreoverer, for as more as he liketh half of Wordsworth and none of Crabbe; moreoverest for as most as he hath written this page of penmanship—he prayeth your Worships to give him a lodging—Witnessed by Rd. Abbey and Co. *cum familiaribus* and *consanguiniis,* (signed) Count de Cockaigne.

The nothing of the day is a machine called the velocipede. It is a wheel carriage to ride cock-horse upon, sitting astride and pushing it along with the toes, a rudder wheel in hand—they will go seven miles an hour. A handsome gelding will come to eight guineas; however they will soon be cheaper, unless the army takes to them. I look back upon the last month, and find nothing to write about; indeed I do not recollect anything particular in it. It's all alike; we keep on breathing. The only amusement is a little scandal, of however fine a shape, a laugh at a pun—and then after all we wonder how we could enjoy the scandal or laugh at the pun.

I have been at different times turning it in my head whether I should go to Edinburgh and study for a physician; I am afraid I should not take kindly to it; I am sure I could not take fees—and yet I should like to do so. It's not worse than writing poems, and hanging them up to be fly-blown on the review-shambles. Everybody is in his own mess. Here is the parson at Hampstead quarrelling with all the world, he is in the wrong by this same token; when the black cloth was put up in the church for the Queen's mourning, he asked the workmen to hang it the wrong side outwards, that it might be better when taken down, it being his perquisite. Parsons will always keep up their character, but as it is said there are some animals the ancients knew which we do not, let us hope our posterity will miss the black badger with tricornered hat; who knows but some reviser of Buffon or Pliny may put an account of the parson in the appendix; no one will then believe it any more than we believe in the Phoenix. I think we may class the lawyer in the same natural history of monsters; a green bag will hold as much as a lawn sleeve. The only difference is that one is fustian and the other flimsy; I am not unwilling to read church history—at present I have Milner in my eye—his is reckoned a very good one.

[18th September 1819—In looking over some of my papers I found the above specimen of my carelessness. It is a sheet you ought to have had long ago—my letter must have appeared very unconnected, but as I number the sheets you must have discovered how the mistake happened. How many things have happened since I wrote it. How have I acted contrary to my resolves. The interval between writing this sheet and the day I put this supplement to it, has been completely filled with generous and most friendly actions of Brown towards me.

How frequently I forget to speak of things which I think of and feel most. 'Tis very singular, the idea about Buffon above has been taken up by Hunt in the Examiner, in some papers which he calls "A Preter-natural History".]

March 12, *Friday*—I went to town yesterday chiefly for the purpose of seeing some young men who were to take some letters for us to you through the medium of Peachey. I was surprised and disappointed at hearing they had changed their minds and did not purpose going so far as Birkbeck's—I was much disappointed; for I had counted upon seeing some persons who were to see you, and upon your seeing some who had seen me. I have not only lost this opportunity, but the sail of the postpacket to New York or Philadelphia, by which last your brothers have sent some letters. The weather in town yesterday was so stifling that I could not remain there though I wanted much to see Kean in Hotspur. I have by me at present Hazlitt's letter to Gifford —perhaps you would like an extract or two from the high-seasoned parts. It begins thus: "Sir, you have an ugly trick of saying what is not true of any one you do not like; and it will be the object of this letter to cure you of it. You say what you please of others; it is time you were told what you are. In doing this give me leave to borrow the familiarity of your style: for the fidelity of the picture I shall be answerable. You are a little person but a considerable cat's paw; and so far worthy of notice. Your clandestine connection with persons high in office constantly influences your opinions and alone gives importance to them. You are the government critic, a character nicely differing from that of a government spy—the invisible link, that connects literature with the police." Again: "Your employers, Mr Gifford, do not pay their hirelings for nothing—for condescending to notice weak and wicked sophistry; for pointing out to contempt what excites no admiration; for cautiously selecting a few specimens of bad taste and bad grammar where nothing else is to be found. They want your invincible pertness, your mercenary malice, your impenetrable dullness, your barefaced impudence, your pragmatical self-sufficiency, your hypocritical zeal, your pious frauds to stand in the gap of their prejudices and pretensions, to fly-blow and taint public opinion, to defeat independent efforts, to apply not the touch of the scorpion but the touch of the torpedo to youthful hopes, to crawl and leave the slimy track of sophistry and lies over every work that does not 'dedicate its sweet leaves' to some luminary of the treasury bench, or is not fostered in the hot bed of corruption. This is your office; 'This is what is looked for at your hands and this you do not baulk'—to sacrifice what little honesty, and prostitute what little intellect you possess to any dirty job you are commissioned to execute. 'They keep you as an ape does an apple in the corner of his jaw, first mouthed to be at last swallowed'. You are by appointment literary toad-eater to greatness and taster to the court. You have a natural aversion to whatever differs from your own pretensions, and an acquired one for what gives offence to your superiors. Your vanity panders to your interest, and your malice truckles only to your love of power. If your instinctive or premeditated abuse of your enviable trust were found wanting in a single instance; if you were to make a single slip in getting up your select committee of enquiry and greenbag report of the state of letters, your occupation would be gone. You would never after obtain a squeeze of the hand from a great man, or a smile from a punk of quality. The great and powerful (whom you call wise and good) do not like to have the privacy of their self-love startled by the obtrusive and unmanageable claims of Literature and Philosophy, except through the intervention of people like you, whom, if they have common penetration, they soon find out to be without any superiority of intellect; or if they do not, whom they can despise for their meanness of soul. You 'have the office opposite to Saint Peter'. You 'keep a corner in the public mind, for foul prejudice and corrupt power to knot and gender in'; you volunteer your services to people of quality to ease scruples of mind and qualms of conscience; you lay the flattering unction of venal prose and laurelled verse to their souls. You persuade them that there is neither purity of morals nor depth of understanding except in themselves and their hangers on; and would prevent the unhallowed names of liberty and humanity from ever being whispered in ears polite! You, sir, do you not do all this? I cry you mercy then: I took you for the editor of the *Quarterly Review*!" This is the sort of *feu de joie* he keeps up. There is another extract or two—one especially which I will copy tomorrow, for the candles are burnt down and I am using the wax taper which has a long snuff on it. The fire is at its last click—I am sitting with my back to it with one foot rather askew upon the rug and the other with the heel a little elevated from the carpet—I am writing this on *The Maid's Tragedy* which I have read since tea with great pleasure. Besides this volume of Beaumont and Fletcher, there are on the table two volumes of Chaucer and a new work of Tom Moore's called *Tom Cribb's Memorial to Congress*—nothing in it. These are trifles but I require nothing so much of you as that you will give me a like description of yourselves, however it may be when you are writing to me. Could I see the same thing done of any great man long since dead it would be a great delight: as to know in what position Shakespeare sat when he began "To be or not to be"—such things become interesting from distance of time or place. I hope you are both now in that sweet sleep which no two beings deserve more than you do—I must fancy you so—and please myself in the fancy of speaking a prayer and blessing over you and your lives—God bless you—I whisper good night in your ears and you will dream of me.

Saturday, 13 *March*—I have written to Fanny this morning; and received a note from Haslam. I was to have dined with him tomorrow: he gives me a bad account of his father who has not been in town for 5 weeks and is not well enough for company. Haslam is well, and from the prosperous state of some love affair he does not mind the double tides he has to work. I have been a walk past West End—and was going to call at Mr Monkhouse's, but did not, not being in the humour. I know not why poetry and I have been so distant lately. I must make some advances soon or she will cut me entirely. Hazlitt has this fine passage in his letter. Gifford, in his review of Hazlitt's characters of Shakespeare's plays, attacks the Coriolanus critique. He says that Hazlitt has slandered Shakespeare in saying that he had a leaning to the arbitrary side of the question. Hazlitt thus defends himself "My words are '*Coriolanus* is a storehouse of political commonplaces. The arguments for and against aristocracy and democracy, on the privileges of the few and the claims of the many, on liberty and slavery, power and the abuse of it, peace and war, are here very ably handled, with the spirit of a poet and the acuteness of a philosopher. Shakespeare himself seems to have had a leaning to the arbitrary side of the question, perhaps from some feeling of contempt for his own origin, and to have spared no occasion of baiting the rabble. *What he says of them is very true; what he says of their betters is also very true, though he dwells less upon it*. I then proceed to account for this by showing how it is that 'the cause of the people is but little calculated for a subject for poetry; or that the language of poetry naturally falls in with the language of power'. I affirm, Sir, that poetry, that the imagination, generally speaking, delights in power, in strong excitement, as well as in truth, in good, in right, whereas pure reason and the moral sense approve only of the true and good. I proceed to show that this general love or tendency to immediate excitement or theatrical effect, no matter how produced, gives a bias to the imagination often inconsistent with the greatest good, that in poetry it triumphs over principle, and bribes the passions to make a sacrifice of common humanity. You say that it does not, that there is no such original sin in poetry, that it makes no such sacrifice or unworthy compromise between poetical effect and still small voice of reason. And how do you prove that there is no such principle giving a bias to the imagination, and a false colouring to poetry? Why, by asking in reply to the instances where this principle operates, and where no other can with much modesty and simplicity—'But are these the only topics that afford delight in poetry, etc?' No; but these objects do afford delight in poetry, and they afford it in proportion to their strong and often tragical effect, and not in proportion to the good produced, or their desirableness in a moral point of view. 'Do we read with more pleasure of the ravages of a beast of prey than of the shepherd's pipe upon the mountain?' No, but we do read with pleasure of the ravages of a beast of prey, and we do so on the principle I have stated, namely from the sense of power abstracted from the sense of good; and it is the same principle that makes us read with admiration and reconciles us in fact to the triumphant progress of the conquerors and mighty hunters of mankind, who come to stop the shepherd's pipe upon the mountains and sweep away his listening flock. Do you mean to deny that there is anything imposing to the imagination in power, in grandeur, in outward show, in the accumulation of individual wealth and luxury, at the expense of equal justice and the common weal? Do you deny that there is anything in the 'Pride, Pomp, and Circumstance of glorious war, that makes ambition virtue!' in the eyes of admiring multitudes? Is this a new theory of the pleasures of the imagination, which says that the pleasures of the imagination do not take rise solely in the calculations of the understanding? Is it a paradox of my making that 'one murder makes a villain, millions a hero!' Or is it not true that here, as in other cases, the enormity of the evil overpowers and makes a convert of the imagination by its very magnitude? You contradict my reasoning, because you know nothing of the question, and you think that no one has a right to understand what you do not. My offence against purity in the passage alluded to, 'which contains the concentrated venom of my malignity', is, that I have admitted that there are tyrants and slaves abroad in the world; and you would hush the matter up, and pretend that there is no such thing in order that there may be nothing else. Farther I have explained the cause, the subtle sophistry of the human mind, that tolerates and pampers the evil in order to guard against its approaches; you would conceal the cause in order to prevent the cure, and to leave the proud flesh about the heart to harden and ossify into one impenetrable mass of selfishness and hypocrisy, that we may not 'sympathize in the distresses of suffering virtue' in any case in which they come in competition with the factitious wants and 'imputed weaknesses of the great'. You ask 'are we gratified by the cruelties of Domitian or Nero?' No, not we—they were too petty and cowardly to strike the imagination at a distance; but the Roman senate tolerated them, addressed their perpetrators, exalted them into gods, the fathers of their people, they had pimps and scribblers of all sorts in their pay, their Senacas, etc, till a turbulent rabble thinking there were no injuries to society greater than the endurance of unlimited and wanton oppression, put an end to the farce and abated the nuisance as well as they could. Had you and I lived in those times we should have been what we are now, I, 'a sour malcontent', and you 'a sweet courtier'."

The manner in which this is managed, the force and innate power with which it yeasts and works up itself, the feeling for the costume of society, is in a style of genius. He hath a demon, as he himself says of

Lord Byron. We are to have a party this evening. The Davenports from Church Row—I don't think you know anything of them—they have paid me a good deal of attention. I like Davenport himself. The names of the rest are Miss Barnes, Miss Winter with the children.

March 17th, Wednesday—On Sunday I went to Davenport's where I dined and had a nap. I cannot bear a day annihilated in that manner—there is a great difference between an easy and an uneasy indolence. An indolent day filled with speculations even of an unpleasant colour is bearable and even pleasant alone, when one's thoughts cannot find out anything better in the world; and experience has told us that locomotion is no change: but to have nothing to do, and to be surrounded with unpleasant human identities, who press upon one just enough to prevent one getting into a lazy position, and not enough to interest or rouse one, is a capital punishment of a capital crime; for is not giving up, through good-nature, one's time to people who have no light and shade a capital crime? Yet what can I do? They have been very kind and attentive to me. I do not know what I did on Monday—nothing—nothing—nothing—I wish this was anything extraordinary. Yesterday I went to town. I called on Mr Abbey; he began again (he has done it frequently lately) about that hat-making concern—saying he wishes you had hearkened to it: he wants to make me a hatmaker—I really believe 'tis all interested: for from the manner he spoke withal and the card he gave me I think he is concerned in hat-making himself. He speaks well of Fanny's health. Hodgkinson is married. From this I think he takes a little latitude—Mr A was waiting very impatiently for his return to the counting house, and meanwhile observed how strange it was that Hodgkinson should have been not able to walk two months ago and that now he should be married. "I do not", says he, "think it will do him any good—I should not be surprised if he should die of a consumption in a year or two. I called at Taylor's, and found that he and Hilton had set out to dine with me: so I followed them immediately back—I walked with them townwards again as far as Camden Town and smoked home a cigar. This morning I have been reading *The False One*. I have been up to Mrs Bentley's—shameful to say I was in bed at ten—I mean this morning. The Blackwood's review has committed themselves in a scandalous heresy—they have been putting up Hogg the Ettrick Shepherd against Burns—the senseless villains. I have not seen Reynolds, Rice or any of our set lately. Reynolds is completely buried in the law: he is not only reconciled to it but hobby-horses upon it. Blackwood wanted very much to see him—the Scotch cannot manage by themselves at all—they want imagination, and that is why they are so fond of Hogg who has a little of it.

Friday, 19th—Yesterday I got a black eye—the first time I took a cricket bat. Brown who is always one's friend in a disaster applied a leech to the eyelid, and there is no inflammation this morning though the ball hit me on the sight—'twas a white ball. I am glad it was not a clout. This is the second black eye I have had since leaving school—during all my school days I never had one at all. We must eat a peck before we die. This morning I am in a sort of temper indolent and supremely careless: I long after a stanza or two of Thomson's *Castle of Indolence*. My passions are all asleep from my having slumbered till nearly eleven and weakened the animal fibre all over me to a delightful sensation about three degrees on this side of faintness—if I had teeth of pearl and the breath of lilies I should call it languor, but as I am* I must call it laziness. In this state of effeminacy the fibres of the brain are relaxed in common with the rest of the body, and to such a happy degree that pleasure has no show of enticement and pain no unbearable frown. Neither poetry, nor ambition, nor love have any alertness of countenance as they pass by me: they seem rather like three figures on a Greek vase—a man and two women whom no one but myself could distinguish in their disguisement. This is the only happiness; and is a rare instance of advantage in the body overpowering the mind. I have this moment received a note from Haslam in which he expects the death of his father, who has been for some time in a state of insensibility—his mother bears up, he says, very well. I shall go to town tomorrow to see him. This is the world—thus we cannot expect to give way many hours to pleasure. Circumstances are like clouds continually gathering and bursting. While we are laughing the seed of some trouble is put into the wide arable land of events, while we are laughing it sprouts, it grows and suddenly bears a poison fruit which we must

---

*Especially as I have a black eye.

pluck. Even so we have leisure to reason on the misfortunes of our friends; our own touch us too nearly for words. Very few men have ever arrived at a complete disinterestedness of mind: very few have been influenced by a pure desire of the benefit of others—in the greater part of the benefactors to humanity some meretricious motive has sullied their greatness, some melodramatic scenery has fascinated them. From the manner in which I feel Haslam's misfortune I perceive how far I am from any humble standard of disinterestedness. Yet this feeling ought to be carried to its highest pitch as there is no fear of its ever injuring society, which it would do I fear, pushed to an extremity. For in wild nature the hawk would lose his breakfast of robins and the robin his of worms—the lion must starve as well as the swallow. The greater part of men make their way with the same instinctiveness, the same unwandering eye from their purposes, the same animal eagerness as the hawk. The hawk wants a mate, so does the man—look at them both, they set about it and procure one in the same manner. They want both a nest and they both set about one in the same manner—they get their food in the same manner. The noble animal man for his amusement smokes his pipe, the hawk balances about the clouds—that is the only difference of their leisures. This it is that makes the amusement of life to a speculative mind. I go among the fields and catch a glimpse of a stoat or a fieldmouse peeping out of the withered grass—the creature hath a purpose and its eyes are bright with it. I go amongst the buildings of a city and I see a man hurrying along—to what? The creature has a purpose and his eyes are bright with it. But then, as Wordsworth says, "We have all one human heart". There is an electric fire in human nature tending to purify, so that among these human creatures there is continually some birth of new heroism. The pity is that we must wonder at it: as we should at finding a pearl in rubbish. I have no doubt that thousands of people never heard of have had hearts completely disinterested: I can remember but two—Socrates and Jesus—their histories evince it. What I heard a little time ago Taylor observe with respect to Socrates may be said of Jesus: that he was so great a man that though he transmitted no writing of his own to posterity, we have his mind and his sayings and his greatness handed to us by others. It is to be lamented that the history of the latter was written and revised by men interested in the pious frauds of religion. Yet through all this I see his splendour. Even here though I myself am pursuing the same instinctive course as the veriest human animal you can think of—I am however young, writing at random, straining at particles of light in the midst of a great darkness, without knowing the bearing of any one assertion of any one opinion. Yet may I not in this be free from sin? May there not be superior beings amused with any graceful, though instinctive attitude my mind may fall into, as I am entertained with the alertness of a stoat or the anxiety of a deer? Though a quarrel in the streets is a thing to be hated, the energies displayed in it are fine; the commonest man shows a grace in his quarrel. By a superior being our reasonings may take the same tone—though erroneous they may be fine. This is the very thing in which consists poetry; and if so it is not so fine a thing as philosophy, for the same reason that an eagle is not so fine a thing as a truth. Give me this credit—Do you not think I strive to know myself? Give me this credit, and you will not think that on my own account I repeat Milton's lines

> How charming is divine Philosophy
> Not harsh and crabbed as dull fools suppose
> But musical as is Apollo's lute

No—not for myself—feeling grateful as I do to have got into a state of mind to relish them properly. Nothing ever becomes real till it is experienced. Even a proverb is no proverb to you till your life has illustrated it. I am ever afraid that your anxiety for me will lead you to fear for the violence of my temperament continually smothered down: for that reason I did not intend to have sent you the following sonnet—but look over the two last pages and ask yourselves whether I have not that in me which will well bear the buffets of the world. It will be the best comment on my sonnet; it will show you that it was written with no agony but that of ignorance; with no thirst of anything but knowledge when pushed to the point though the first steps to it were through my human passions. They went away, and I wrote with my mind, and perhaps I must confess a little bit of my heart:

TO GEORGE AND GEORGIANA KEATS

    Why did I laugh tonight? No voice will tell,
      No god no demon of severe response
    Deigns to reply from heaven or from hell.
    Then to my human heart I turn at once—
    Heart! thou and I are here sad and alone;
      Say, wherefore did I laugh? O mortal pain!
    O darkness! darkness! ever must I moan
      To question heaven and hell and heart in vain!
    Why did I laugh? I know this being's lease
      My fancy to its utmost blisses spreads:
    Yet could I on this very midnight cease
      And the world's gaudy ensigns see in shreds.
    Verse, fame and beauty are intense indeed
    But death intenser—death is life's high mead.

I went to bed and enjoyed an uninterrupted sleep. Sane I went to bed and sane I arose.

This the 15th April—you see what a time it is since I wrote. All that time I have been day by day expecting letters from you. I write quite in the dark—in the hopes of a letter daily, I have deferred that I might write in the light. I was in town yesterday and at Taylor's heard that young Birkbeck had been in town and was to set forward in six or seven days, so I shall dedicate that time to making up this parcel ready for him. I wish I could hear from you to make me "whole and general as the casing air". A few days after the 19th of March I received a note from Haslam containing the news of his father's death. The family has all been well—Haslam has his father's situation. The Framptons have behaved well to him. The day before yesterday I went to a rout at Sawrey's; it was made pleasant by Reynolds being there, and our getting into conversation with one of the most beautiful girls I ever saw. She gave a remarkable prettiness to all those commonplaces which most women who talk must utter. I liked Mrs Sawrey very well. The Sunday before last your brothers were to come by a long invitation... so long that for the time I forgot it when I promised Mrs Brawne to dine with her on the same day. On recollecting my engagement with your brothers, I immediately excused myself with Mrs Brawne but she would not hear of it and insisted on my bringing my friends with me. So we all dined at Mrs Brawne's. I have been to Mrs Bentley's this morning and put all the letters to and from you and poor Tom and me . . . I have found some of the correspondence between him and that degraded Wells and Amena. It is a wretched business. I do not know the rights of it, but what I do know would I am sure affect you so much that I am in two minds whether I will tell you anything about it. And yet I do not see why, for anything tho' it be unpleasant, that calls to mind those we still love, has a compensation in itself for the pain it occasions—so very likely tomorrow I may set about copying the whole of what I have heard about it: with no sort of a Richardson self-satisfaction—I hate it to a sickness—and I am afraid more from indolence of mind than anything else. I wonder how people exist with all their worries. I have not been to Westminster but once lately and that was to see Dilke in his new lodgings—I think of living somewhere in the neighbourhood myself. Your mother was well by your brother's account. I shall see her perhaps tomorrow—yes I shall. We have had the boys here lately—they make a bit of a racket—I shall not be sorry when they go. I found also this morning in a note from George to you, my dear sister, a lock of your hair which I shall this moment put in the miniature case. A few days ago Hunt dined here and Brown invited Davenport to meet him. Davenport from a sense of weakness thought it incumbent on him to show off, and pursuant to that never ceased talking and boring all day, till I was completely fagged out. Brown grew melancholy, but Hunt perceiving what a complimentary tendency all this had bore it remarkably well. Brown grumbled about it for two or three days. I went with Hunt to Sir John Leicester's gallery: there I saw Northcote, Hilton, Bewick and many more of great and little note. Haydon's picture is of very little progress this last year. He talks about finishing it next year. Wordsworth is going to publish a poem called "Peter Bell"—what a perverse fellow it is! Why wilt he talk about Peter Bells? I was told not to tell—but to you it will not be telling. Reynolds hearing that said "Peter Bell" was coming out, took it into his head to write a skit upon it called "Peter Bell". He did it as soon as thought on, it is to be published this morning, and comes out before the real "Peter Bell", with this admirable motto from *The Bold Stroke for a Wife*, "I am the real Simon Pure". It would be just as well to trounce Lord Byron in the same manner. I am still at a stand in versifying—I cannot do it yet with any pleasure. I mean however to look round at my resources and means and see what I can do without poetry. To that end I shall live in Westminster. I have no doubt of making by some means a little to help on or I shall be left in the lurch—with the burden of a little pride. However I look in time. The Dilkes like their lodging in Westminster tolerably well. I cannot help thinking what a shame it is that poor Dilke should give up his comfortable house and garden for his son, whom he will certainly ruin with too much care. The boy has nothing in his ears all day but himself and the importance of his education. Dilke has continually in his mouth "My Boy". This is what spoils princes: it may have the same effect with commoners. Mrs Dilke has been very well lately. But what a shameful thing it is that for that obstinate boy Dilke should stifle himself in town lodgings and wear out his life by his continual apprehension of his boy's fate in Westminster School with the rest of the boys and the masters. Everyone has some wear and tear. One would think Dilke ought to be quiet and happy—but no—this one boy makes his face pale, his society silent and his vigilance jealous. He would I have no doubt quarrel with anyone who snubbed his boy. With all this he has no notion how to manage him. O what a farce is our greatest cares! Yet one must be in the pother for the sake of clothes, food and lodging. There has been a squabble between Kean and Mr Bucke. There are faults on both sides—on Bucke's the faults are positive to the question: Kean's fault is a want of genteel knowledge and high policy—the former writes knavishly foolish and the other silly bombast. It was about a tragedy written by said Mr Bucke, which it appears Mr Kean kicked at—it was so bad. After a little struggle of Mr Bucke's against Kean, Drury Lane had the policy to bring it on and Kean the impolicy not to appear in it. It was damned. The people in the pit had a favourite call on the night of "Buck, Buck, rise up" and "Buck, Buck, how many horns do I hold up". Kotzebue the German dramatist and traitor to his country was murdered lately by a young student whose name I forget—he stabbed himself immediately after crying out "Germany! Germany!" I was unfortunate to miss Richards the only time I have been for many months to see him. Shall I treat you with a little extempore?

> When they were come unto the Faery's Court,
> They rang—no one at home—all gone to sport
> And dance and kiss and love as faeries do
> For faeries be as humans' lovers true—
> Amid the woods they were so lone and wild
> Where even the Robin feels himself exiled,
> And where the very brooks as if afraid
> Hurry along to some less magic shade.
> "No one at home!" the fretful princess cried
> "And all for nothing such a dreary ride
> And all for nothing my new diamond cross
> No one to see my persian feathers toss
> No one to see my Ape, my Dwarf, my Fool
> Or how I pace my otaheitan mule—
> Ape, Dwarf and Fool why stand you gaping there
> Burst the door open, quick—or I declare,
> I'll switch you soundly and in pieces tear."
> The Dwarf began to tremble and the Ape
> Star'd at the Fool, the Fool was all agape
> The Princess grasp'd her switch but just in time
> The dwarf with piteous face began to rhyme.
> "O mighty Princess, did you ne'er hear tell
> What your poor servants know but too, too well;
> Know you the three great crimes in faery land:
> The first alas! poor Dwarf I understand,
> I made a whipstock of a faery's wand;
> The next is snoring in their company;
> The next, the last, the direst of the three
> Is making free when they are not at home.
> I was a Prince—a baby prince—my doom
> You see; I made a whipstock of a wand,
> My top, has henceforth slept in faery land.
> He was a Prince, the Fool a grown up Prince

But he has never been a King's son since
He fell a snoring at a faery ball—
Your poor Ape was a Prince, and he poor thing
Picklock'd a faery's boudoir—now no king
But ape—so pray your highness stay awhile
'Tis sooth indeed. We know it to our sorrow—
Persist and *you* may be an ape tomorrow—"
While the Dwarf spake the Princess all for spite
Peal'd the brown hazel twig to lily white
Clench'd her small teeth, and held her lips apart,
Tried to look unconcern'd with beating heart.
They saw her highness had made up her mind
A-quavering like the reeds before the wind—
And they had had it, but O happy chance
The Ape for very fear began to dance
And grin'd as all his ugliness did ache—
She stayed her vixen fingers for his sake,
He was so very ugly: then she took
Her pocket mirror and began to look
First at herself and then at him and then
She smil'd at her own beauteous face again.
Yet for all this—for all her pretty face—
She took it in her head to see the place.
Women gain little from experience
Either in lovers, husbands or expense
The more the beauty, the more fortune too.
Beauty before the wide world never knew
So each Fair reasons—though it oft miscarries.
She thought *her* pretty face would please the faeries
"My darling Ape, I won't whip you today
Give me the picklock sirrah and go play"—
They all three wept—but counsel was as vain
As crying cup biddy to drops of rain.
Yet lingeringly did the sad Ape forth draw
The picklock from the pocket in his jaw.
The Princess took it and dismounting straight

Tripped in blue silver'd slippers to the gate
And touch'd the wards, the door full courteously
Opened—she enter'd with her servants three
Again it clos'd and there was nothing seen
But the Mule grazing on the herbage green.

Canto the xiii

The Mule no sooner saw himself alone
Than he prick'd up his ears—and said "Well done
At least unhappy Prince I may be free—
No more a Princess shall side-saddle me
O King of Otaheite—though a Mule
'Aye every inch a King'—though—'Fortune's fool'
Well done—for by what Mr Dwarfy said
I would not give a sixpence for her head."
Even as he spake he trotted in high glee
To the knotty side of an old pollard tree
And rub'd his sides against the mossed bark
Till his girths burst and left him naked stark
Except his bridle—how get rid of that
Buckled and tied with many a twist and plait.
At last it struck him to pretend to sleep
And then the thievish Monkeys down would creep
And filch the unpleasant trammels quite away.
No sooner thought of than adown he lay
Shammed a good snore—the Monkey-men descended
And whom they thought to injure they befriended.
They hung his bridle on a topmost bough
And off he went run, trot, or any how.

Brown is gone to bed—and I am tired of rhyming. There is a north wind blowing, playing young gooseberry with the trees. I don't care so it helps even with a side wind a letter to me, for I cannot put faith in any reports I hear of the settlement: some are good, some bad. Last Sunday I took a walk towards Highgate and in the lane that winds by the side of Lord Mansfield's park I met Mr Green, our demonstrator at

Guy's, in conversation with Coleridge. I joined them, after enquiring by a look whether it would be agreeable. I walked with him at his alderman-after-dinner pace for near two miles I suppose. In those two miles he broached a thousand things—let me see if I can give you a list—nightingales, poetry, on poetical sensation, metaphysics, different genera and species of dreams, nightmare, a dream accompanied by a sense of touch, single and double touch, dream related, first and second consciousness, the difference explained between will and volition, so many metaphysicians from a want of smoking the second consciousness, monsters, the Kraken, mermaids—Southey believes in them—Southey's belief too much diluted, a ghost story—good morning. I heard his voice as he came towards me, I heard it as he moved away, I had heard it all the interval—if it may be called so. He was civil enough to ask me to call on him at Highgate. Good night!

It looks so much like rain I shall not go to town to-day, but put it off till tomorrow. Brown this morning is writing some Spenserian stanzas against Mrs, Miss Brawne and me; so I shall amuse myself with him a little, in the manner of Spenser:

> He is to weet a melancholy carle
> Thin in the waist, with bushy head of hair
> As hath the seeded thistle when in parle
> It holds the zephyr ere it sendeth fair
> Its light balloons into the summer air
> Therto his beard had not begun to bloom
> No brush had touch'd his chin or razor sheer
> No care had touch'd his cheek with mortal doom
> But new he was and bright as scarf from Persian loom.
>
> Ne cared he for wine, or half and half
> Ne cared he for fish or flesh or fowl
> And sauces held he worthless as the chaff
> He 'sdeign'd the swine herd at the wassail bowl
> Ne with lewd ribbalds sat he cheek by jowl
> Ne with sly lemans in the scorner's chair
> But after water brooks this pilgrim's soul

> Panted, and all his food was woodland air
> Though he would ofttimes feast on gilliflowers rare.
>
> The slang of cities in no wise he knew
> *Tipping the wink* to him was heathen Greek
> He sipp'd no olden Tom or ruin blue
> Or nantz or cheery brandy drank full meek
> By many a damsel hoarse and rouge of cheek
> Nor did he know each aged watchman's beat—
> Nor in obscured purlieus would he seek
> For curled Jewesses with ankles neat
> Who as they walk abroad make tinkling with their feet.

This character would ensure him a situation in the establishment of patient Griselda. The servant has come for the little Browns this morning—they have been a toothache to me which I shall enjoy the riddance of. Their little voices are like wasps' stings—"Sometimes am I all wound with Browns". We had a claret feast some little while ago. There were Dilke, Reynolds, Skinner, Mancur, John Brown, Martin, Brown and I. We all got a little tipsy—but pleasantly so—I enjoy claret to a degree. I have been looking over the correspondence of the pretended Amena and Wells this evening—I now see the whole cruel deception. I think Wells must have had an accomplice in it—Amena's letters are in a man's language, and in a man's hand imitating a woman's. The instigations to this diabolical scheme were vanity, and the love of intrigue. It was no thoughtless hoax—but a cruel deception on a sanguine temperament, with every show of friendship. I do not think death too bad for the villain. The world would look upon it in a different light should I expose it—they would call it a frolic—so I must be wary, but I consider it my duty to be prudently revengeful. I will hang over his head like a sword by a hair. I will be opium to his vanity—if I cannot injure his interests. He is a rat and he shall have ratsbane to his vanity—I will harm him all I possibly can—I have no doubt I shall be able to do so. Let us leave him to his misery alone except when we can throw in a little more. The fifth canto of Dante pleases me more and more—it is that one in which he meets

TO GEORGE AND GEORGIANA KEATS

with Paulo and Francesca. I had passed many days in rather a low state of mind, and in the midst of them I dreamt of being in that region of Hell. The dream was one of the most delightful enjoyments I ever had in my life—I floated about the whirling atmosphere as it is described with a beautiful figure to whose lips mine were joined as it seemed for an age, and in the midst of all this cold and darkness I was warm—even flowery tree tops sprang up and we rested on them, sometimes with the lightness of a cloud till the wind blew us away again. I tried a sonnet upon it—there are fourteen lines but nothing of what I felt in it. O that I could dream it every night:

> As Hermes once took to his feathers light
> When lulled Argus, baffled, swoon'd and slept
> So on a delphic reed my idle spright
> So play'd, so charm'd, so conquer'd, so bereft
> The dragon world of all its hundred eyes
> And seeing it asleep so fled away:
> Not to pure Ida with its snow-cold skies
> Nor unto Tempe where Jove grieved that day,
> But to that second circle of sad hell,
> Where in the gust, the whirlwind and the flaw
> Of rain and hailstones lovers need not tell
> Their sorrows—Pale were the sweet lips I saw
> Pale were the lips I kiss'd and fair the form
> I floated with about that melancholy storm.

I want very, very much a little of your wit my dear sister—a letter or two of yours just to bandy back a pun or two across the Atlantic and send a quibble over the Floridas. Now you have by this time crumpled up your large bonnet, what do you wear—a cap? Do you put your hair in papers of a night? Do you pay the Miss Birkbecks a morning visit—have you any tea? Or do you milk and water with them? What place of worship do you go to—the Quakers, the Moravians, the Unitarians or the Methodists? Are there any flowers in bloom you like—any beautiful heaths, any streets full of corset makers? What sort of shoes have you to fit those pretty feet of yours? Do you desire Comp[ts] to one another? Do you ride on horseback? What do you have for breakfast, dinner and supper?—without mentioning lunch and bever and wet and snack and a bit to stay one's stomach. Do you get any spirits? Now you might easily distil some whisky and going into the woods set up a whisky shop for the monkeys. Do you and the Miss Birkbecks get groggy on anything—a little so-so-ish so as to be obliged to be seen home with a lantern? You may perhaps have a game at puss in the corner. Ladies are warranted to play at this game though they have not whiskers. Have you a fiddle in the settlement—or at any rate a jew's harp—which will play in spite of one's teeth. When you have nothing else to do for a whole day I tell you how you may employ it— first get up and when you are dressed, as it would be pretty early with a high wind in the woods, give George a cold pig with my compliments. Then you may saunter into the nearest coffee house and after taking a dram and a look at the chronicle, go and frighten the wild boars upon the strength—you may as well bring one home for breakfast serving up the hooves garnished with bristles and a grunt or two to accompany the singing of the kettle—then if George is not up give him a colder pig always with my compliments. When you are both set down to breakfast I advise you to eat your full share—but leave off immediately on feeling yourself inclined to anything on the other side of the puffy—avoid that for it does not become young women. After you have eaten your breakfast keep your eye upon dinner—it is the safest way. You should keep a hawk's eye over your dinner and keep hovering over it till due time, then pounce, taking care not to break any plates. While you are hovering with your dinner, in prospect you may do a thousand things—put a hedgehog into George's hat—pour a little water into his rifle—soak his boots in a pail of water—cut his jacket round into shreds like a Roman kilt or the back of my grandmother's stays—sew *off* his buttons.

Yesterday I could not write a line I was so fatigued, for the day before I went to town in the morning, called on your mother, and returned in time for a few friends we had to dinner. There were Taylor, Woodhouse, Reynolds—we began cards at about 9 o'clock, and the night coming on and continuing dark and rainy they could not think of returning to town. So we played at cards till very daylight—and yesterday I was not worth sixpence. Your mother was very well but anxious for a letter. We had half an hour's talk and no more for I was obliged to be home. Mrs and Miss Millar were well—and so was Miss Waldegrave—I have asked your brothers here for next Sunday. When Reynolds was here on Monday he asked me to give Hunt a hint to take notice of his "Peter Bell" in the *Examiner*—the best thing I can do is to write a little notice of it myself which I will do here and copy it out if it should suit my purpose.

Peter Bell—There have been lately advertised two books both "Peter Bell" by name; what stuff the one was made of might be seen by the motto "I am the real Simon Pure". This false Florimell has hurried from the press and obtruded herself into public notice while for aught we know the real one may be still wandering about the woods and mountains. Let us hope she may soon appear and make good her right to the magic girdle. The pamphleteering Archimage we can perceive has rather a splenetic love than a downright hatred to real Florimells— if indeed they had been so christened, or had even a pretension to play at bob cherry with Barbara Lewthwaite: but he has a fixed aversion to those three rhyming Graces Alice Fell, Susan Gale and Betty Foy; and now at length especially to Peter Bell—fit Apollo. It may be seen from one or two passages in this little skit that the writer of it has felt the finer parts of Mr Wordsworth, and perhaps expatiated with his more remote and sublimer muse. This as far as it relates to Peter Bell is unlucky. The more he may love the sad embroidery of *The Excursion*, the more he will hate the coarse samplers of Betty Foy and Alice Fell; and as they come from the same hand, the better will be able to imitate that which can be imitated—to wit "Peter Bell"—as far as can be imagined from the obstinate name. We repeat, it is very unlucky— this real Simon Pure is in parts the very man—there is a pernicious likeness in the scenery, a "pestilent humour" in the rhymes and an inveterate cadence in some of the stanzas that must be lamented. If we are one part amused at this we are three parts sorry that an appreciator of Wordsworth should show so much temper at this really provoking name of Peter Bell—!

This will do well enough—I have copied it and enclosed it to Hunt. You will call it a little politic—seeing I keep clear of all parties. I say something for and against both parties—and suit it to the tune of the

Examiner—I mean to say I do not unsuit it, and I believe I think what I say, nay I am sure I do. I and my conscience are in luck to-day—which is an excellent thing. The other night I went to the play with Rice, Reynolds and Martin. We saw a new dull and half damned opera called *The Heart of Midlothian*—that was on Saturday. I stopped at Taylor's on Sunday with Woodhouse, and passed a quiet sort of pleasant day. I have been very much pleased with the panorama of the ships at the north pole, with the icebergs, the mountains, the bears, the walrus, the seals, the penguins—and a large whale floating back above water. It is impossible to describe the place—Wednesday evening:

LA BELLE DAME SANS MERCI

O, what can ail thee, knight at arms,
    Alone and palely loitering?
The sedge has withered from the lake
    And no birds sing!

O, what can ail thee, knight at arms
    So haggard, and so woe-begone?
The squirrel's granary is full
    And the harvest's done.

I see a lily on thy brow
    With anguish moist and fever-dew,
And on thy cheek a fading rose
    Fast withereth too.

I met a lady in the meads
    Full beautiful, a faery's child,
Her hair was long, her foot was light,
    And her eyes were wild.

I made a garland for her head,
    And bracelets too, and fragrant zone;
She look'd at me as she did love,
    And made sweet moan.

TO GEORGE AND GEORGIANA KEATS

I set her on my pacing steed,
  And nothing else saw all day long;
For sidelong would she bend and sing
  A faery's song.

She found me roots of relish sweet,
  And honey wild, and manna dew;
And sure in language strange she said—
  I love thee true.

She took me to her elfin grot
  And there she wept and sigh'd full sore,
And there I shut her wild, wild eyes
  With kisses four.

And there she lulled me asleep
  And there I dream'd—Ah woe betide!
The latest dream I ever dreamt
  On the cold hill side.

I saw pale kings and princes too,
  Pale warriors, death-pale were they all;
They cried "La belle Dame sans Merci
  Thee hath in thrall."

I saw their starv'd lips in the gloam
  With horrid warning gaped wide
And I awoke and found me here
  On the cold hill's side.

And this is why I sojourn here
  Alone and palely loitering;
Though the sedge is wither'd from the lake
  And no birds sing.

Why four kisses, you will say. Why, four because I wish to restrain the headlong impetuosity of my muse—she would have fain said "score" without hurting the rhyme, but we must temper the imagination, as the critics say, with judgment. I was obliged to choose an even number that both eyes might have fair play: and to speak truly I think two a-piece quite sufficient. Suppose I had said seven; there would have been three and a half a-piece—a very awkward affair, and well got out of on my side.

CHORUS OF FAERIES, 4 FIRE, AIR, EARTH AND WATER
SALAMANDER, ZEPHYR, DUSKETHA, BREAMA

Sal. Happy, happy glowing fire!
Zep. Fragrant air, delicious light!
Dusk. Let me to my glooms retire
Bream. I to greenweed rivers bright.

Salam.

Happy, happy glowing fire
Dazzling bowers of soft retire!
Ever let my nourish'd wing
Like a bat's still wandering
Faintless fan your fiery spaces
Spirit sole in deadly places
In unhaunted roar and blaze
Open eyes that never daze
Let me see the myriad shapes
Of men and beasts and fish and apes
Portray'd in many a fiery den,
And wrought by spumy bitumen
On the deep intenser roof
Arched every way aloof.
Let me breathe upon my skies
And anger their live tapestries
Free from cold and every care
Of chilly rain and shiv'ring air.

Zephyr

Spright of fire—away away!
Or your very roundelay

Will sear my plumage newly budded
From its quilled sheath all studded
With the selfsame dews that fell
On the May-grown asphodel.
Spright of fire, away away!

Breama

Spright of fire, away away!
Zephyr, blue-eyed faery, turn
And see my cool sedge-shaded urn
Where it rests its mossy brim
Mid water mint and cresses dim
And the flowers in sweet troubles
Lift their eyes above the bubbles
Like our Queen when she would please
To sleep and Oberon will tease.
Love me blue-eyed Faery true
Soothly I am sick for you.

Zephyr

Gentle Breama by the first
Violet young nature nurst
I will bathe myself with thee
So you sometime follow me
To my home far, far in west
Far beyond the search and quest
Of the golden-browed sun—
Come with me o'er tops of trees
To my fragrant palaces
Where they ever-floating are
Beneath the cherish of a star
Call'd Vesper—who with silver veil
Ever hides his brilliance pale
Ever gently drows'd doth keep
Twilight of the Fays to sleep

Fear not that your wat'ry hair
Will thirst in drouthy ringlets there—
Clouds of stored summer rains
Thou shalt taste before the stains
Of the mountain soil they take
And too unlucent for thee make
I love thee chrystal faery true
Sooth I am as sick for you.

Salam.

Out, ye agueish Faeries, out!
Chilly Lovers what a rout,
Keep ye with your frozen breath
Colder than the mortal death—
Adder-eyed Dusketha, speak
Shall we leave these and go seek
In the earth's wide entrails old
Couches warm as theirs is cold
O for a fiery gloom and thee
Dusketha so enchantingly
Freckle-wing'd and lizard-sided!

Dusketha

By thee Spright will I be guided,
I care not for cold or heat.
Frost and flame or sparks or sleet
To my essence are the same—
But I honour more the flame—
Spright of fire I follow thee
Wheresoever it may be,
To the torrid spouts and fountains
Underneath earth-quaked mountains
Or at thy supreme desire
Touch the very pulse of fire
With my bare unlidded eyes.

Salam.

Sweet Dusketha: Paradise!
Off ye icy Spirits—fly
Frosty creatures of the sky.

Dusketha

Breathe upon them, fiery Spright.

Zephyr and Breama [to each other]

Away away to our delight.

Salam.

Go feed on icicles while we
Bedded in tongued flames will be.

Dusketha

Lead me to those fevrous glooms
Spright of fire—

Breama

    Me to the blooms
Blue-eyed Zephyr of those flowers
Far in the west where the May-cloud lours
And the beams of still vesper, where winds are all wist
Are shed through the rain and the milder mist
    And twilight your floating bowers.

I have been reading lately two very different books, Robertson's *America* and Voltaire's *Le Siècle de Louis XIV*. It is like walking arm and arm between Pizarro and the great-little monarch. In how lamentable a case do we see the great body of the people in both instances: in the first, where men might seem to inherit quiet of mind from unsophisticated senses, from uncontamination of civilization, and especially from their being as it were estranged from the mutual helps of society and its mutual injuries—and thereby more immediately under the protection of providence—even there they had mortal pains to bear as bad or even worse than bailiffs, debts and poverties of civilized life. The whole appears to resolve into this—that man is originally "a poor forked creature" subject to the same mischances as the beasts of the forest, destined to hardships and disquietude of some kind or other. If he improves by degrees his bodily accommodations and comforts, at each stage, at each ascent there are waiting for him a fresh set of annoyances—he is mortal and there is still a heaven with its stars above his head. The most interesting question that can come before us is, how far by the persevering endeavours of a seldom appearing Socrates mankind may be made happy—I can imagine such happiness carried to an extreme—but what must it end in? Death—and who could in such a case bear with death? The whole troubles of life which are now frittered away in a series of years, would then be accumulated for the last days of a being who instead of hailing its approach, would leave this world as Eve left Paradise. But in truth I do not at all believe in this sort of perfectibility—the nature of the world will not admit of it—the inhabitants of the world will correspond to itself. Let the fish philosophize the ice away from the rivers in winter time and they shall be at continual play in the tepid delight of summer. Look at the poles and at the sands of Africa, whirlpools and volcanoes—let men exterminate them and I will say that they may arrive at earthly happiness. The point at which man may arrive is as far as the parallel state in inanimate nature and no further. For instance, suppose a rose to have sensation, it blooms on a beautiful morning, it enjoys itself—but there comes a cold wind, a hot sun—it cannot escape it, it cannot destroy its annoyances—they are as native to the world as itself: no more can man be happy in spite, the worldly elements will prey upon his nature. The common cognomen of this world among the misguided and superstitious is "a vale of tears" from which we are to be redeemed by a certain arbitrary interposition of God and taken to heaven. What a little circumscribed straightened notion! Call the world if you please "The vale of soul-making". Then you will find out the use of the world (I am speaking now in the highest terms for human nature admitting it to be immortal which I will here take for granted for the purpose of showing a thought which has struck me concerning it). I say *"Soul making"*, soul as distinguished from an intelligence. There may be intelligences or sparks of the divinity in millions—but they are not souls till they acquire identities, till each one is personally itself. Intelligences are atoms of perception—they know and they see and they are pure, in short they are God. How then are souls to be made? How then are these sparks which are God to have identity given them —so as ever to possess a bliss peculiar to each one's individual existence? How, but by the medium of a world like this? This point I sincerely wish to consider because I think it a grander system of salvation than the Christian religion—or rather it is a system of spirit-creation. This is effected by three grand materials acting the one upon the other for a series of years. These three materials are the *intelligence*, the *human heart* (as distinguished from intelligence or mind) and the *world* or *elemental space* suited for the proper action of *mind and heart* on each other for the purpose of forming the *soul* or *intelligence destined to possess the sense of identity*. I can scarcely express what I but dimly perceive—and yet I think I perceive it—that you may judge the more clearly I will put it in the most homely form possible—I will call the *world* a school instituted for the purpose of teaching little children to read—I will call the *human heart* the *horn book* used in that school— and I will call the *child able to read, the soul* made from that *school* and its *horn book*. Do you not see how necessary a world of pains and troubles is to school an intelligence and make it a soul? A place where the heart must feel and suffer in a thousand diverse ways! Not merely is the heart a horn book, it is the mind's Bible, it is the mind's experience, it is the teat from which the mind or intelligence sucks its identity. As various as the lives of men are—so various become their souls, and thus does God make individual beings, souls, identical souls of the sparks of his own essence. This appears to me a faint sketch of a system of salvation which does not affront our reason and humanity. I am convinced that many difficulties which Christians labour under would vanish before it—there is one which even now strikes me—the salvation of children. In them the spark or intelligence returns to God without any identity—it having had no time to learn of and be altered by the heart—or seat of the human passions. It is pretty generally suspected that the Christian scheme has been copied from the ancient Persian and Greek philosophers. Why may they not have made this simple thing even more simple for common apprehension by introducing mediators and personages in the same manner as in the heathen mythology abstractions are personified? Seriously I think it probable that this system of soul-making may have been the parent of all the more palpable and personal schemes of redemption among the Zoroastrians, the Christians and the Hindus. For as one part of the human species must have their carved Jupiter, so another part must have the palpable and named mediator and saviour, their Christ, their Oromanes and their Vishnu. If what I have said should not be plain enough, as I fear it may not be, I will put you in the place where I began in this series of thoughts—I mean, I began by seeing how man was formed by circumstances. And what are circumstances but touchstones of his heart? And what are touchstones but provings of his heart? And what are provings of his heart but fortifiers or alterers of his nature? And what is his altered nature but his soul? And what was his soul before it came into the world and had these provings and alterations and perfectionings? An intelligence—without identity. And how is this identity to be made? Through the medium of the heart? And how is the heart to become this medium but in a world of circumstances? There now I think what with poetry and theology you may thank your stars that my pen is not very long-winded. Yesterday I received two letters from your mother and Henry which I shall send by young Birkbeck with this.

Friday, April 30—Brown has been here rummaging up some of my old sins—that is to say sonnets. I do not think you remember them, so I will copy them out as well as two or three lately written—I have just written one on Fame which Brown is transcribing and he has his book and mine. I must employ myself perhaps in a sonnet on the same subject:

ON FAME

You cannot eat your cake and have it too (proverb)

How fevered is that man who cannot look
   Upon his mortal days with temperate blood
Who vexes all the leaves of his life's book
   And robs his fair name of its maidenhood!

TO GEORGE AND GEORGIANA KEATS

It is as if the rose should pluck herself
   Or the ripe plum finger its misty bloom,
As if a clear lake meddling with itself
   Should cloud its pureness with a muddy gloom;
But the rose leaves herself upon the briar
For winds to kiss and grateful bees to feed,
And the ripe plum still wears its dim attire,
The undisturbed lake has crystal space.
Why then should man teasing the world for grace,
Spoil his salvation by a fierce miscreed?

ANOTHER ON FAME

Fame like a wayward girl will still be coy
   To those who woo her with too slavish knees,
   But makes surrender to some thoughtless boy
And dotes the more upon a heart at ease—
She is a gipsy will not speak to those
   Who have not learnt to be content without her
A jilt whose ear was never whispered close
   Who think they scandal her who talk about her—
A very gipsy is she Nilus born,
Sister in law to jealous Potiphar.
Ye lovesick bards, repay her scorn for scorn—
Ye lovelorn artists madmen that ye are,
Make your best bow to her and bid adieu
Then if she likes it she will follow you.

TO SLEEP

O soft embalmer of the still midnight
   Shutting with careful fingers and benign
Our gloom-pleased eyes embowered from the light,
   Enshaded in forgetfulness divine—
O soothest sleep, if so it please thee close
   In midst of this thine hymn my willing eyes,
Or wait the amen, ere thy poppy throws
   Around my bed its dewy charities—

> Then save me or the passed day will shine
> Upon my pillow breeding many woes;
> Save me from curious conscience that still lords
> Its strength for darkness, burrowing like a mole—
> Turn the key deftly in the oiled wards
> And seal the hushed casket of my soul.

The following poem—the last I have written, is the first and the only one with which I have taken even moderate pains. I have for the most part dashed off my lines in a hurry. This I have done leisurely—I think it reads the more richly for it and will I hope encourage me to write other things in even a more peaceable and healthy spirit. You must recollect that Psyche was not embodied as a goddess before the time of Apuleius the Platonist who lived after the Augustan age, and consequently the goddess was never worshipped or sacrificed to with any of the ancient fervour, and perhaps never thought of in the old religion. I am more orthodox than to let a heathen goddess be so neglected.

ODE TO PSYCHE

> O Goddess hear these tuneless numbers, wrung
>   By sweet enforcement and remembrance dear,
> And pardon that thy secrets should be sung
>   Even into thine own soft-conched ear!
> Surely I dreamt today; or did I see
> The winged Psyche, with awaked eyes?
> I wandered in a forest thoughtlessly,
> And on the sudden, fainting with surprise,
> Saw two fair creatures couched side by side
> In deepest grass beneath the whisp'ring fan
> Of leaves and trembled blossoms, where there ran
>   A brooklet scarce espied
> 'Mid hushed, cool-rooted flowers, fragrant eyed,
> Blue, freckle-pink, and budded Syrian
> They lay, calm-breathing on the bedded grass:
> Their arms embraced and their pinions too;

TO GEORGE AND GEORGIANA KEATS

Their lips touched not, but had not bid adieu,
As if disjoined by soft-handed slumber,
And ready still past kisses to outnumber,
At tender eye dawn of aurorian love.
The winged boy I knew:
But who wast thou O happy, happy dove?
His Psyche true?

O lastest born, and loveliest vision far
   Of all Olympus' faded hierarchy!
Fairer than Phoebe's sapphire-regioned star,
   Or Vesper, amorous glow worm of the sky;
Fairer than these though temple thou hadst none,
   Nor altar heap'd with flowers;
Nor virgin choir to make delicious moan
   Upon the midnight hours;
No voice, no lute, no pipe, no incense sweet
   From chain-swung censer teeming
No shrine, no grove, no oracle, no heat
   Of pale-mouth'd prophet dreaming!

O bloomiest! though too late for antique vows;
   Too, too late for the fond believing lyre,
When holy were the haunted forest boughs,
   Holy the air, the water and the fire:
Yet even in these days so far retir'd
From happy pieties, thy lucent fans,
Fluttering among the faint Olympians,
I see, and sing by my own eyes inspired.
O let me be thy choir and make a moan
   Upon the midnight hours;
Thy voice, thy lute, thy pipe, thy incense sweet
   From swinged censer teeming;
Thy shrine, thy grove, thy oracle, thy heat
   Of pale-mouthed prophet dreaming!
Yes I will be thy priest and build a fane

In some untrodden region of my mind,
Where branched thoughts new grown with pleasant pain,
Instead of pines shall murmur in the wind.
Far, far around shall those dark cluster'd trees
Fledge the wild-ridged mountains steep by steep,
And there by Zephyr's streams and birds and bees
The moss-lain Dryads shall be lull'd to sleep.
And in the midst of this wide-quietness
A rosy sanctuary will I dress
With the wreath'd trellis of a working brain;
With buds and bells and stars without a name;
With all the gardener fancy e'er could feign
Who breeding flowers will never breed the same—
And there shall be for thee all soft delight
That shadowy thought can win;
A bright torch, and a casement ope at night
To let the warm Love in.

        Here endethe ye Ode to Psyche

Incipit altera Sonneta

I have been endeavouring to discover a better sonnet stanza than we have. The legitimate does not suit the language over-well from the pouncing rhymes, the other kind appears too elegiac, and the couplet at the end of it has seldom a pleasing effect. I do not pretend to have succeeded—it will explain itself:

> If by dull rhymes our English must be chain'd
> And, like Andromeda, the sonnet sweet,
> Fetter'd, in spite of pained loveliness;
> Let us find out, if we must be constrain'd,
> Sandals more interwoven and complete
> To fit the naked foot of poesy;
> Let us inspect the lyre, and weigh the stress
> Of every chord, and see what may be gained
> By ear industrious, and attention meet;
> Misers of sound and syllable, no less

> Than Midas of his coinage, let us be
> Jealous of dead leaves in the bay wreath crown,
> So, if we may not let the muse be free,
> She will be bound with garlands of her own.

Here endeth the other sonnet

This is the third of May, and everything is in delightful forwardness; the violets are not withered before the peeping of the first rose. You must let me know everything—how parcels go and come—what papers you have, and what newspapers you want, and other things. God bless you, my dear brother and sister.

Your ever affectionate brother,
John Keats

LETTER 37

To Sarah Jeffrey *Between* 31 *May and* 9 *June* 1819

Wentworth Place

My dear young lady,

I am exceedingly obliged by your two letters. Why I did not answer your first immediately was that I have had a little aversion to the south of Devon from the continual remembrance of my brother Tom. On that account I do not return to my old lodgings in Hampstead though the people of the house have become friends of mine. This however I could think nothing of, it can do no more than keep one's thoughts employed for a day or two. I like your description of Bradley very much and I daresay shall be there in the course of the summer; it would be immediately but that a friend with ill health and to whom I am greatly attached called on me yesterday and proposed my spending a month with him at the back of the Isle of Wight. This is just the thing at present—the morrow will take care of itself. I do not like the name of Bishopsteignton. I hope the road from Teignmouth to Bradley does not lie that way. Your advice about the Indiaman is a very wise advice, because it just suits me, though you are a little in the wrong concerning its destroying the energies of mind: on the contrary it would be the finest thing in the world to strengthen them—to be thrown among people who care not for you, with whom you have no sympathies, forces the mind upon its own resources, and leaves it free to make its speculations of the differences of human character and to class them with the calmness of a botanist. An Indiaman is a little world. One of the great reasons that the English have produced the finest writers in the world is that the English world has ill-treated them during their lives and fostered them after their deaths. They have in general been trampled aside into the bye paths of life and seen the festerings of society. They have not been treated like the Raphaels of Italy. And where is the Englishman and poet who has given a magnificent entertainment at the christening of one of his hero's horses as Boiardo did? He had a castle in the Appennine. He was a noble poet of romance, not a miserable and mighty poet of the human heart. The middle age of Shakespeare was all clouded over; his days were not more happy than Hamlet's who is perhaps more like Shakespeare himself in his common everyday life than any other of his characters. Ben Jonson was a common soldier and, in the Low Countries, in the face of two armies, fought a single combat with a French trooper and slew him. For all this I will not go on board an Indiaman, nor for example's sake run my head into dark alleys: I daresay my discipline is to come, and plenty of it too. I have been very idle lately, very averse to writing; both from the overpowering idea of our dead poets and from abatement of my love of fame. I hope I am a little more of a philosopher than I was, consequently a little less of a versifying petlamb. I have put no more in print or you should have had it. You will judge of my 1819 temper when I tell you that the thing I have most enjoyed this year has been writing an ode to Indolence. Why did you not make your long-haired sister put her great brown hard fist to paper and cross your letter? Tell her when you write again that I expect chequer-work. My friend Mr Brown is sitting opposite me employed in writing a Life of David. He reads me passages as he writes them, stuffing my infidel mouth as though I were a young rook. Infidel rooks do not provender with Elisha's ravens. If he goes on as he has begun your new church had better not proceed, for parsons will be superseded—and of course the clerks must follow. Give my love to your Mother with the assurance that I can never forget her anxiety for my brother Tom. Believe also that I shall ever remember our leave-taking with *you*.

Ever sincerely yours,
John Keats

LETTER 38

To Fanny Brawne *Thursday, 1 July* 1819
Shanklin,
Isle of Wight, Thursday

My dearest lady,

I am glad I had not an opportunity of sending off a letter which I wrote for you on Tuesday night—'twas too much like one out of Rousseau's *Héloise*. I am more reasonable this morning. The morning is the only proper time for me to write to a beautiful girl whom I love so much; for at night, when the lonely day has closed, and the lonely, silent, unmusical chamber is waiting to receive me as into a sepulchre, then believe me my passion gets entirely the sway, then I would not have you see those rhapsodies which I once thought it impossible I should ever give way to, and which I have often laughed at in another, for fear you should think me either too unhappy or perhaps a little mad. I am now at a very pleasant cottage window, looking on to a beautiful hilly country, with a glimpse of the sea; the morning is very fine. I do not know how elastic my spirit might be, what pleasure I might have in living here and breathing and wandering as free as a stag about this beautiful coast if the remembrance of you did not weigh so upon me. I have never known any unalloyed happiness for many days together: the death or sickness of someone has always spoilt my hours—and now when none such troubles oppress me, it is you must confess very hard that another sort of pain should haunt me. Ask yourself, my love, whether you are not very cruel to have so entrammelled me, so destroyed my freedom. Will you confess this in the letter you must write immediately and do all you can to console me in it—make it rich as a draught of poppies to intoxicate me—write the softest words and kiss them that I may at least touch my lips where yours have been. For myself I know not how to express my devotion to so fair a form: I want a brighter word than bright, a fairer word than fair. I almost wish we were butterflies and lived but three summer days—three such days with you I could fill with more delight than fifty common years could ever contain. But however selfish I may feel, I am sure I would never act selfishly: as I told you a day or two before I left Hampstead, I will never return to London if my fate does not turn up Pam or at least a Court-card. Though I could centre my happiness in you, I cannot expect to engross your heart so entirely—indeed if I thought you felt as much for me as I do for you at this moment I do not think I could restrain myself from seeing you again tomorrow, for the delight of one embrace. But no—I must live upon hope and chance. In case of the worst that can happen, I shall still love you—but what hatred shall I have for another! Some lines I read the other day are continually ringing a peal in my ears:

> To see those eyes I prize above mine own
> Dart favours on another—
> And those sweet lips (yielding immortal nectar)
> Be gently press'd by any but myself—
> Think, think Francesca, what a cursed thing
> It were beyond expression!

J.

Do write immediately. There is no post from this place, so you must address Post Office, Newport, Isle of Wight. I know before night I shall curse myself for having sent you so cold a letter; yet it is better to do it as much in my senses as possible.

Be as kind as the distance will permit to your

J. Keats

Present my compliments to your mother, my love to Margaret and best remembrances to your brother—if you please so.

LETTER 39

To Fanny Brawne   *Thursday, 8 July* 1819
Miss Brawne, Wentworth Place, Hampstead, Middx.

July 8th
My sweet girl,
 Your letter gave me more delight than anything in the world but yourself could do; indeed I am almost astonished that any absent one should have that luxurious power over my senses which I feel. Even when I am not thinking of you I receive your influence and a tenderer nature stealing upon me. All my thoughts, my unhappiest days and nights have, I find, not at all cured me of my love of beauty, but made it so intense that I am miserable that you are not with me: or rather breathe in that dull sort of patience that cannot be called life. I never knew before what such a love as you have made me feel, was; I did not believe in it; my fancy was afraid of it, lest it should burn me up. But if you will fully love me, though there may be some fire, 'twill not be more than we can bear when moistened and bedewed with pleasures. You mention "horrid people" and ask me whether it depend upon them whether I see you again. Do understand me, my love, in this. I have so much of you in my heart that I must turn mentor when I see a chance of harm befalling you. I would never see anything but pleasure in your eyes, love on your lips, and happiness in your steps. I would wish to see you among those amusements suitable to your inclinations and spirits; so that our loves might be a delight in the midst of pleasures agreeable enough, rather than a resource from vexations and cares. But I doubt much, in case of the worst, whether I shall be philosopher enough to follow my own lessons: if I saw my resolution give you a pain I could not. Why may I not speak of your beauty, since without that I could never have loved you. I cannot conceive any beginning of such love as I have for you but beauty. There may be a sort of love for which, without the least sneer at it, I have the highest respect and can admire it in others: but it has not the richness, the bloom, the full form, the enchantment of love after my

own heart. So let me speak of your beauty, though to my own endangering, if you could be so cruel to me as to try elsewhere its power. You say you are afraid I shall think you do not love me—in saying this you make me ache the more to be near you. I am at the diligent use of my faculties here, I do not pass a day without sprawling some blank verse or tagging some rhymes; and here I must confess that (since I am on that subject) I love you the more in that I believe you have liked me for my own sake and for nothing else. I have met with women whom I really think would like to be married to a poem and to be given away by a novel. I have seen your comet, and only wish it was a sign that poor Rice would get well whose illness makes him rather a melancholy companion: and the more so as so to conquer his feelings and hide them from me, with a forced pun. I kissed your writing over in the hope you had indulged me by leaving a trace of honey. What was your dream? Tell it me and I will tell you the interpretation thereof.   Ever yours, my love!

John Keats

Do not accuse me of delay—we have not here an opportunity of sending letters every day. Write speedily.

LETTER 40

To Fanny Brawne   *Thursday, 15 July* 1819

Shanklin
Thursday Evening

My love,

 I have been in so irritable a state of health these two or three last days, that I did not think I should be able to write this week. Not that I was so ill, but so much so as only to be capable of an unhealthy teasing letter. Tonight I am greatly recovered only to feel languor I have felt after you touched with ardency. You say you perhaps might have made me better: you would then have made me worse: now you could quite effect a cure: what fee, my sweet physician, would I not give you to do so. Do not call it folly, when I tell you I took your letter last night to bed with me. In the morning I found your name on the sealing wax obliterated. I was startled at the bad omen till I recollected that it must have happened in my dreams, and they, you know, fall out by contraries. You must have found out by this time I am a little given to bode ill like the raven; it is my misfortune not my fault; it has proceeded from the general tenor of the circumstances of my life, and rendered every event suspicious. However I will no more trouble either you or myself with sad prophecies, though so far I am pleased at it as it has given me opportunity to love your disinterestedness towards me. I can be a raven no more; you and pleasure take possession of me at the same moment. I am afraid you have been unwell. If through me illness have touched you (but it must be with a very gentle hand) I must be selfish enough to feel a little glad at it. Will you forgive me this? I have been reading lately an oriental tale of a very beautiful colour. It is of a city of melancholy men, all made so by this circumstance. Through a series of adventures each one of them by turns reaches some gardens of Paradise where they meet with a most enchanting lady; and just as they are going to embrace her, she bids them shut their eyes—they shut them—and on opening their eyes again find themselves descending to the earth in a magic basket. The remembrance of this lady and their delights lost beyond all recovery render them melancholy ever after. How I applied this to you, my dear; how I palpitated at it; how the certainty that you were in the same world with myself, and though as beautiful, not so talismanic as that lady; how I could not bear you should be so, you must believe because I swear it by yourself. I cannot say when I shall get a volume ready. I have three or four stories half done, but as I cannot write for the mere sake of the press, I am obliged to let them progress or lie still as my fancy chooses. By Christmas perhaps they may appear, but I am not yet sure they ever will. 'Twill be no matter, for poems are as common as newspapers and I do not see why it is a greater crime in me than in another to let the verses of a half-fledged brain tumble into the reading-rooms and drawing room windows. Rice has been better lately than usual: he is not suffering from any neglect of his parents who have for some years been able to appreciate him better than they did in his first youth, and are now devoted to his comfort.

Tomorrow I shall, if my health continues to improve during the night, take a look farther about the country, and spy at the parties about here who come hunting after the picturesque like beagles. It is astonishing how they raven down scenery like children do sweetmeats. The wondrous Chine here is a very great lion: I wish I had as many guineas as there have been spy-glasses in it. I have been, I cannot tell why, in capital spirits this last hour. What reason? when I have to take my candle and retire to a lonely room, without the thought as I fall asleep, of seeing you tomorrow morning, or the next day, or the next—it takes on the appearance of impossibility and eternity—I will say a month—I will say I will see you in a month at most, though no one but yourself should see me; if it be but for an hour. I should not like to be so near you as London without being continually with you; after having once more kissed you, Sweet, I would rather be here alone at my task than in the bustle and hateful literary chit-chat. Meantime you must write to me—as I will every week—for your letters keep me alive. My sweet girl I cannot speak my love for you.

Good night! and ever yours,
John Keats

LETTER 41

To Fanny Brawne   *Sunday, 25 July* 1819

Sunday Night

My sweet girl,

I hope you did not blame me much for not obeying your request of a letter on Saturday: we have had four in our small room playing at cards night and morning leaving me no undisturbed opportunity to write. Now Rice and Martin are gone I am at liberty. Brown to my sorrow confirms the account you give of your ill health. You cannot conceive how I ache to be with you: how I would die for one hour—for what is in the world? I say you cannot conceive; it is impossible you should look with such eyes upon me as I have upon you: it cannot be. Forgive me if I wander a little this evening, for I have been all day employed in a very abstract poem and I am in deep love with you—

two things which must excuse me. I have, believe me, not been an age in letting you take possession of me; the very first week I knew you I wrote myself your vassal; but burnt the letter as the very next time I saw you I thought you manifested some dislike to me. If you should ever feel for man at the first sight what I did for you, I am lost. Yet I should not quarrel with you, but hate myself if such a thing were to happen—only I should burst if the thing were not as fine as a man as you are as a woman. Perhaps I am too vehement, then fancy me on my knees, especially when I mention a part of your letter which hurt me; you say speaking of Mr Severn "but you must be satisfied in knowing that I admired you much more than your friend". My dear love, I cannot believe there ever was or ever could be anything to admire in me especially as far as sight goes—I cannot be admired, I am not a thing to be admired. You are, I love you; all I can bring you is a swooning admiration of your beauty. I hold that place among men which snubnosed brunettes with meeting eyebrows do among women —they are trash to me—unless I should find one among them with a fire in her heart like the one that burns in mine. You absorb me in spite of myself—you alone: for I look not forward with any pleasure to what is called being settled in the world; I tremble at domestic cares—yet for you I would meet them, though if it would leave you the happier I would rather die than do so. I have two luxuries to brood over in my walks, your loveliness and the hour of my death. O that I could have possession of them both in the same minute. I hate the world: it batters too much the wings of my self-will, and would I could take a sweet poison from your lips to send me out of it. From no others would I take it. I am indeed astonished to find myself so careless of all charms but yours—remembering as I do the time when even a bit of ribband was a matter of interest with me. What softer words can I find for you after this—what it is I will not read. Nor will I say more here, but in a postscript answer anything else you may have mentioned in your letter in so many words—for I am distracted with a thousand thoughts. I will imagine you Venus to-night and pray, pray, pray to your star like a heathen.

Yours ever, fair star,
John Keats

My seal is marked like a family table cloth with my mother's initial F for Fanny, put between my Father's initials. You will soon hear from me again. My respectful compliments to your Mother. Tell Margaret I'll send her a reef of best rocks and tell Sam I will give him my light bay hunter if he will tie the Bishop hand and foot and pack him in a hamper and send him down for me to bathe him for his health with a necklace of good snubby stones about his neck.

LETTER 42

To Benjamin Bailey   *Saturday, 14 August 1819*
The Revd. B. Bailey, St. Andrews, N.B.

... We removed to Winchester for the convenience of a library and find it an exceeding pleasant town, enriched with a beautiful cathedral and surrounded by a fresh-looking country. We are in tolerably good and cheap lodgings. Within these two months I have written 1,500 lines, most of which besides many more of prior composition you will probably see by next winter. I have written two tales, one from Boccaccio called the "Pot of Basil"; and another called "St Agnes' Eve" on a popular superstition; and a third called "Lamia"—half finished. I have also been writing parts of my "Hyperion" and completed four acts of a tragedy. It was the opinion of most of my friends that I should never be able to write a scene. I will endeavour to wipe away the prejudice—I sincerely hope you will be pleased when my labours since we last saw each other shall reach you. One of my ambitions is to make as great a revolution in modern dramatic writing as Kean has done in acting—another to upset the drawling of the bluestocking literary world. If in the course of a few years I do these two things I ought to die content, and my friends should drink a dozen claret on my tomb. I am convinced more and more every day that (excepting the human friend philosopher) a fine writer is the most genuine being in the world. Shakespeare and the *Paradise Lost* every day become greater wonders to me. I look upon fine phrases like a lover. I was glad to see, by a passage in one of Brown's letters some time ago from the north, that you were in such good spirits. Since that you have been married and in congratulating you I wish you every continuance of them. Present my respects to Mrs Bailey. This sounds oddly to me, and I daresay I do it awkwardly enough: but I suppose by this time it is nothing new to you. Brown's remembrances to you. As far as I know we shall remain at Winchester for a goodish while.

Ever your sincere friend,
John Keats

LETTER 43

To Fanny Brawne   *Monday,* 16 *August* 1819
Miss Brawne, Wentworth Place, Hampstead, Middx.

Winchester, August 17th

My dear girl,

What shall I say for myself? I have been here four days and not yet written you—'tis true I have had many teasing letters of business to dismiss—and I have been in the claws, like a serpent in an eagle's, of the last act of our Tragedy. This is no excuse; I know it; I do not presume to offer it. I have no right either to ask a speedy answer to let me know how lenient you are—I must remain some days in a mist—I see you through a mist, as I daresay you do me by this time. Believe in the first letters I wrote you: I assure you I felt as I wrote—I could not write so now. The thousand images I have had pass through my brain—my uneasy spirits—my unguessed fate—all spread as a veil between me and you—remember I have had no idle leisure to brood over you—'tis well perhaps I have not. I could not have endured the throng of jealousies that used to haunt me before I had plunged so deeply into imaginary interests. I would fain, as my sails are set, sail on without an interruption for a brace of months longer. I am in complete cue—in the fever; and shall in these four months do an immense deal. This page as my eye skims over it I see is excessively unloverlike and ungallant—I cannot help it—I am no officer in yawning quarters; no parson-romeo. My mind is heaped to the full; stuffed like a cricket ball—if I strive to fill it more it would burst. I know the generality of women would hate me for this, that I should have so unsoftened, so hard a mind as to forget them; forget the brightest realities for the dull imaginations of my own brain. But I conjure you to give it a fair thinking; and ask yourself whether 'tis not better to explain my feelings to you, than write artificial passion. Besides you would see through it. It would be vain to strive to deceive you. 'Tis harsh, harsh, I know it. My heart seems now made of iron— I could not write a proper answer to an invitation to Idalia. You are my judge: my forehead is on the ground. You seem offended at a little simple innocent childish playfulness in my last. I did not seriously mean to say that you were endeavouring to make me keep my promise. I beg your pardon for it. 'Tis but *just* your pride should take the alarm—*seriously*. You say I may do as I please—I do not think with any conscience I can; my cash resources are for the present stopped, I fear for some time. I spend no money but it increases my debts. I have all my life thought very little of these matters—they seem not to belong to me. It may be a proud sentence; but, by heaven, I am as entirely above all matters of interest as the sun is above the earth— and though of my own money I should be careless, of my friends I must be spare. You see how I go on—like so many strokes of a hammer. I cannot help it—I am impelled, driven to it. I am not happy enough for silken phrases, and silver sentences. I can no more use soothing words to you than if I were at this moment engaged in a charge of cavalry. Then you will say I should not write at all. Should I not? This Winchester is a fine place: a beautiful cathedral and many other ancient buildings in the environs. The little coffin of a room at Shanklin is changed for a large room, where I can promenade at my pleasure— looks out on to a beautiful, blank side of a house. It is strange I should like it better than the view of the sea from our window at Shanklin. I began to hate the very posts there—the voice of the old lady over the way was getting a great plague. The fisherman's face never altered any more than our black teapot—the nob however was knocked off to my little relief. I am getting a great dislike of the picturesque, and can only relish it over again by seeing you enjoy it. One of the pleasantest things I have seen lately was at Cowes. The Regent in his yacht was anchored opposite—a beautiful vessel—and all the yachts and boats on the coast were passing and repassing it, and circuiting and tacking about it in every direction—I never beheld anything so silent, light, and graceful. As we passed over to Southampton, there was nearly an accident. There came by a boat well manned, with two naval officers at the stern. Our bowlines took the top of their little mast and snapped it off close by the board. Had the mast been a little stouter they would have been upset. In so trifling an event I could not help admiring our seamen—neither officer nor man in the whole boat moved a muscle—they scarcely noticed it even with words. Forgive me for this flint-worded letter, and believe and see that I cannot think of you without some sort of energy—though *mal à propos*. Even as I leave off it seems to me that a few more moments' thought of you would uncrystallize and dissolve me. I must not give way to it, but turn to my writing again—if I fail I shall die hard. O my love, your lips are growing sweet again to my fancy—I must forget them.

Ever your affectionate
Keats

LETTER 44

To J. H. Reynolds   *Tuesday, 24 August* 1819
Mr J. H. Reynolds, Little Britain, Christ's Hospital

Winchester, August 25th

My dear Reynolds,

By this post I write to Rice, who will tell you why we have left Shanklin, and how we like this place. I have indeed scarcely anything else to say, leading so monotonous a life, except I was to give you a history of sensations, and day-nightmares. You would not find me at all unhappy in it, as all my thoughts and feelings which are of the selfish nature, home speculations every day continue to make me more iron. I am convinced more and more, day by day, that fine writing is, next to fine doing, the top thing in the world; the *Paradise Lost* beomes a greater wonder. The more I know what my diligence may in time probably effect, the more does my heart distend with pride and obstinacy—I feel it in my power to become a popular writer—I feel it in my strength to refuse the poisonous suffrage of a public. My own being which I know to be becomes of more consequence to me than the crowds of shadows in the shape of men and women that inhabit a kingdom. The soul is a world of itself, and has enough to do in its own home. Those whom I know already, and who have grown as it were a part of myself, I could not do without: but for the rest of mankind, they are as much a dream to me as Milton's Hierarchies. I think if I had a free and healthy and lasting organization of heart, and lungs as strong as an ox's so as to be able to bear unhurt the shock of extreme thought and sensation without weariness, I could pass my life very nearly alone though it should last eighty years. But I feel my body too weak to support me to the height, I am obliged continually to check myself and strive to be nothing. It would be vain for me to endeavour after a more reasonable manner of writing to you. I have nothing to speak of but myself—and what can I say but what I feel? If you should have any reason to regret this state of excitement in me, I will turn the tide of your feelings in the right channel, by mentioning that it is the only state for the best sort of poetry—that is all I care for, all I live for. Forgive me for not filling up the whole sheet; letters become so irksome to me that the next time I leave London I shall petition them all to be spared me. To give me credit for constancy, and at the same time waive letter writing will be the highest indulgence I can think of.

Ever your affectionate friend,
John Keats

LETTER 45

To Fanny Keats   *Saturday,* 28 *August* 1819
Miss Keats, R^d Abbey's Esq, Walthamstow, near London

                        Winchester, August 28th
My dear Fanny,
  You must forgive me for suffering so long a space to elapse between the dates of my letters. It is more than a fortnight since I left Shanklin, chiefly for the purpose of being near a tolerable library which, after all, is not to be found in this place. However we like it very much: it is the pleasantest town I ever was in, and has the most recommendations of any. There is a fine cathedral which to me is always a source of amusement, part of it built 1400 years ago; and the more modern by a magnificent man, you may have read of in our history, called William of Wickham. The whole town is beautifully wooded. From the hill at the eastern extremity you see a prospect of streets, and old buildings mixed up with trees. Then there are the most beautiful streams about I ever saw—full of trout. There is the foundation of St Croix about half a mile in the fields—a charity greatly abused. We have a Collegiate School, a Roman Catholic School, a chapel ditto and a nunnery! And what improves it all is the fashionable inhabitants are all gone to Southampton. We are quiet—except a fiddle that now and then goes like a gimlet through my ears, our landlady's son not being quite a proficient. I have still been hard at work, having completed a tragedy I think I spoke of to you. But there I fear all my labour will be thrown away for the present, as I hear Mr Kean is going to America. For all I can guess I shall remain here till the middle of October—when Mr Brown will return to his house at Hampstead: whither I shall return with him. I some time since sent the letter I told you I had received from George to Haslam with a request to let you and Mrs Wylie see it. He sent it back to me for very insufficient reasons without doing so, and I was so irritated by it that I would not send it travelling about by the post any more; besides the postage is very expensive.

I know Mrs Wylie will think this a great neglect. I am sorry to say my temper gets the better of me—I will not send it again. Some correspondence I have had with Mr Abbey about George's affairs—and I must confess he has behaved very kindly to me as far as the wording of his letter went. Have you heard any further mention of his retiring from business? I am anxious to hear whether Hodgkinson, whose name I cannot bear to write, will in any likelihood be thrown upon himself. The delightful weather we have had for two months is the highest gratification I could receive—no chilled red noses, no shivering, but fair atmosphere to think in, a clean towel marked with mangle and a basin of clear water to drench one's face with ten times a day: no need of much exercise, a mile a day being quite sufficient. My greatest regret is that I have not been well enough to bathe, though I have been two months by the sea side and live now close to delicious bathing. Still I enjoy the weather, I adore fine weather as the greatest blessing I can have. Give me books, fruit, French wine and fine weather and a little music out of doors, played by somebody I do not know—not pay the price of one's time for a gig—but a little chance music; and I can pass a summer very quietly without caring much about fat Louis, fat Regent or the Duke of Wellington. Why have you not written to me? Because you were in expectation of George's letter and so waited? Mr Brown is copying out our tragedy of Otho the Great in a superb style—better than it deserves. There as I said is labour in vain for the present. I had hoped to give Kean another opportunity to shine. What can we do now? There is not another actor of tragedy in all London or Europe. The Covent Garden Company is execrable. Young is the best among them and he is a ranting, coxcombical tasteless actor—a disgust, a nausea—and yet the very best after Kean. What a set of barren asses are actors! I should like now to promenade round your gardens—apple-tasting—pear-tasting—plum-judging—apricot-nibbling—peach-scrunching—nectarine-sucking and meloncarving. I have also a great feeling for antiquated cherries full of sugar cracks—and a white currant tree kept for company. I admire lolling on a lawn by a water-lilied pond to eat white currants and see gold fish: and go to the Fair in the evening if I'm good. There is not hope for that—one is sure to get into some mess before evening. Have these hot days I brag of so much been well or ill for your health? Let me hear soon.

Your affectionate brother,
John

LETTER 46

To J. H. Reynolds Tuesday, 21 September 1819
Mr J. H. Reynolds, 8 Duke Street, Bath

Winchester, Tuesday

My dear Reynolds,

I was very glad to hear from Woodhouse that you would meet in the country. I hope you will pass some pleasant time together. Which I wish to make pleasanter by a brace of letters, very highly to be estimated, as really I have had very bad luck with this sort of game this season. I "kepen in solitarinesse", for Brown has gone a-visiting. I am surprised myself at the pleasure I live alone in. I can give you no news of the place here, or any other idea of it but what I have to this effect written to George. Yesterday I say to him was a grand day for Winchester. They elected a Mayor. It was indeed high time the place should receive some sort of excitement. There was nothing going on: all asleep: not an old maid's sedan returning from a card party: and if any old woman got tipsy at christenings they did not expose it in the streets. The first night, tho', of our arrival here there was a slight uproar took place at about 10 o' the clock. We heard distinctly a noise patting down the High Street as of a walking cane of the good old dowager breed; and a little minute after we heard a less voice observe "What a noise the ferrule made—it must be loose". Brown wanted to call the constables, but I observed 'twas only a little breeze, and would soon pass over. The side streets here are excessively maiden-lady like: the door-steps always fresh from the flannel. The knockers have a staid serious, nay almost awful quietness about them. I never saw so quiet a collection of lions' and rams' heads—the doors most part black, with a little brass handle just above the keyhole, so that in Winchester a man may very quietly shut himself out of his own house. How beautiful the season is now, how fine the air. A temperate sharpness about it. Really, without joking, chaste weather—Dian skies—I never liked stubble fields so much as now. Aye better than the chilly green of the spring. Somehow a stubble-plain looks warm—in the same way that some pictures look warm. This struck me so much in my Sunday's walk that I composed upon it.

I hope you are better employed than in gaping after weather. I have been at different times so happy as not to know what weather it was. No, I will not copy a parcel of verses. I always somehow associate Chatterton with autumn. He is the purest writer in the English language. He has no French idiom, or particles like Chaucer—'tis genuine English idiom in English words. I have given up "Hyperion" —there were too many Miltonic inversions in it. Miltonic verse cannot be written but in an artful or rather artist's humour. I wish to give myself up to other sensations. English ought to be kept up. It may be interesting to you to pick out some lines from Hyperion and put a mark × to the false beauty proceeding from art, and one ‖ to the true voice of feeling. Upon my soul 'twas imagination, I cannot make the distinction. Every now and then there is a Miltonic intonation— but I cannot make the division properly. The fact is I must take a walk, for I am writing so long a letter to George, and have been employed at it all the morning. You will ask, have I heard from George. I am sorry to say not the best news—I hope for better. This is the reason among others that if I write to you it must be in such a scraplike way. I have no meridian to date interests from, or measure circumstances. To-night I am all in a mist; I scarcely know what's what. But you knowing my unsteady and vagarish disposition, will guess that all this turmoil will be settled by to-morrow morning. It strikes me to-night that I have led a very odd sort of life for the two or three last years—here and there—no anchor. I am glad of it. If you can get a peep at Babbacombe before you leave the country, do. I think it the finest place I have seen, or is to be seen in the south. There is a cottage there I took warm water at, that made up for the tea. I have lately shirked some friends of ours and I advise you to do the same, I mean the blue-devils—I am never at home to them. You need not fear them while you remain in Devonshire. There will be some of the family waiting for you at the coach office—but go by another coach.

I shall beg leave to have a third opinion in the first discussion you have with Woodhouse—just half-way—between both. You know I will not give up my argument. In my walk to-day I stooped under a railway that lay across my path, and asked myself "Why I did not get over?" "Because", answered I, "no one wanted to force you under". I would give a guinea to be a reasonable man—good sound sense—a says what he thinks, and does what he says, man, and did not take snuff. They say men near death, however mad they may have been, come to their senses. I hope I shall here in this letter—there is a decent space to be very sensible in—many a good proverb has been in less. Nay, I have heard of the statutes at large being changed into the statutes at small and printed for a watch paper.

Your sisters by this time must have got the Devonshire *ees*—short *ees*—you know 'em—they are the prettiest *ees* in the language. O how I admire the middle-sized delicate Devonshire girls of about 15. There was one at an inn door holding a quartern of brandy—the very thought of her kept me warm a whole stage—and a 16 miler too—"You'll pardon me for being jocular".

Ever your affectionate friend,
John Keats

LETTER 47

To Richard Woodhouse   *Tuesday, 21 September* 1819
Mr Richd. Woodhouse, 8 Duke Street, Bath

Tuesday

Dear Woodhouse,

If you see what I have said to Reynolds before you come to your own dose you will put it between the bars unread; provided they have begun fires in Bath. I should like a bit of fire to-night—one likes a bit of fire. How glorious the blacksmiths' shops look now. I stood to-night before one till I was very near listing for one. Yes I should like a bit of fire—at a distance about 4 feet, "not quite hob nob" as Wordsworth says. The fact was I left town on Wednesday—determined to be in a hurry. You don't eat travelling—you're wrong—beef—beef— I like the look of a sign. The coachman's face says eat, eat, eat. I never feel more contemptible than when I am sitting by a good-looking coachman. One is nothing. Perhaps I eat to persuade myself I am somebody. You must be when slice after slice—but it won't do—the coachman nibbles a bit of bread—He's favoured—he's had a call—a Hercules Methodist. Does he live by bread alone? O that I were a Stage Manager—perhaps that's as old as "doubling the Cape". "How are ye, old 'un? Hey! Why don't 'e speak?" O that I had so sweet a breast to sing as the coachman hath! I'd give a penny for his whistle— and bow to the girls on the road—bow—nonsense—'tis a nameless graceful slang action. Its effect on the women suited to it must be delightful. It touches 'em in the ribs—*en passant*—very off hand—very fine—*Sed thongum formosa vale vale inquit* Heigh ho la! You like poetry better—so you shall have some I was going to give Reynolds.

> Season of mists and mellow fruitfulness,
>   Close bosom friend of the maturing sun;
> Conspiring with him how to load and bless
>   The vines with fruit that round the thatch eaves run;
> To bend with apples the moss'd cottage trees,
>   And fill all fruit with ripeness to the core;
>   To swell the gourd, and plump the hazel-shells
> With a white kernel; to set budding more,
>   And still more later flowers for the bees
>   Until they think warm days will never cease
>   For summer has o'er brimm'd their clammy cells.
>
> Who hath not seen thee oft, amid thy store?
>   Sometimes, whoever seeks abroad may find
> Thee sitting careless on a granary floor,
>   Thy hair soft-lifted by the winnowing wind;

TO RICHARD WOODHOUSE

Or on a half reap'd furrow sound asleep,
  Dazed with the fume of poppies, while thy hook
    Spares the next swath and all its twined flowers;
And sometimes like a gleaner thou dost keep
  Steady thy laden head across a brook;
Or by a cyder press, with patient look,
  Thou watchest the last oozings hours by hours.

Where are the songs of spring? Aye, where are they?
  Think not of them, thou hast thy music too.
While barred clouds bloom the soft-dying day
  And touch the stubble plains with rosy hue:
Then in a wailful quire the small gnats mourn
  Among the river sallows, borne aloft
    Or sinking as the light wind lives and dies;
And full grown lambs loud bleat from hilly bourne:
  Hedge crickets sing, and now with treble soft
  The redbreast whistles from a garden croft
    And gathered swallows twitter in the skies.

I will give you a few lines from "Hyperion" on account of a word in the last line of a fine sound:

  Mortal! that thou may'st understand aright
  I humanize my sayings to thine ear,
  Making comparisons of earthly things;
  Or thou might'st better listen to the wind
  Though it blows *legend-laden* through the trees.

I think you will like the following description of the Temple of Saturn:

  I look'd around upon the carved sides
  Of an old sanctuary, with roof august
  Builded so high, it seem'd that filmed clouds
  Might sail beneath, as o'er the stars of heaven.
  So old the place was I remember none
  The like upon the earth; what I had seen

>   Of grey cathedrals, buttress'd walls, rent towers
>   The superannuations of sunk realms,
>   Or nature's rocks hard toil'd in winds and waves,
>   Seem'd but the failing of decrepit things
>   To that eternal-domed monument.
>   Upon the marble, at my feet, there lay
>   Store of strange vessels and large draperies
>   Which needs had been of dyed asbestos wove,
>   Or in that place the moth could not corrupt,
>   So white the linen, so, in some, distinct
>   Ran imageries from a sombre loom.
>   All in a mingled heap confused there lay
>   Robes, golden tongs, censer and chafing dish
>   Girdles, and chains and holy jewelries.
>   Turning from these, with awe once more I rais'd
>   My eyes to fathom the space every way;
>   The embossed roof, the silent massive range
>   Of columns north and south, ending in mist
>   Of nothing; then to the eastward where black gates
>   Were shut against the sunrise evermore.

I see I have completely lost my direction. So I even make you pay double postage. I had begun a sonnet in French of Ronsard—on my word 'tis very capable of poetry—I was stopped by a circumstance not worth mentioning—I intended to call it *La Platonique Chevalresque*—I like the second line—

>   Non ne suis si audace à languire
>   De m'empresser au coeur vos tendres mains . . . etc.

Here is what I had written for a sort of induction—

>   Fanatics have their dreams wherewith they weave
>   A paradise for a sect; the savage too
>   From forth the loftiest fashion of his sleep
>   Guesses at heaven: pity these have not
>   Traced upon vellum or wild indian leaf
>   The shadows of melodious utterance:

TO RICHARD WOODHOUSE

> But bare of laurel they live, dream, and die,
> For poesy alone can tell her dreams,
> With the fine spell of words alone can save
> Imagination from the sable charm
> And dumb enchantment—

   My poetry will never be fit for anything—it doesn't cover its ground well. You see he, she is off her guard and doesn't move a peg though prose is coming up in an awkward style enough. Now a blow in the spondee will finish her. But let it get over this line of circumvallation if it can. These are unpleasant phrases.

   Now for all this you two must write me a letter apiece—for as I know you will inter-read one another. I am still writing to Reynolds as well as yourself. As I say to George I am writing *to* you but *at* your wife. And don't forget to tell Reynolds of the fairy tale *Undine*. Ask him if he has read any of the American Brown's novels that Hazlitt speaks so much of—I have read one called *Wieland*—very powerful—something like Godwin. Between Schiller and Godwin. A domestic prototype of Schiller's *Armenian*. More clever in plot and incident than Godwin. A strange American scion of the German trunk. Powerful genius—accomplished horrors—I shall proceed tomorrow.

   Wednesday—I am all in a mess here—embowelled in Winchester. I wrote two letters to Brown, one from said place, and one from London, and neither of them has reached him. I have written him a long one this morning and am so perplexed as to be an object of curiosity to you quiet people. I hire myself a show wagon and trumpeter. Here's the wonderful man whose letters won't go! All the infernal imaginary thunderstorms from the Post Office are beating upon me—so that "unpoeted I write". Some curious body has detained my letters. I am sure of it. They know not what to make of me—not an acquaintance in the place—what can I be about? So they open my letters. Being in a lodging house, and not so self-willed, but I am a little cowardly, I dare not spout my rage against the ceiling. Besides I should be run through the body by the major in the next room. I don't think his wife would attempt such a thing.

   Now I am going to be serious. After revolving certain circumstances in my mind, chiefly connected with a late American letter, I have determined to take up my abode in a cheap lodging in town and get employment in some of our elegant periodical works. I will no longer live upon hopes. I shall carry my plan into execution speedily. I shall live in Westminster, from which a walk to the British Museum will be noisy and muddy, but otherwise pleasant enough. I shall enquire of Hazlitt how the figures of the market stand. O that I could write something agrest-rural, pleasant, fountain-voiced—not plague you with unconnected nonsense. But things won't leave me *alone*. I shall be in town as soon as either of you. I only wait for an answer from Brown: if he receives mine which is now a very moot point. I will give you a few reasons why I shall persist in not publishing "The Pot of Basil". It is too smokeable. I can get it smoked at the carpenter's shaving chimney much more cheaply. There is too much inexperience of life, and simplicity of knowledge in it, which might do very well after one's death—but not while one is alive. There are very few would look to the reality. I intend to use more finesse with the public. It is possible to write fine things which cannot be laughed at in any way. "Isabella" is what I should call were I a reviewer, "A weak-sided poem" with an amusing sober-sadness about it. Not that I do not think Reynolds and you are quite right about it—it is enough for me. But this will not do to be public. If I may so say, in my dramatic capacity I enter fully into the feeling: but *in propria persona* I should be apt to quiz it myself. There is no objection of this kind to "Lamia"—a good deal to "St Agnes' Eve"—only not so glaring. Would, as I say, I could write you something sylvestran. But I have no time to think: I am an *otiosus-peroccupatus* man. I think upon crutches like the folks in your Pump Room. Have you seen old Bramble yet—they say he's on his last legs. The gout did not treat the old man well so the physician superseded it, and put the dropsy in office, who gets very fat upon his new employment, and behaves worse than the other to the old man. But he'll have his house about his ears soon. We shall have another fall of siege-arms. I suppose Mrs Humphrey persists in a big-belly—poor thing, she little thinks how she is spoiling the corners of her mouth—and making her nose quite a piminy. Mr Humphrey I hear was giving a lecture in the gaming-room, when someone called out "Spousey!" I hear too he has received a challenge from a gentleman who lost that evening. The fact is Mr H is a mere nothing out of his bedroom. Old Tabitha died in being bolstered up for a whist-party. They had to cut again—Chowder died long ago. Mrs H laments that the last time they *put him* (i.e. to breed) he didn't take. They say he was a direct descendant of Cupid and Veney in *The Spectator*. This may be easily known by the Parish Books. If you do not write in the course of a day or two—direct to me at Rice's. Let me know how you pass your times and how you are.

Your sincere friend,
John Keats

Haven't heard from Taylor.

LETTER 48

To Charles Brown   *Thursday, 23 September* 1819

. . . Do not suffer me to disturb you unpleasantly: I do not mean that you should not suffer me to occupy your thoughts, but to occupy them pleasantly; for, I assure you, I am as far from being unhappy as possible. Imaginary grievances have always been more my torment than real ones. You know this well. Real ones will never have any other effect upon me than to stimulate me to get out of or avoid them. This is easily accounted for. Our imaginary woes are conjured up by our passions, and are fostered by passionate feeling: our real ones come of themselves, and are opposed by an abstract exertion of mind. Real grievances are displacers of passion. The imaginary nail a man down for a sufferer, as on a cross; the real spur him up into an agent. I wish, at one view, you would see my heart towards you. 'Tis only from a high tone of feeling that I can put that word upon paper—out of poetry. I ought to have waited for your answer to my last before I wrote this.

I felt, however, compelled to make a rejoinder to yours. I had written to [Dilke] on the subject of my last, I scarcely know whether I shall send my letter now. I think he would approve of my plan; it is so evident. Nay, I am convinced, out and out, that by prosing for a while in periodical works, I may maintain myself decently . . .

LETTER 49

To Fanny Brawne   Monday, 11 October 1819
Miss Brawne, Wentworth Place, Hampstead

College Street

My sweet girl,

    I am living to-day in yesterday: I was in a complete fascination all day. I feel myself at your mercy. Write me ever so few lines and tell me you will never for ever be less kind to me than yesterday. You dazzled me. There is nothing in the world so bright and delicate. When Brown came out with that seemingly true story against me last night, I felt it would be death to me if you had ever believed it—though against any one else I could muster up my obstinacy. Before I knew Brown could disprove it I was for the moment miserable. When shall we pass a day alone? I have had a thousand kisses, for which with my whole soul I thank love—but if you should deny me the thousand and first—'twould put me to the proof how great a misery I could live through. If you should ever carry your threat yesterday into execution—believe me 'tis not my pride, my vanity or any petty passion would torment me—really 'twould hurt my heart—I could not bear it. I have seen Mrs Dilke this morning; she says she will come with me any fine day.

Ever yours,
John Keats

Ah hertè mine!

LETTER 50

To Fanny Brawne   *Wednesday, 13 October 1819*
Miss Brawne, Wentworth Place, Hampstead

                                  25 College Street

My dearest girl,
  This moment I have set myself to copy some verses out fair. I cannot proceed with any degree of content. I must write you a line or two and see if that will assist in dismissing you from my mind for ever so short a time. Upon my soul I can think of nothing else. The time is passed when I had power to advise and warn you against the unpromising morning of my life. My love has made me selfish. I cannot exist without you. I am forgetful of everything but seeing you again—my life seems to stop there—I see no further. You have absorbed me. I have a sensation at the present moment as though I was dissolving—I should be exquisitely miserable without the hope of soon seeing you. I should be afraid to separate myself far from you. My sweet Fanny, will your heart never change? My love, will it? I have no limit now to my love. Your note came in just here—I cannot be happier away from you. 'Tis richer than an argosy of pearls. Do not threat me even in jest. I have been astonished that men could die martyrs for religion—I have shuddered at it. I shudder no more—I could be martyred for my religion—Love is my religion—I could die for that. I could die for you. My creed is Love and you are its only tenet. You have ravished me away by a power I cannot resist; and yet I could resist till I saw you; and even since I have seen you I have endeavoured often "to reason against the reasons of my love". I can do that no more—the pain would be too great. My love is selfish. I cannot breathe without you.

                                      Yours for ever,
                                         John Keats

LETTER 51

To John Taylor   *Wednesday, 17 November 1819*
John Taylor Esq, Taylor and Hessey's, Fleet Street

Wentworth Place, Wednesday

My dear Taylor,

 I have come to a determination not to publish anything I have now ready written; but for all that to publish a poem before long and that I hope to make a fine one. As the marvellous is the most enticing and the surest guarantee of harmonious numbers, I have been endeavouring to persuade myself to untether fancy and let her manage for herself. I and myself cannot agree about this at all. Wonders are no wonders to me. I am more at home amongst men and women. I would rather read Chaucer than Ariosto. The little dramatic skill I may as yet have, however badly it might show in a drama, would, I think, be sufficient for a poem. I wish to diffuse the colouring of St Agnes Eve throughout a poem in which character and sentiment would be the figures to such drapery. Two or three such poems, if God should spare me, written in the course of the next six years, would be a famous *gradus ad Parnassum altissimum*. I mean they would nerve me up to the writing of a few fine plays—my greatest ambition—when I do feel ambitious. I am sorry to say that is very seldom. The subject we have once or twice talked of appears a promising one, the Earl of Leicester's history. I am this morning reading Holinshed's Elizabeth. You had some books awhile ago you promised to lend me, illustrative of my subject. If you can lay hold of them or any others which may be serviceable to me I know you will encourage my low-spirited muse by sending them—or rather by letting me know when our errand cart man shall call with my little box. I will endeavour to set myself selfishly at work on this poem that is to be.

Your sincere friend,
John Keats

LETTER 52

To Fanny Keats *Sunday, 6 February* 1820
Miss Keats, R^d Abbey Esq, Pancras Lane, Queen Street, Cheapside

Wentworth Place
Sunday Morning

My dear Sister,
I should not have sent those letters without some notice if Mr Brown had not persuaded me against it on account of an illness with which I was attacked on Thursday. After that I was resolved not to write till I should be on the mending hand: thank God, I am now so. From imprudently leaving off my great coat in the thaw I caught cold which flew to my lungs. Every remedy that has been applied has taken the desired effect, and I have nothing now to do but stay within doors for some time. If I should be confined long I shall write to Mr Abbey to ask permission for you to visit me. George has been running great chance of a similar attack, but I hope the sea air will be his physician in case of illness—the air out at sea is always more temperate than on land. George mentioned, in his letters to us, something of Mr Abbey's regret concerning the silence kept up in his house. It is entirely the fault of his manner. You must be careful always to wear warm clothing not only in frost but in a thaw.

I have no news to tell you. The half-built houses opposite us stand just as they were and seem dying of old age before they are brought up. The grass looks very dingy, the celery is all gone, and there is nothing to enliven one but a few cabbage stalks that seem fixed on the superannuated list. Mrs Dilke has been ill but is better. Several of my friends have been to see me. Mrs Reynolds was here this morning and the two Mr Wylies. Brown has been very alert about me, though a little wheezy himself this weather. Everybody is ill. Yesterday evening Mr Davenport, a gentleman of Hampstead, sent me an invitation to supper, instead of his coming to see us, having so bad a cold he could not stir out—so you see 'tis the weather and I am among a thousand. Whenever you have an inflammatory fever never mind about eating. The day on which I was getting ill I felt this fever to a great height, and therefore almost entirely abstained from food the whole day. I have no doubt experienced a benefit from so doing. The papers I see are full of anecdotes of the late King: how he nodded to a coal heaver and laughed with a Quaker and liked boiled leg of mutton. Old Peter Pindar is just dead: what will the old King and he say to each other? Perhaps the King may confess that Peter was in the right, and Peter maintain himself to have been wrong. You shall hear from me again on Tuesday.

Your affectionate brother,
John

LETTER 53

To Fanny Keats   *Tuesday, 8 February* 1820
Miss Keats, R^d Abbey Esq, Pancras Lane, Queen Street, Cheapside

Wentworth Place
Tuesday Morn

My dear Fanny,

    I had a slight return of fever last night, which terminated favourably, and I am now tolerably well, though weak from small quantity of food to which I am obliged to confine myself: I am sure a mouse would starve upon it. Mrs Wylie came yesterday. I have a very pleasant room for a sick person. A sofa bed is made up for me in the front parlour which looks on to the grass plot as you remember Mrs Dilke's does. How much more comfortable than a dull room upstairs, where one gets tired of the pattern of the bed curtains. Besides I see all that passes—for instance now, this morning, if I had been in my own room I should not have seen the coals brought in. On Sunday between the hours of twelve and one I descried a pot boy. I conjectured it might be the one o'clock beer. Old women with bobbins and red cloaks and unpresuming bonnets I see creeping about the heath. Gipsies after hare skins and silver spoons. Then goes by a fellow with a wooden clock under his arm that strikes a hundred and more. Then comes the old French emigrant, (who has been very well-to-do in France) with his hands joined behind on his hips, and his face full of political schemes.

Then passes Mr David Lewis, a very good-natured, good-looking old gentleman who has been very kind to Tom and George and me. As for those fellows the brickmakers they are always passing to and fro. I mustn't forget the two old maiden ladies in Well Walk who have a lap dog between them that they are very anxious about. It is a corpulent little beast whom it is necessary to coax along with an ivory-tipped cane. Carlo our neighbour Mrs Brawne's dog and it meet sometimes. Lappy thinks Carlo a devil of a fellow and so do his mistresses. Well they may—he would sweep them all down at a run; all for the joke of it. I shall desire him to peruse the fable of the boys and the frogs; though he prefers the tongues and the bones. You shall hear from me again the day after tomorrow.

Your affectionate brother,
John Keats

LETTER 54

To Fanny Brawne (?) *10 February* 1820
Miss Brawne

My dearest girl,

If illness makes such an agreeable variety in the manner of your eyes I should wish you sometimes to be ill. I wish I had read your note before you went last night that I might have assured you how far I was from suspecting any coldness. You had a just right to be a little silent to one who speaks so plainly to you. You must believe—you shall, you will—that I can do nothing, say nothing, think nothing of you but what has its spring in the love which has so long been my pleasure and torment. On the night I was taken ill—when so violent a rush of blood came to my lungs that I felt nearly suffocated—I assure you I felt it possible I might not survive, and at that moment thought of nothing but you. When I said to Brown "this is unfortunate" I thought of you. 'Tis true that since the first two or three days other subjects have entered my head. I shall be looking forward to health and the spring and a regular routine of our old walks.

Your affectionate,
J.K.

LETTER 55

To Fanny Brawne (?) *February* 1820
Miss Brawne

My dearest girl, how could it ever have been my wish to forget you? How could I have said such a thing? The utmost stretch my mind has been capable of was to endeavour to forget you for your own sake seeing what a chance there was of my remaining in a precarious state of health. I would have borne it as I would bear death if fate was in that humour: but I should as soon think of choosing to die as to part from you. Believe too my love that our friends think and speak for the best, and if their best is not our best it is not their fault. When I am better I will speak with you at large on these subjects, if there is any occasion—I think there is none. I am rather nervous to-day, perhaps from being a little recovered and suffering my mind to take little excursions beyond the doors and windows. I take it for a good sign, but as it must not be encouraged you had better delay seeing me till to-morrow. Do not take the trouble of writing much: merely send me my good night.

Remember me to your mother and Margaret.

Your affectionate,

J.K.

TO JAMES RICE

LETTER 56

To James Rice   *Monday–Wednesday, 14–16 February 1820*
Mr James Rice, 50 Poland Street, Oxford Street
                              Wentworth Place
                                Monday Morn

My dear Rice,
   I have not been well enough to make any tolerable rejoinder to your kind letter. I will, as you advise, be very chary of my health and spirits. I am sorry to hear of your relapse and hypochondriac symptoms attending it. Let us hope for the best as you say. I shall follow your example in looking to the future good rather than brooding upon present ill. I have not been so worn with lengthened illnesses as you have, therefore cannot answer you on your own ground with respect to those haunting and deformed thoughts and feelings you speak of. When I have been or supposed myself in health I have had my share of them, especially within this last year. I may say that for 6 months before I was taken ill I had not passed a tranquil day. Either that gloom overspread me or I was suffering under some passionate feeling, or if I turned to versify that acerbated the poison of either sensation. The beauties of nature had lost their power over me. How astonishingly (here I must premise that illness as far as I can judge in so short a time has relieved my mind of a load of deceptive thoughts and images and makes me perceive things in a truer light)—how astonishingly does the chance of leaving the world impress a sense of its natural beauties on us. Like poor Falstaff though I do not babble, I think of green fields. I muse with the greatest affection on every flower I have known from my infancy—their shapes and colours are as new to me as if I had just created them with a superhuman fancy. It is because they are connected with the most thoughtless and happiest moments of our lives. I have seen foreign flowers in hothouses of the most beautiful nature, but I do not care a straw for them. The simple flowers of our spring are what I want to see again.
   Brown has left the inventive and taken to the imitative art—he is

doing his forte, which is copying Hogarth's heads. He has just made a purchase of the Methodist meeting picture, which gave me a horrid dream a few nights ago. I hope I shall sit under the trees with you again in some such place as the Isle of Wight. I do not mind a game at cards in a saw pit or wagon; but if ever you catch me on a stage coach in the winter full against the wind bring me down with a brace of bullets and I promise not to "peach". Remember me to Reynolds and say how much I should like to hear from him; that Brown returned immediately after he went on Sunday, and that I was vexed at forgetting to ask him to lunch for as he went towards the gate I saw he was fatigued and hungry.

I am, my dear Rice,
ever most sincerely yours,
John Keats

I have broken this open to let you know I was surprised at seeing it on the table this morning, thinking it had gone long ago.

LETTER 57

To Fanny Keats *Saturday, 19 February 1820*
Miss Keats, R^d Abbey Esq, Pancras Lane, Queen Street, Cheapside

My dear Fanny,

Being confined almost entirely to vegetable food and the weather being at the same time so much against me, I cannot say I have much improved since I wrote last. The doctor tells me there are no dangerous symptoms about me and that quietness of mind and fine weather will restore me. Mind my advice to be very careful to wear warm clothing in a thaw. I will write again on Tuesday when I hope to send you good news.

Your affectionate brother,
John

LETTER 58

To Fanny Brawne (?) *February* 1820

My dear Fanny,

Do not let your mother suppose that you hurt me by writing at night. For some reason or other your last night's note was not so treasurable as former ones. I would fain that you call me *Love* still. To see you happy and in high spirits is a great consolation to me—still let me believe that you are not half so happy as my restoration would make you. I am nervous, I own, and may think myself worse than I really am; if so you must indulge me, and pamper with that sort of tenderness you have manifested towards me in different letters. My sweet creature, when I look back upon the pains and torments I have suffered for you from the day I left you to go to the Isle of Wight; the ecstasies in which I have passed some days and the miseries in their turn, I wonder the more at the beauty which has kept up the spell so fervently. When I send this round I shall be in the front parlour watching to see you show yourself for a minute in the garden. How illness stands as a barrier betwixt me and you! Even if I was well—I must make myself as good a philosopher as possible. Now I have had opportunities of passing nights anxious and awake I have found other thoughts intrude upon me. "If I should die", said I to myself, "I have left no immortal work behind me—nothing to make my friends proud of my memory—but I have loved the principle of beauty in all things, and if I had had time I would have made myself remembered." Thoughts like these came very feebly whilst I was in health and every pulse beat for you—now you divide with this (may *I* say it?) "last infirmity of noble minds" all my reflection.

God bless you, love.
J. Keats

LETTER 59

To Fanny Brawne (?) *24 February* 1820
Miss Brawne

My dearest girl,
  Indeed I will not deceive you with respect to my health. This is the fact as far as I know. I have been confined three weeks and am not yet well—this proves that there is something wrong about me which my constitution will either conquer or give way to. Let us hope for the best. Do you hear the thrush singing over the field? I think it is a sign of mild weather—so much the better for me. Like all sinners, now I am ill, I philosophize aye out of my attachment to everything, trees, flowers, thrushes, spring, summer, claret, etc, etc—aye everything but you—my sister would be glad of my company a little longer. That thrush is a fine fellow, I hope he was fortunate in his choice this year. Do not send any more of my books home. I have a great pleasure in the thought of you looking on them.
                                    Ever yours,
                                       my sweet Fanny,
                                          J.K.

LETTER 60

To Fanny Brawne (?) *27 February* 1820
Miss Brawne

My dearest Fanny,
  I had a better night last night than I have had since my attack, and this morning I am the same as when you saw me. I have been turning over two volumes of letters written between Rousseau and two ladies in the perplexed strain of mingled finesse and sentiment in which the ladies and gentlemen of those days were so clever, and which is still prevalent among ladies of this country who live in a state of reasoning romance. The likeness however only extends to the mannerism, not

TO FANNY BRAWNE

to the dexterity. What would Rousseau have said at seeing our little correspondence! What would his ladies have said! I don't care much—I would sooner have Shakespeare's opinion about the matter. The common gossiping of washerwomen must be less disgusting than the continual and eternal fence and attack of Rousseau and these sublime petticoats. One calls herself Clara and her friend Julia, two of Rousseau's heroines—they at the same time christen poor Jean Jacques St Preux—who is the pure cavalier of his favous novel. Thank God I am born in England with our own great men before my eyes. Thank God that you are fair and can love me without being letter-written and sentimentalized into it. Mr Barry Cornwall has sent me another book, his first, with a polite note. I must do what I can to make him sensible of the esteem I have for his kindness. If this north-east would take a turn it would be so much the better for me. Good bye, my love, my dear love, my beauty.

Love me for ever.

J.K.

LETTER 61

To Fanny Brawne (*date unknown*)
Miss Brawne

My dear Fanny,

I think you had better not make any long stay with me when Mr Brown is at home—whenever he goes out you may bring your work. You will have a pleasant walk to-day. I shall see you pass. I shall follow you with my eyes over the Heath. Will you come towards evening instead of before dinner—when you are gone, 'tis past. If you do not come till the evening I have something to look forward to all day. Come round to my window for a moment when you have read this. Thank your mother, for the preserves, for me. The raspberry will be too sweet not having any acid; therefore as you are so good a girl I shall make you a present of it. Good bye,

My sweet Love!

J. Keats

LETTER 62

To Fanny Brawne (?) *March* 1820
Miss Brawne

My dearest Fanny,
I slept well last night and am no worse this morning for it. Day by day if I am not deceived I get a more unrestrained use of my chest. The nearer a racer gets to the goal the more his anxiety becomes, so I, lingering upon the borders of health, feel my impatience increase. Perhaps on your account I have imagined my illness more serious than it is: how horrid was the chance of slipping into the ground instead of into your arms—the difference is amazing, Love. Death must come at last; man must die, as Shallow says, but before that is my fate I fain would try what more pleasures than you have given, so sweet a creature as you can give. Let me have another opportunity of years before me and I will not die without being remembered. Take care of yourself, dear, that we may both be well in the summer. I do not at all fatigue myself with writing, having merely to put a line or two here and there, a task which would worry a stout state of the body and mind, but which just suits me as I can do no more.

Your affectionate,
J.K.

LETTER 63

To Fanny Keats Monday, 20 *March* 1820
Miss Keats, Rd. Abbey Esq., Walthamstow

My dear Fanny,
According to your desire I write to-day. It must be but a few lines for I have been attacked several times with a palpitation at the heart and the doctor says I must not make the slightest exertion. I am much

the same to-day as I have been for a week past. They say 'tis nothing but debility and will entirely cease on my recovery of my strength, which is the object of my present diet. As the doctor will not suffer me to write I shall ask Mr Brown to let you hear news of me for the future if I should not get stronger soon. I hope I shall be well enough to come and see your flowers in bloom.

Ever your most affectionate brother,
John

LETTER 64

To Fanny Brawne   *(?) March* 1820
Miss Brawne

My dearest girl,
   In consequence of our company I suppose I shall not see you before to-morrow. I am much better to-day, indeed all I have to complain of is want of strength and a little tightness in the chest. I envied Sam's walk with you to-day; which I will not do again as I may get very tired of envying. I imagine you now sitting in your new black dress which I like so much and if I were a little less selfish and more enthusiastic I should run round and surprise you with a knock at the door. I fear I am too prudent for a dying kind of lover. Yet, there is a great difference between going off in warm blood like Romeo, and making one's exit like a frog in a frost. I had nothing particular to say to-day, but not intending that there shall be any interruption to our correspondence (which at some future time I propose offering to Murray) I write something! God bless you my sweet love! Illness is a long lane, but I see you at the end of it, and shall mend my pace as well as possible.

J.K.

LETTER 65

To Fanny Brawne   (?) April 1820
Miss Brawne

My dear Fanny,
   I am much better this morning than I was a week ago: indeed I improve a little every day. I rely upon taking a walk with you upon the first of May; in the meantime, undergoing a Babylonish captivity I shall not be Jew enough to hang up my harp upon a willow, but rather endeavour to clear up my arrears in versifying and with returning health begin upon something new: pursuant to which resolution it will be necessary to have my, or rather Taylor's, manuscript, which you, if you please, will send by my messenger either to-day or tomorrow. Is Mr D with you to-day? You appeared very much fatigued last night: you must look a little brighter this morning. I shall not suffer my little girl ever to be obscured like glass breathed upon but always bright as it is her *nature to*. Feeding upon sham victuals and sitting by the fire will completely annul me. I have no need of an enchanted wax figure to duplicate me for I am melting in my proper person before the fire. If you meet with anything better (worse) than common in your magazines let me see it.
                              Good bye my sweetest girl.
                                                J.K.

LETTER 66

To Fanny Keats   Thursday, 4 May 1820
Miss Keats, Rd. Abbey Esq, Walthamstow

                                                Wentworth Place
                                                Thursday
My dear Fanny,
   I went for the first time into the City the day before yesterday, for before I was very disinclined to encounter the scuffle, more from

nervousness than real illness; which notwithstanding I should not have suffered to conquer me if I had not made up my mind not to go to Scotland, but to remove to Kentish Town till Mr Brown returns. Kentish Town is a mile nearer to you than Hampstead—I have been getting gradually better but am not so well as to trust myself to the casualties of rain and sleeping out which I am liable to in visiting you. Mr Brown goes on Saturday and by that time I shall have settled in my new lodging when I will certainly venture to you. You will forgive me I hope when I confess that I endeavour to think of you as little as possible and to let George dwell upon my mind but slightly. The reason being that I am afraid to ruminate on anything which has the shade of difficulty or melancholy in it, as that sort of cogitation is so pernicious to health, and it is only by health that I can be enabled to alleviate your situation in future. For some time you must do what you can of yourself for relief, and bear your mind up with the consciousness that your situation cannot last for ever, and that for the present you may console yourself against the reproaches of Mrs Abbey. Whatever obligations you may have had to her you have none now as she has reproached you. I do not know what property you have, but I will enquire into it: be sure however that beyond the obligations that a lodger may have to a landlord you have none to Mr Abbey—Let the surety of this make you laugh at Mrs A's foolish tattle. Mrs Dilke's brother has got your dog. She is not very well—still liable to illness. I will get her to come and see you if I can make up my mind on the propriety of introducing a stranger into Abbey's house. Be careful to let no fretting injure your health as I have suffered it—health is the greatest of blessings—with *health* and *hope* we should be content to live, and so you will find as you grow older.

      I am, my dear Fanny,
        Your affectionate brother,
           John

LETTER 67

To Fanny Brawne (?) *late May* 1820
Tuesday Morn

My dearest girl,
  I wrote a letter for you yesterday expecting to have seen your mother. I shall be selfish enough to send it though I know it may give you a little pain, because I wish you to see how unhappy I am for love of you, and endeavour as much as I can to entice you to give up your whole heart to me whose whole existence hangs upon you. You could not step or move an eyelid but it would shoot to my heart— I am greedy of you. Do not think of anything but me. Do not live as if I was not existing. Do not forget me—but have I any right to say you forget me? Perhaps you think of me all day. Have I any right to wish you to be unhappy for me? You would forgive me for wishing it, if you knew the extreme passion I have that you should love me— and for you to love me as I do you, you must think of no one but me, much less write that sentence. Yesterday and this morning I have been haunted with a sweet vision—I have seen you the whole time in your shepherdess dress. How my senses have ached at it! How my heart has been devoted to it! How my eyes have been full of tears at it! Indeed I think a real love is enough to occupy the widest heart. Your going to town alone, when I heard of it was a shock to me—yet I expected it—*promise me you will not for sometime, till I get better*. Promise me this and fill the paper full of the most endearing names. If you cannot do so with good will, do my love tell me—say what you think —confess if your heart is too much fastened on the world. Perhaps then I may see you at a greater distance, I may not be able to appropriate you so closely to myself. Were you to loose a favourite bird from the cage, how would your eyes ache after it as long as it was in sight; when out of sight you would recover a little. Perhaps if you would, if so it is, confess to me how many things are necessary to you besides me, I might be happier, by being less tantalized. Well may you exclaim, how selfish, how cruel, not to let me enjoy my youth! To wish me to

be unhappy! You must be so if you love me—upon my soul I can be contented with nothing else. If you could really what is called enjoy yourself at a party—if you can smile in people's faces, and wish them to admire you *now*, you never have nor ever will love me. I see *life* in nothing but the certainty of your love—convince me of it my sweetest. If I am not somehow convinced I shall die of agony. If we love we must not live as other men and women do—I cannot brook the wolfsbane of fashion and foppery and tattle. You must be mine to die upon the rack if I want you. I do not pretend to say I have more feeling than my fellows—but I wish you seriously to look over my letters kind and unkind and consider whether the person who wrote them can be able to endure much longer the agonies and uncertainties which you are so peculiarly made to create. My recovery of bodily health will be of no benefit to me if you are not all mine when I am well. For God's sake save me—or tell me my passion is of too awful a nature for you. Again God bless you.

J.K.

No—my sweet Fanny—I am wrong. I do not want you to be unhappy —and yet I do, I must while there is so sweet a beauty—my loveliest, my darling! Good bye! I kiss you—O the torments!

LETTER 68

To Fanny Brawne   *(?) June* 1820
Mrs Brawne

My dearest Fanny,
   My head is puzzled this morning, and I scarce know what I shall say though I am full of a hundred things. 'Tis certain I would rather be writing to you this morning, notwithstanding the alloy of grief in such an occupation, than enjoy any other pleasure, with health to boot, unconnected with you. Upon my soul I have loved you to the extreme. I wish you could know the tenderness with which I con-

tinually brood over your different aspects of countenance, action and dress. I see you come down in the morning: I see you meet me at the window—I see everything over again eternally that I ever have seen. If I get on the pleasant clue I live in a sort of happy misery, if on the unpleasant 'tis miserable misery. You complain of my ill-treating you in word, thought and deed—I am sorry—at times I feel bitterly sorry that I ever made you unhappy—my excuse is that those words have been wrung from me by the sharpness of my feelings. At all events and in any case I have been wrong; could I believe that I did it without any cause, I should be the most sincere of penitents. I could give way to my repentant feelings now, I could recant all my suspicions, I could mingle with you heart and soul though absent, were it not for some parts of your letters. Do you suppose it possible I could ever leave you? You know what I think of myself and what of you. You know that I should feel how much it was my loss and how little yours. My friends laugh at you! I know some of them—when I know them all I shall never think of them again as friends or even acquaintances. My friends have behaved well to me in every instance but one, and there they have become tattlers, and inquisitors into my conduct: spying upon a secret I would rather die than share it with anybody's confidence. For this I cannot wish them well, I care not to see any of them again. If I am the theme, I will not be the friend of idle gossips. Good gods, what a shame it is our loves should be so put into the microscope of a coterie. Their laughs should not affect you (I may perhaps give you reasons some day for these laughs, for I suspect a few people to hate me well enough, *for reasons I know of*, who have pretended a great friendship for me) when in competition with one, who if he never should see you again would make you the saint of his memory. These laughers, who do not like you, who envy you for your beauty, who would have God-blessed-me from you for ever, who were plying me with disencouragements with respect to you eternally. People are revengeful—do not mind them—do nothing but love me—if I knew that for certain life and health will in such event be a heaven, and death itself will be less painful. I long to believe in immortality. I shall never be able to bid you an entire farewell. If I am destined to be happy with you here—how short is the longest life. I wish to believe in immortality—I wish to live with you for ever. Do not let my name ever pass between you and those laughers, if I have no other merit than the great love for you, that were sufficient to keep me sacred and unmentioned in such society. If I have been cruel and unjust I swear my love has ever been greater than my cruelty which lasts but a minute whereas my love, come what will, shall last for ever. If concession to me has hurt your pride, God knows I have had little pride in my heart when thinking of you. Your name never passes my lips—do not let mine pass yours. Those people do not like me. After reading my letter you even then wish to see me. I am strong enough to walk over—but I dare not. I shall feel so much pain in parting with you again. My dearest love, I am afraid to see you, I am strong but not strong enough to see you. Will my arm be ever round you again? And if so shall I be obliged to leave you again? My sweet love! I am happy whilst I believe your first letter. Let me be but certain that you are mine heart and soul, and I could die more happily than I could otherwise live. If you think me cruel—if you think I have slighted you—do muse it over again and see into my heart. My love to you is "true as truth's simplicity and simpler than the infancy of truth" as I think I once said before. How could I slight you? How threaten to leave you? Not in the spirit of a threat to you—no—but in the spirit of wretchedness in myself. My fairest, my delicious, my angel Fanny! Do not believe me such a vulgar fellow. I will be as patient in illness and as believing in love as I am able.

                                      Yours for ever, my dearest,
                                                         John Keats

LETTER 69

To John Taylor (?) 11 *June* 1820
John Taylor Esq, Taylor & Hessey, Booksellers etc, Fleet Street,
The first Bookseller on the left hand, from St. Paul's, past
Bridge Street, Blackfriars

My dear Taylor,
  In reading over the proof of "St Agnes' Eve" since I left Fleet Street, I was struck with what appears to me an alteration in the 7th stanza very much for the worse. The passage I mean stands thus:

>   her maiden eyes incline
>   Still on the floor, while many a sweeping train
>   Pass by—

'Twas originally written:

>   her maiden eyes divine
>   Fix'd on the floor saw many a sweeping train
>   Pass by—

My meaning is quite destroyed in the alteration. I do not use *train* for *concourse of passers by* but for *skirts* sweeping along the floor.
  In the first stanza my copy reads—2nd line—

>   bitter *chill* it was

to avoid the echo *cold* in the next line.

            Ever yours sincerely,
                 John Keats

LETTER 70

To Fanny Brawne (?) *June* 1820
Mrs Brawne

My dearest Girl,
 I endeavour to make myself as patient as possible. Hunt amuses me very kindly—besides I have your ring on my finger and your flowers on the table. I shall not expect to see you yet because it would be so much pain to part with you again. When the books you want come you shall have them. I am very well this afternoon. My dearest . . .

LETTER 71

To Fanny Brawne (?) 5 *July* 1820
  Wednesday Morng.

My dearest girl,
 I have been a walk this morning with a book in my hand, but as usual I have been occupied with nothing but you; I wish I could say in an agreeable manner. I am tormented day and night. They talk of my going to Italy. 'Tis certain I shall never recover if I am to be so long separate from you yet with all this devotion to you I cannot persuade myself into any confidence of you. Past experience connected with the fact of my long separation from you gives me agonies which are scarcely to be talked of. When your mother comes I shall be very sudden and expert in asking her whether you have been to Mrs Dilke's, for she might say no to make me easy. I am literally worn to death, which seems my only recourse. I cannot forget what has passed. What? Nothing with a man of the world, but to me deathful. I will get rid of this as much as possible. When you were in the habit of flirting with Brown you would have left off, could your own heart have felt one half of one pang mine did. Brown is a good sort of man

—he did not know he was doing me to death by inches. I feel the effect of every one of those hours in my side now; and for that cause, though he has done me many services, though I know his love and friendship for me, though at this moment I should be without pence were it not for his assistance, I will never see or speak to him until we are both old men, if we are to be. I *will* resent my heart having been made a football. You will call this madness. I have heard you say that it was not unpleasant to wait a few years—you have amusements—your mind is away—you have not brooded over one idea as I have, and how should you? You are to me an object intensely desirable—the air I breathe in a room empty of you is unhealthy. I am not the same to you—no—you can wait—you have a thousand activities—you can be happy without me. Any party, anything to fill up the day has been enough. How have you passed this month? Who have you smiled with? All this may seem savage in me. You do not feel as I do—you do not know what it is to love—one day you may—your time is not come. Ask yourself how many unhappy hours Keats has caused you in loneliness. For myself I have been a martyr the whole time, and for this reason I speak; the confession is forced from me by the torture. I appeal to you by the blood of that Christ you believe in: do not write to me if you have done anything this month which it would have pained me to have seen. You may have altered—if you have not—if you still behave in dancing rooms and other societies as I have seen you—I do not want to live— if you have done so I wish this coming night may be my last. I cannot live without you, and not only you but *chaste you; virtuous you*. The sun rises and sets, the day passes, and you follow the bent of your inclination to a certain extent—you have no conception of the quantity of miserable feeling that passes through me in a day. Be serious! Love is not a plaything—and again do not write unless you can do it with a crystal conscience. I would sooner die for want of you than—

Yours for ever,
J. Keats

LETTER 72

To Fanny Keats *Wednesday, 5 July 1820*
Miss Keats, Rd. Abbey Esq, Walthamstow

Mortimer Terrace
Wednesday

My dear Fanny,
 I have had no return of the spitting of blood, and for two or three days have been getting a little stronger. I have no hopes of an entire re-establishment of my health under some months of patience. My physician tells me I must contrive to pass the winter in Italy. This is all very unfortunate for us—we have no recourse but patience, which I am now practising better than I ever thought it possible for me. I have this moment received a letter from Mr Brown, dated Dunvegan Castle, Island of Skye. He is very well in health and spirits. My new publication has been out for some days and I have directed a copy to be bound for you, which you will receive shortly. No one can regret Mr Hodgkinson's ill fortune: I must own illness has not made such a saint of me as to prevent my rejoicing at his reverse. Keep yourself in as good hopes as possible; in case my illness should continue an unreasonable time many of my friends would I trust for my sake do all in their power to console and amuse you, at the least word from me. You may depend upon it that in case my strength returns I will do all in my power to extricate you from the Abbeys. Be above all things careful of your health which is the corner stone of all pleasure.
Your affectionate brother,
John

LETTER 73

To Fanny Keats *Saturday, 22 July 1820*
Miss Keats, Rd. Abbey Esq, Walthamstow

My dear Fanny,
 I have been gaining strength for some days: it would be well if I could at the same time say I am gaining hopes of a speedy recovery. My constitution has suffered very much for two or three years past, so as to be scarcely able to make head against illness, which the natural activity and impatience of my mind renders more dangerous. It will at all events be a very tedious affair, and you must expect to hear very little alteration of any sort in me for some time. You ought to have received a copy of my book ten days ago. I shall send another message to the booksellers. One of the Mr Wylies will be here to-day or tomorrow when I will ask him to send you George's letter. Writing the smallest note is so annoying to me that I have waited till I shall see him. Mr Hunt does everything in his power to make the time pass as agreeably with me as possible. I read the greatest part of the day, and generally take two half hour walks a day up and down the terrace which is very much pestered with cries, ballad singers, and street music. We have been so unfortunate for so long a time, every event has been of so depressing a nature, that I must persuade myself to think some change will take place in the aspect of our affairs. I shall be upon the look out for a trump card.
                                        Your affectionate brother,
                                                  John

LETTER 74

To Fanny Brawne (?) *early August* 1820
            (I do not write this till the last
            that no eye may catch it.)

My dearest girl,
   I wish you could invent some means to make me at all happy without you. Every hour I am more and more concentrated in you; everything else tastes like chaff in my mouth. I feel it almost impossible to go to Italy—the fact is I cannot leave you, and shall never taste one minute's content until it pleases chance to let me live with you for good. But I will not go on at this rate. A person in health as you are can have no conception of the horrors that nerves and a temper like mine go through. What island do your friends propose retiring to? I should be happy to go with you there alone, but in company I should object to it; the backbitings and jealousies of new colonists who have nothing else to amuse themselves is unbearable. Mr Dilke came to see me yesterday, and gave me a very great deal more pain than pleasure. I shall never be able any more to endure the society of any of those who used to meet at Elm Cottage and Wentworth Place. The last two years taste like brass upon my palate. If I cannot live with you I will live alone. I do not think my health will improve much while I am separated from you. For all this I am averse to seeing you— I cannot bear flashes of light and return into my glooms again. I am not so unhappy now as I should be if I had seen you yesterday. To be happy with you seems such an impossibility! It requires a luckier star than mine! It will never be. I enclose a passage from one of your letters which I want you to alter a little—I want (if you will have it so) the matter expressed less coldly to me. If my health would bear it, I could write a poem which I have in my head, which would be a consolation for people in such a situation as mine. I would show someone in love as I am, with a person living in such liberty as you do. Shakespeare always sums up matters in the most sovereign manner. Hamlet's heart was full of such misery as mine is when he said to Ophelia "Go to

a Nunnery, go, go!" Indeed I should like to give up the matter at once—I should like to die. I am sickened at the brute world which you are smiling with. I hate men and women more. I see nothing but thorns for the future—wherever I may be next winter in Italy or nowhere, Brown will be living near you with his indecencies—I see no prospect of any rest. Suppose me in Rome—well, I should there see you as in a magic glass going to and from town at all hours—I wish you could infuse a little confidence in human nature into my heart. I cannot muster any—the world is too brutal for me—I am glad there is such a thing as the grave—I am sure I shall never have any rest till I get there. At any rate I will indulge myself by never seeing any more Dilke or Brown or any of their friends. I wish I was either in your arms full of faith or that a thunderbolt would strike me.

God bless you.

J.K.

LETTER 75

To Fanny Keats
Miss Keats, Rd. Abbey's Esq, Walthamstow

13 *August* 1820

Wentworth Place

My dear Fanny,

Tis a long time since I received your last. An accident of an unpleasant nature occurred at Mr Hunt's and prevented me from answering you, that is to say made me nervous. That you may not suppose it worse I will mention that someone of Mr Hunt's household opened a letter of mine—upon which I immediately left Mortimer Terrace, with the intention of taking to Mrs Bentley's again; fortunately I am not in so lone a situation, but am staying a short time with Mrs Brawne who lives in the house which was Mrs Dilke's. I am excessively nervous: a person I am not quite used to entering the room half chokes me. 'Tis not yet consumption I believe, but it would be were I to remain in this climate all the winter: so I am thinking of either voyaging or travelling to Italy. Yesterday I received an invitation from Mr Shelley, a gentleman residing at Pisa, to spend the winter with him: if I go I must be away in a month or even less. I am glad you like the poems, you must hope with me that time and health will produce you some more. This is the first morning I have been able to sit to the paper and have many letters to write if I can manage them. God bless you my dear sister.

Your affectionate brother,
John

LETTER 76

To John Taylor   13 *August* 1820
John Taylor Esq, Taylor & Hessey, Booksellers, Fleet Street

Wentworth Place
Saturday Morn

My dear Taylor,

My chest is in so nervous a state, that anything extra such as speaking to an unaccustomed person or writing a note half suffocates me. This journey to Italy wakes me at daylight every morning and haunts me horribly. I shall endeavour to go though it be with the sensation of marching up against a battery. The first step towards it is to know the expense of a journey and a year's residence; which if you will ascertain for me and let me know early you will greatly serve me. I have more to say but must desist for every line I write increases the tightness of the chest, and I have many more to do. I am convinced that this sort of thing does not continue for nothing. If you can come with any of our friends, do.

Your sincere friend,
John Keats

LETTER 77

To John Taylor   Monday, 14 *August* 1820
John Taylor Esq, Taylor & Hessey, Booksellers, Fleet Street
                                           Wentworth Place

My dear Taylor,
   I do not think I mentioned anything of a passage to Leghorn by sea. Will you join that to your enquiries and, if you can, give a peep at the berth if the vessel is in our river?
                                  Your sincere friend,
                                           John Keats

                                                     [*over*]

P.S. Somehow a copy of Chapman's Homer, lent to me by Haydon, has disappeared from my lodgings—it has quite flown I am afraid, and Haydon urges the return of it so that I must get one at Longman's and send it to Lisson Grove—or you must—or as I have given you a job on the river—ask Mistessey. I had written a note to this effect to Hessey sometime since but crumpled it up in hopes that the book might come to light. This morning Haydon has sent another messenger. The copy was in good condition, with the head. Damn all thieves! Tell Woodhouse I have not lost his Blackwood.
   In case of my death this scrap of paper may be serviceable in your possession.
   All my estate real and personal consists in the hopes of the sale of books published or unpublished. Now I wish *Brown* and you to be the first paid creditors—the rest is *in nubibus*—but in case it should shower pay my tailor the few pounds I owe him.
   My chest of books divide among my friends.

LETTER 78

To Charles Brown 14 *August* 1820

My dear Brown,
  You may not have heard from XXX, or XXX, or in any way, that an attack of spitting of blood, and all its weakening consequences, has prevented me from writing for so long a time. I have matter now for a very long letter, but not news; so I must cut everything short. I shall make some confession, which you will be the only person, for many reasons, I shall trust with. A winter in England would, I have not a doubt, kill me; so I have resolved to go to Italy, either by sea or land. Not that I have any great hopes of that, for, I think, there is a core of disease in me not easy to pull out. . . . If I should die. . . . I shall be obliged to set off in less than a month. Do not, my dear Brown, tease yourself about me. You must fill up your time as well as you can, and as happily. You must think of my faults as lightly as you can. When I have health I will bring up the long arrears of letters I owe you. . . . My book has had good success among literary people, and I believe has a moderate sale. I have seen very few people we know. XXX has visited me more than anyone. I would go to XXX and make some enquiries after you, if I could with any bearable sensation; but a person I am not quite used to causes an oppression on my chest. Last week I received a letter from Shelley, at Pisa, of a very kind nature, asking me to pass the winter with him. Hunt has behaved very kindly to me. You shall hear from me again shortly.
                                    Your affectionate friend,
                                         John Keats

LETTER 79

To Percy Bysshe Shelley   *Wednesday, 16 August* 1820
P. B. Shelley Esq
                            Hampstead August 16

My dear Shelley,
   I am very much gratified that you, in a foreign country, and with a mind almost over-occupied, should write to me in the strain of the letter beside me. If I do not take advantage of your invitation it will be prevented by a circumstance I have very much at heart to prophesy. There is no doubt that an English winter would put an end to me, and do so in a lingering hateful manner, therefore I must either voyage or journey to Italy as a soldier marches up to a battery. My nerves at present are the worst part of me, yet they feel soothed when I think that come what extreme may, I shall not be destined to remain in one spot long enough to take a hatred of any four particular bedposts. I am glad you take any pleasure in my poor poem, which I would willingly take the trouble to unwrite, if possible, did I care so much as I have done about reputation. I received a copy of *The Cenci*, as from yourself from Hunt. There is only one part of it I am judge of; the poetry, and dramatic effect, which by many spirits nowadays is considered the mammon. A modern work it is said must have a purpose, which may be the God—*an artist* must serve Mammon—he must have "self concentration", selfishness perhaps. You I am sure will forgive me for sincerely remarking that you might curb your magnanimity and be more of an artist, and "load every rift" of your subject with ore. The thought of such discipline must fall like cold chains upon you, who perhaps never sat with your wings furled for six months together. And is not this extraordinary talk for the writer of *Endymion*! Whose mind was like a pack of scattered cards—I am picked up and sorted to a pip. My imagination is a monastery and I am its monk—you must explain my metaphors to yourself. I am in expectation of *Prometheus* every day. Could I have my own wish for its interest effected you would have it still in manuscript—or be but now putting an end to the second act. I remember you advising me not to publish

TO CHARLES BROWN

my first-blights, on Hampstead Heath—I am returning advice upon your hands. Most of the poems in the volume I send you have been written above two years, and would never have been published but from a hope of gain; so you see I am inclined enough to take your advice now. I must express once more my deep sense of your kindness, adding my sincere thanks and respects for Mrs Shelley. In the hope of soon seeing you, I remain,

Most sincerely yours,
John Keats

LETTER 80

To Charles Brown   *(?) August or September* 1820

My dear Brown,

* ... I ought to be off at the end of this week, as the cold winds begin to blow towards evening; but I will wait till I have your answer to this. I am to be introduced, before I set out, to a Dr Clark, a physician settled at Rome, who promises to befriend me in every way there. The sale of my book is very slow, though it has been very highly rated. One of the causes, I understand from different quarters, of the unpopularity of this new book, and the others also, is the offence the ladies take at me. On thinking that matter over, I am certain that I have said nothing in a spirit to displease any woman I would care to please; but still there is a tendency to class women in my books with roses and sweetmeats—they never see themselves dominant. If ever I come to publish "Lucy Vaughan Lloyd", there will be some delicate picking for squeamish stomachs. I will say no more but, waiting in anxiety for your answer, doff my hat, and make a purse as long as I can.

Your affectionate friend,
John Keats

* Note [by Brown]. The commencement is a continuation of the secret in his former letter, ending with a request that I would accompany him to Italy.

LETTER 81

To Fanny Keats   *Wednesday, 23 August* 1820
Miss Keats, Rd. Abbey's Esq, Walthamstow

Wentworth Place
Wednesday Morning

My dear Fanny,

  It will give me great pleasure to see you here, if you can contrive it; though I confess I should have written instead of calling upon you before I set out on my journey, from the wish of avoiding unpleasant partings. Meantime I will just notice some parts of your letter. The seal-breaking business is overblown. I think no more of it. A few days ago I wrote to Mr Brown, asking him to befriend me with his company to Rome. His answer is not yet come, and I do not know when it will, not being certain how far he may be from the Post Office to which my communication is addressed. Let us hope he will go with me. George certainly ought to have written to you: his troubles, anxieties and fatigues are not quite a sufficient excuse. In the course of time you will be sure to find that this neglect is not forgetfulness. I am sorry to hear you have been so ill and in such low spirits. Now you are better, keep so. Do not suffer your mind to dwell on unpleasant reflections—that sort of thing has been the destruction of my health. Nothing is so bad as want of health—it makes one envy scavengers and cinder-sifters. There are enough real distresses and evils in wait for every one to try the most vigorous health. Not that I would say yours are not real—but they are such as to tempt you to employ your imagination on them, rather than endeavour to dismiss them entirely. Do not diet your mind with grief, it destroys the constitution; but let your chief care be of your health, and with that you will meet with your share of pleasure in the world—do not doubt it. If I return well from Italy I will turn over a new leaf for you. I have been improving lately, and have very good hopes of "turning a neuk" and cheating the consumption. I am not well enough to write to George myself—Mr Haslam will do it for me, to whom I shall write to-day, desiring him to mention as gently as possible your complaint. I am, my dear Fanny,

Your affectionate brother,
John

LETTER 82

To Fanny Keats   *Monday, 11 September 1820*
Miss Keats, R^d Abbey's Esq, Walthamstow

                                        Monday Morn^g

My dear Fanny,

In the hope of entirely re-establishing my health I shall leave England for Italy this week, and of course I shall not be able to see you before my departure. It is not illness that prevents me from writing but as I am recommended to avoid every sort of fatigue I have accepted the assistance of a friend, who I have desired to write to you when I am gone and to communicate any intelligence she may hear of me. I am as well as I can expect and feel very impatient to get on board as the sea air is expected to be of great benefit to me. My present intention is to stay some time at Naples and then to proceed to Rome where I shall find several friends or at least several acquaintances. At any rate it will be a relief to quit this cold, wet, uncertain climate. I am not very fond of living in cities but there will be too much to amuse me, as soon as I am well enough to go out, to make me feel dull. I have received your parcel and intend to take it with me. You shall hear from me as often as possible; if I feel too tired to write myself I shall have some friend to do it for me. I have not yet heard from George nor can I expect to receive any letters from him before I leave.

                             Your affectionate brother,
                                               John

LETTER 83

To Charles Brown   *Saturday, 30 September 1820*
Mr C. Brown, Wentworth Place, Hampstead, Middx.

Saturday Sept. [30]
Maria Crowther
off Yarmouth, Isle of Wight

My dear Brown,

    The time has not yet come for a pleasant letter from me. I have delayed writing to you from time to time because I felt how impossible it was to enliven you with one heartening hope of my recovery; this morning in bed the matter struck me in a different manner; I thought I would write "while I was in some liking" or I might become too ill to write at all, and then if the desire to have written should become strong it would be a great affliction to me. I have many more letters to write and I bless my stars that I have begun, for time seems to press—this may be my best opportunity. We are in a calm and I am easy enough this morning. If my spirits seem too low you may in some degree impute it to our having been at sea a fortnight without making any way. I was very disappointed at not meeting you at Bedhampton, and am very provoked at the thought of you being at Chichester to-day. I should have delighted in setting off for London for the sensation merely—for what should I do there? I could not leave my lungs or stomach or other worse things behind me. I wish to write on subjects that will not agitate me much—there is one I must mention and have done with it. Even if my body would recover of itself, this would prevent it. The very thing which I want to live most for will be a great occasion of my death. I cannot help it. Who can help it? Were I in health it would make me ill, and how can I bear it in my state? I daresay you will be able to guess on what subject I am harping—you know what was my greatest pain during the first part of my illness at your house. I wish for death every day and night to deliver me from these pains, and then I wish death away, for death would destroy even those pains which are better than nothing. Land and sea, weakness and decline are great separators but death is the great divorcer

TO CHARLES BROWN

for ever. When the pang of this thought has passed through my mind, I may say the bitterness of death is passed. I often wish for you that you might flatter me with the best. I think without my mentioning it for my sake you would be a friend to Miss Brawne when I am dead. You think she has many faults—but, for my sake, think she has not one—if there is anything you can do for her by word or deed I know you will do it. I am in a state at present in which woman merely as woman can have no more power over me than stocks and stones, and yet the difference of my sensations with respect to Miss Brawne and my sister is amazing. The one seems to absorb the other to a degree incredible. I seldom think of my brother and sister in America. The thought of leaving Miss Brawne is beyond everything horrible—the sense of darkness coming over me—I eternally see her figure eternally vanishing. Some of the phrases she was in the habit of using during my last nursing at Wentworth Place ring in my ears. Is there another life? Shall I awake and find all this a dream? There must be: we cannot be created for this sort of suffering. The receiving of this letter is to be one of yours. I will say nothing about our friendship or rather yours to me more than that as you deserve to escape you will never be so unhappy as I am. I should think of—you in my last moments. I shall endeavour to write to Miss Brawne if possible to-day. A sudden stop to my life in the middle of one of these letters would be no bad thing for it keeps one in a sort of fever awhile. Though fatigued with a letter longer than any I have written for a long while, it would be better to go on for ever than awake to a sense of contrary winds. We expect to put into Portland Roads to-night. The Captain, the crew and the passengers are all ill-tempered and weary. I shall write to Dilke. I feel as if I was closing my last letter to you—My dear Brown,

Your affectionate friend,
John Keats

LETTER 84

To Mrs Brawne   *Tuesday, 24 October* 1820
Mrs Brawne, Wentworth Place, Hampstead, Middx, England
                        Octr. 24, Naples Harbour
                                  care Giovanni

My dear Mrs Brawne,
   A few words will tell you what sort of a passage we had, and what situation we are in, and few they must be on account of the quarantine, our letters being liable to be opened for the purpose of fumigation at the Health Office. We have to remain in the vessel ten days and are at present shut in a tier of ships. The sea air has been beneficial to me about to as great an extent as squally weather and bad accommodation and provisions has done harm—So I am about as I was—Give my love to Fanny and tell her, if I were well there is enough in this port of Naples to fill a quire of paper—but it looks like a dream—every man who can row his boat and walk and talk seems a different being from myself—I do not feel in the world—It has been unfortunate for me that one of the passengers is a young lady in a consumption—her imprudence has vexed me very much—the knowledge of her complaint—the flushings in her face, all her bad symptoms have preyed upon me—they would have done so had I been in good health. Severn now is a very good fellow but his nerves are too strong to be hurt by other people's illnesses—I remember poor Rice wore me in the same way in the Isle of Wight—I shall feel a load off me when the lady vanishes out of my sight. It is impossible to describe exactly in what state of health I am—at this moment I am suffering from indigestion very much, which makes such stuff of this letter. I would always wish you to think me a little worse than I really am; not being of a sanguine disposition I am likely to succeed. If I do not recover your regret will be softened, if I do your pleasure will be doubled—I dare not fix my mind upon Fanny, I have not dared to think of her. The only comfort I have had that way has been in thinking for hours together of having the knife she gave me put in a silver case—the hair in a locket—and the pocket book in a gold net—Show her this. I dare say no more—

Yet you must not believe I am so ill as this letter may look for if ever there was a person born without the faculty of hoping I am he. Severn is writing to Haslam, and I have just asked him to request Haslam to send you his account of my health. O what an account I could give you of the Bay of Naples if I could once more feel myself a citizen of this world—I feel a spirit in my brain would lay it forth pleasantly—O what a misery it is to have an intellect in splints! My love again to Fanny—Tell Tootts I wish I could pitch her a basket of grapes—and tell Sam the fellows catch here with a line a little fish much like an anchovy, pull them up fast. Remember me to Mrs and Mr Dilke—mention to Brown that I wrote him a letter at Portsmouth which I did not send and am in doubt if he ever will see it.

    My dear Mrs Brawne,
      Yours sincerely and affectionately,
              John Keats

Good bye Fanny! God bless you.

LETTER 85

To Charles Brown   *Wednesday, 1 November* 1820
            Wednesday, first in November

My dear Brown,
 Yesterday we were let out of quarantine, during which my health suffered more from bad air and the stifled cabin than it had done the whole voyage. The fresh air revived me a little, and I hope I am well enough this morning to write to you a short calm letter—if that can be called one, in which I am afraid to speak of what I would the fainest dwell upon. As I have gone thus far into it, I must go on a little—perhaps it may relieve the load of WRETCHEDNESS which presses upon me. The persuasion that I shall see her no more will kill me. I cannot q— — My dear Brown, I should have had her when I was in health, and I should have remained well. I can bear to die—I cannot bear to leave her. O, God! God! God! Everything I have in

my trunks that reminds me of her goes through me like a spear. The silk lining she put in my travelling cap scalds my head. My imagination is horribly vivid about her—I see her—I hear her. There is nothing in the world of sufficient interest to divert me from her a moment. This was the case when I was in England; I cannot recollect, without shuddering, the time that I was a prisoner at Hunt's, and used to keep my eyes fixed on Hampstead all day. Then there was a good hope of seeing her again—Now!—O that I could be buried near where she lives! I am afraid to write to her—to receive a letter from her—to see her handwriting would break my heart—even to hear of her anyhow, to see her name written, would be more than I can bear. My dear Brown, what am I to do? Where can I look for consolation or ease? If I had any chance of recovery, this passion would kill me. Indeed, through the whole of my illness, both at your house and at Kentish Town, this fever has never ceased wearing me out. When you write to me, which you will do immediately, write to Rome (*poste restante*) —if she is well and happy, put a mark thus +, —if— Remember me to all. I will endeavour to bear my miseries patiently. A person in my state of health should not have such miseries to bear. Write a short note to my sister, saying you have heard from me. Severn is very well. If I were in better health I should urge your coming to Rome. I fear there is no one can give me any comfort. Is there any news of George? O, that something fortunate had ever happened to me or my brothers!—then I might hope—but despair is forced upon me as a habit. My dear Brown, for my sake, be her advocate for ever. I cannot say a word about Naples; I do not feel at all concerned in the thousand novelties around me. I am afraid to write to her. I should like her to know that I do not forget her. Oh, Brown, I have coals of fire in my breast. It surprises me that the human heart is capable of containing and bearing so much misery. Was I born for this end? God bless her, and her mother, and my sister, and George, and his wife, and you, and all!

Your ever affectionate friend,
John Keats

Thursday. I was a day too early for the courier. He sets out now. I have been more calm today, though in a half dread of not continuing so. I said nothing of my health; I know nothing of it; you will hear Severn's account from Haslam. I must leave off. You bring my thoughts too near to—

God bless you!

LETTER 86

To Charles Brown   *Thursday*, 30 *November* 1820
                                                       Rome, 30 November 1820

My dear Brown,
'Tis the most difficult thing in the world to me to write a letter. My stomach continues so bad, that I feel it worse on opening any book—yet I am much better than I was in quarantine. Then I am afraid to encounter the proing and conning of anything interesting to me in England. I have an habitual feeling of my real life having passed, and that I am leading a posthumous existence. God knows how it would have been—but it appears to me—however, I will not speak of that subject. I must have been at Bedhampton nearly at the time you were writing to me from Chichester—how unfortunate—and to pass on the river too! There was my star predominant! I cannot answer anything in your letter, which followed me from Naples to Rome, because I am afraid to look it over again. I am so weak (in mind) that I cannot bear the sight of any handwriting of a friend I love so much as I do you. Yet I ride the little horse and, at my worst, even in quarantine, summoned up more puns, in a sort of desperation, in one week than in any year of my life. There is one thought enough to kill me—I have been well, healthy, alert etc, walking with her—and now—the knowledge of contrast, feeling for light and shade, all that information (primitive sense) necessary for a poem, are great enemies to the recovery of the stomach. There, you rogue, I put you to the torture—but you must bring your philosophy to bear—as I do mine, really—or how should I be able to live? Dr Clark is very attentive to me; he says, there is very little the matter with my lungs, but my

stomach, he says, is very bad. I am well disappointed in hearing good news from George—for it runs in my head we shall all die young. I have not written to XXX yet, which he must think very neglectful; being anxious to send him a good account of my health, I have delayed it from week to week. If I recover, I will do all in my power to correct the mistakes made during sickness; and if I should not, all my faults will be forgiven. I shall write to XXX tomorrow, or next day. I will write to XXX in the middle of next week. Severn is very well, though he leads so dull a life with me. Remember me to all friends, and tell XXX I should not have left London without taking leave of him, but from being so low in body and mind. Write to George as soon as you receive this, and tell him how I am, as far as you can guess; and also a note to my sister—who walks about my imagination like a ghost —she is so like Tom. I can scarcely bid you goodbye, even in a letter. I always made an awkward bow.

God bless you!
John Keats

NOTES

NOTES

LETTER I

p. 47   *Sonnet to the Sun* (lines 3-4). Almost certainly *To the Setting Sun* by Horace Smith. Clarke told Woodhouse in 1823 that "one of the first things J. K. wrote was a *Sonnet to the Moon* which he gave" to Clarke.
Darwin (line 6). See Introduction, p. 19.
the Borough (line 15), i.e. Southwark.
Dean Street (line 16). Now Stainer Street, and an arch of the railway at London Bridge Station.
a Meeting (line 19), i.e. a Baptist chapel.

LETTER 2

p. 48   *Haydon* (line 2). B. R. Haydon, the artist, whom Keats met at Leigh Hunt's in October 1816, and at once idolized. In return there were "the laudations that Haydon trowelled on to the young poet". There was trouble in 1819 over money Keats had lent Haydon, and by January 1820 Keats was weary of "Haydon's worn out discourses of poetry and painting". Haydon irritated Keats during his last illness with advice on how to take care of his health. He committed suicide in 1846.

LETTER 3

p. 49   *every head* (line 20). The heads of Wordsworth, Keats, Hazlitt and others in Haydon's picture *Christ's Triumphal Entry*.

p. 50   *Wilkinson's plan* (line 3). Keats presented a copy of *Poems* (1817) "to C. Wilkinson", possibly a London lawyer. He also lent one Wilkinson money which George Keats thought was still owing in 1825.

LETTER 5

p. 53   *Miss Caley's School*. Miss Caley, an assistant at the Ladies' Boarding Academy, took over the school when the Misses Tuckey died. This is the earliest letter we have from Keats to his sister.

p. 54   *King Pepin* (lines 4–5). A commonplace figure in children's tales.
a young man (line 16), i.e. Benjamin Bailey.
a poem (line 19). "It was during this visit, and in my room, that he wrote the third book of *Endymion*" (Bailey to Milnes, 1849).

p. 55   (line 21) *Essays in Rhyme, or Morals and Manners* by Jane Taylor (1816). A copy was bought in Madrid in 1924 inscribed "John Keats to his dear sister".
(line 23) *Original Poems for Infant Minds* by Jane and Ann Taylor (1804).
the poorest . . . spoken (line 26). By September 1819 Keats had come to think French "very capable of poetry".

LETTER 6

p. 56   *the two Rs* (line 4), i.e. Rice and Reynolds.
Johnny Martin (line 5). A publishing acquaintance of Keats, much later librarian at Woburn Abbey.

p. 57   *Gleig* (line 6). G. R. Gleig became Bailey's brother-in-law. He was a writer, and many years later Chaplain General to the Forces.
as many lines (line 8), i.e. of *Endymion*.

p. 58   *Hazlitt's essay on commonplace people* (line 22), i.e. "On Commonplace Critics". Hazlitt wrote: "Mr Wordsworth . . . has made an attack on a set of gipsies for having done nothing in four and twenty hours. . . . What had he himself been doing in these four and twenty hours?"

p. 59   *Crips* (line 4). Charles Crips, a young artist whom Keats had been asked by Haydon to get in touch with. Haydon had high-flown ideas for training Crips which, typically, evaporated.
like a son of Niobe's (line 10), i.e. "all tears".
I shall . . . off-hand (lines 11–12). Bailey's writing was almost illegible.
Peona (line 17), see *Endymion*, Book I, line 408.
Coleridge's Lays (line 25), i.e. *Lay Sermons*.

LETTER 7

p. 60   *your disappointment* (line 1). Some delay in Bailey's ordination, related to his taking up a curacy, was blamed on the Bishop of Lincoln.

p. 61   *the* Edinburgh Magazine (line 31). Blackwood's *Edinburgh Magazine* launched repeated attacks on Keats and his associates, of which this was the sighting shot in October 1817. The attacks did not stop with Keats's death.

NOTES

p. 62 *Cornelius Webb* (line 1), a poet and author now famous only for his invention of the description "the Muse's son of promise" for Keats. The phrase was repeated endlessly by later writers.
the following advertisement (line 7). The only effect of the advertisement was more anonymous abuse from "Z" upon Hunt.

LETTER 8

p. 65 *the little song* (line 8), i.e. "O Sorrow".
consequitive (line 13). This is what Keats wrote.
O for a life of sensations, etc. (lines 15–16). The ideas are discussed at length by N. F. Ford in *The Prefigurative Imagination of John Keats* (Stanford University Press: O.U.P., 1951).

p. 66 *years ... philosophic mind* (line 4). cf. Wordsworth, "Ode: Intimations of Immortality".
to wind up my poem (line 33). "Burford Bridge, November 28 1817." is written at the end of the first draft of *Endymion*. Keats stayed at the foot of Box Hill at the Fox and Hounds (now Burford Bridge Hotel).
Christie (line 35), i.e. J. H. Christie, found not guilty in April 1821 of the murder of John Scott, editor of the *London Magazine*, whom he had mortally wounded in a duel arising from J. G. Lockhart's reviews in what Bailey called "that most odious publication of Blackwood's".

LETTER 9

Transcript by Jeffrey of part of a journal letter. The omissions indicated are Jeffrey's.

p. 67 *Luke in* Riches (line 3), i.e. Luke Traffic in *Riches*, by J. B. Burges.
proper ... entirely lost (lines 5–7). A reference to articles by Leigh Hunt.
Hone the publisher's ... service (lines 7–8). William Hone, writer and bookseller, was tried for libel and acquitted by Lord Chief Justice Ellenborough who had sent Leigh Hunt to prison; and Thomas Wooler, journalist, had been acquitted by a different judge.
Wells (line 15), i.e. Charles Wells, school friend of Tom Keats, with whom Keats was familiar until he fooled Tom by sending him mock love-letters signed Amena. Wells later regretted it bitterly.
West's age (line 17). Benjamin West (1738–1820), fashionable painter, was President of the Royal Academy. Leigh Hunt attacked him.

p. 68 *Horace Smith* (line 10), close friend of Shelley and Hunt, author of *Rejected Addresses*.

Hill and Kingston, and one Du Bois (lines 10–11). Thomas Hill was a book collector. Keats later called Kingston "the thing Kingston" but enjoyed "a book of Dubois's", *My Pocket Book*.
penetralium (line 27). A "Latin" word coined by Keats.
Shelley's poem . . . objected to (lines 32–3). C. & J. Ollier, the publishers, tried to recall copies of Shelley's *Laon and Cythna* because of its "immoral" nature, and after extensive changes it was re-issued as *The Revolt of Islam*. The Olliers also published Keats's *Poems* 1817.

LETTER 10

p. 69   *one from Haydon* (line 4), in which Haydon offers eternal friendship to Keats, and an engagement "every Sunday at 3."
three things superior (line 12). Haydon in his reply added a fourth—"John Keats' genius".

p. 70   *the Drury Lane ticket* (line 19). Brown had a life admission that Keats often used.
from Hampstead (line 33). It should read either "from Hampshire" or "to Hampstead". Brown had been visiting Dilke's sister and her husband, John Snook, at Bedhampton.
has returned . . . style (lines 33–4), i.e. an answer, no doubt, to Reynolds.
Bewick (line 36), pupil and close friend of Haydon.

p. 71   *my first book* (line 3), i.e. of *Endymion*.

LETTER 11

dish of filberts . . . two pence (lines 1–2). Woodhouse noted "2 sonnets on Robin Hood sent by R. by the 2nd post".
"tender and true" (line 12). In 1821 Reynolds altered the line "His greenwood beauty sits, tender and true", to "young as the dew".

p. 72   *Sancho* (line 3), in *Don Quixote*.
"Matthew with a bough of wilding . . ." (lines 22–3). See Wordsworth, "The Two April Mornings".
4th Book of Childe Harold (line 33), published April 1818.

p. 75   *2nd book* (line 22), i.e. of *Endymion*.

LETTER 13

p. 78   *soberly* (line 3). *Endymion*, Book I, line 149.
quiet (line 4). *Endymion*, Book I, line 247.

NOTES

p. 79   "*raft ... ash top*" (lines 19–20). *Endymion*, Book I, line 334.
"*Dryope's ... child*" (line 23). *Endymion*, Book I, line 495.

LETTER 14

p. 81   pulvis ... *strong dose* (line 4). An emetic.
Acrasian (line 16). From Acrasia, "a false enchantress" in *The Faerie Queene*.
the cruel emperor (line 34), i.e. Caligula, who wished the Roman people had one head, that he might cut it off.

p. 82   "*consecrate ... look upon*" (lines 19–20), cf. Shelley, "Hymn to Intellectual Beauty", line 13.

LETTER 15

p. 83   *Brown's accident* (line 2). Years before, Brown had a narrow escape when a parapet stone fell and struck the calf of his leg.

p. 84   *Lydia Languish* (line 12), in Sheridan's *The Rivals*.
Damosel Radcliffe (line 18), i.e. Mrs Ann Radcliffe, famous for her Gothic novels.
where I ... Kean (line 32). The actor was ill the previous winter.

p. 85   *fourth Book* (line 6), of *Endymion*.

LETTER 16

p. 86   *the thing* (line 1), i.e. the rejected preface to *Endymion*.

p. 87   *Thomas Chatterton* (lines 4–5), the poet, born 1752, dead before he was 18 and buried in a pauper's shell at Shoe Lane Workhouse. He deceived the critics with his mock medieval poems. "It is wonderful how the whelp has written such things", said Dr Johnson. Wordsworth called him "the marvellous Boy", and he enjoyed a considerable posthumous vogue with many besides Keats.
Kents Cave (line 15). Prehistoric remains were found in Kents cavern.
We go ... Bailey (lines 17–18). Keats left Teignmouth on 4 or 5 May, and did not go through Bath. Bailey was at Oxford.

LETTER 17

p. 88   *Sir Andrew ... head*" (lines 9–10). Keats seems to be recollecting Slender's quibble in *The Merry Wives of Windsor*, Act I, Scene i, line 126, and

LETTERS OF JOHN KEATS

attributing it to Sir Andrew Aguecheek, who also had his head "broke across" (*Twelfth Night*, Act V, Scene i, line 178) and *might* have said it.
"*Notus* . . . *Sierraleona*" (line 18). *Paradise Lost*, Book X, line 702.
breathe worsted stockings (line 19), be back at Well Walk, among the family of Bentley the postman.

p. 89   *Parson Hugh . . . canary* (lines 1–2). Parson Hugh in *The Merry Wives of Windsor* finished off dinner with "pippins and seese", Act I, Scene ii, line 13. There is possibly also a pun on King Pepin, used by the Elizabethans as a symbol of antiquity. A Canary was a brisk Spanish dance and the word was used by Mistress Quickly in the same play as a mistake for "quandary", but the whole reference is obscure.
pip-civilian (line 10), little lawyer.
burden . . . mystery (line 12), See Wordsworth's "Tintern Abbey", line 38.

p. 90   "*Knowledge is Sorrow*" (line 30), see *Manfred*, Act I, Scene i, line 10.
p. 91   *Patmore* (line 13), i.e. P. G. Patmore, father of Coventry Patmore.
Colman (line 14), i.e. George Colman (1762–1836) playwright.
fly the garter (line 15), leap-frog from beyond a "garter" or line of stones.
Little (line 16), the pen-name of Thomas Moore.
I may dip (line 21). Woodhouse explains that the letter is crossed here, and the word "dip" is "the first that *dips* into the former writing".
chequer work (line 23). The term Keats often used for crossing (i.e. writing across) a letter. That the term reminds him of chequer-work on an apron, hence of a milkmaid, is clear from the reference to "pulling an apron-string".

p. 93   *Moore's present* (line 15). Not Thomas Moore, to whom Hazlitt was unfriendly, but Peter Moore, one of the rich managers of Drury Lane, as Holman shows.

LETTER 18

p. 94   *letters in the Oxford paper* (lines 1–2). Bailey wrote two on *Endymion*.
a Petrarchal coronation (line 11). A coronation as a poet, like Petrarch.
p. 95   *those minute volumes of Cary* (line 20). Cary's translation of the *Divine Comedy*, published by Taylor and Hessey in 32mo.
the Edinburgh . . . Mister Keats" (lines 24–5). Lockhart in *Blackwood's*, called him an "amiable but infatuated bardling, Mister John Keats".
"*Foliage*" (line 27). A reference to Leigh Hunt's *Foliage* reviewed in January 1818.

244

NOTES

LETTER 19

p. 96   *canvassing . . . Brougham* (lines 19-20). William Lowther, later Ear Lonsdale, the Whig, defeated Henry Brougham, later Baron Brougham, the Tory.

LETTER 20

p. 104   *a sheet of parliament* (line 24). A thin ginger-bread cake.
lady's fingers (line 26). Large mints.

LETTER 21

p. 106   *Now . . . Fanny* (line 23), i.e. to writing the previous letter.
p. 108   *the Hummums* (line 24), a hotel in Great Russell Street.

LETTER 22

p. 110   *Laputan printing press* (line 3), See *Gulliver's Travels*, Book III, chapter 5.
p. 111   *a sonnet* (line 19), i.e. "This mortal body of a thousand days".
Caliph Vathek (line 26), in *Vathek*, by William Beckford.
p. 112   *my little nephews* (line 10). None was born till Keats was dead.
your lovely wife (line 11). Eliza Drewe, whom Reynolds married in 1822.
the book (line 34). *Endymion*. Keats wrote "from the author" on a scrap of paper, which he asked to be pasted in the book.

LETTER 23

p. 114   *Jessie of Dunblane* (line 22). "Jessie the flower of Dunblane" was a popular song.
Icolmkill (line 28), i.e. Iona.

LETTER 26

p. 117   *the voice . . . woman* (lines 7-8). Jane Cox, called Charmian.
p. 118   *Sawrey* (line 5). Solomon Sawrey, the surgeon who attended Tom Keats.

LETTER 29

p. 120   *I shall call . . . again* (lines 14-15). Abbey passed £20 to Keats when he called. Fanny was not permitted to come.

LETTER 30

p. 121   *Saturn and Ops* (line 24). They appear in "Hyperion". Woodhouse noted that this letter "was in answer to one I addressed to Keats on 21 Oct, in occasion of the malicious and unjust article in the *Quarterly Review*". Keats at a dinner "about six weeks back" had "seemed very doubtful of his continuing to write".

Woodhouse wrote very soon to Taylor, commenting on Keats's views in this important letter:

> I believe him to be right with regard to his own poetical character. And I perceive clearly the distinction he draws between himself and those of the Wordsworth school. There are gradations in poetry and in poets. One is purely descriptive, confining himself to external nature and visible objects. Another describes in addition the effects of the thoughts of which he is conscious (and the effects he has produced in others by such like thoughts) and which others are affected by. Another will soar so far into the regions of imagination as to conceive beings and substances in situations different from what he has ever seen them, but still such as either have actually occurred or may possibly occur. (Such is the tragedian). Another will reason in poetry, another be witty. Another will imagine things that never did or probably never will occur, or such as cannot in nature occur and yet he will describe them so that you may recognize nothing very unnatural in the descriptions when certain principles or powers or conditions are admitted. Another will throw himself into various characters and make them speak as the passions would naturally incite them to do. The highest order of poet will not only possess all the above powers but will have as high an imagination that he will be able to throw his own soul into any object he sees or imagines, so as to feel and be sensible of, and express, all that the object itself would see, feel and be sensible of or express—and he will speak out of that object—so that his own self will with the exception of the mechanical part be "annihilated". And it is the excess of this power that I suppose Keats speaks, when he says he has no identity. As a poet, and when the fit is upon him, this is true—and it is a fact that he does by the power of his imagination create ideal personages, substances and powers—that he lives for a time in their souls or essences or ideas—and that occasionally so intensely as to lose consciousness of what is around him. We all do the same, in a degree, when we fall into a reverie.

If then his imagination has such power, and he is continually cultivating it, and giving it play, it will acquire strength by the indulgence and exercise. This in excess is the case of mad persons. And this may be carried to that extent that he may lose sight of his identity so far as to give him a habit of speaking generally in an assumed character—so that what he says shall be tinged with the sentiments proper to the character which at the time has possessed itself of his imagination.

This being his idea of the poetical character, he may well say that a poet has no identity. As a man he must have identity. But as a poet he need not. And in this sense a poet is "the most unpoetical of God's creatures", for his soul has no distinctive characteristic—it cannot be itself made the subject of poetry, that is another person's soul cannot be thrown into the poet's, for there is no identity or personal impulse to be acted upon.

Shakespeare was a poet of the kind above mentioned—and he was perhaps the only one besides Keats who possessed this power in an extraordinary degree, so as to be a feature in his works. He gives a description of his idea of a poet.

The poet's eye, etc.

Lord Byron does not come up to this character. He can certainly conceive and describe a dark accomplished villain in love—and a female tender and kind who loves him. Or a sated and palled sensualist, misanthrope and deist—but here his power ends. The true poet cannot only conceive this, but can assume any character, essence, idea or substance at pleasure. And he has this imaginative faculty not in a limited manner, but in full universality.

Let us pursue speculation on these matters: and we shall soon be brought to believe in the truth of every syllable of Keats's letter, taken as a description of himself and his own ideas and feelings.

Note. The power of his imagination is apparent in every page of his *Endymion*—and he had affirmed that he can conceive of a billiard ball that it may have a sense of delight from its own roundness, smoothness and very volubility and the rapidity of its motion.

Take page 69—only, and look at the qualities with which in that one page (*Endymion*, Book II, line 344, ff.) he endues inane beings and even imagined ideas, as silence, a channel of a stream, a shallow by water side and the sense of refreshment.

LETTER 31

p. 122 *Poor Tom* (line 1). He died the next morning.

LETTER 33

p. 123 *the music* (line 12), i.e. piano.
p. 124 *for I . . . steps* (line 3). Keats could dance, however.

LETTER 34

p. 124 *our . . . cousin's* (line 7). The "cousin" was Mary Millar, of Henrietta Street, where Mrs Wylie sometimes stayed, and the brothers-in-law, Henry and Charles Wylie.
a Tassie (line 11). James Tassie kept a shop at 20 Leicester Square, selling "pastes and impressions from ancient and modern gems".
pp. 124–5 *motto ones . . . letter* (line 15, line 1). A lyre and the legend "Qui me néglige me désole".
p. 125 *who came with me* (line 34), i.e. on 13 December 1818.

LETTER 35

p. 126 *so long . . . Tottenham* (line 3). About 8 miles.
it is . . . pit (lines 4–5). Because the only way by coach was into London and out again.
one of Birkbeck's sons (line 8). Taylor and Hessey published *Letters from Illinois* (1818) by Maurice Birkbeck, and Taylor provided George with a letter of introduction to him.

LETTER 36

p. 128 *Peachey* (line 3), a school friend.
a poem . . . born (line 22). *Human Life* by Samuel Rogers.
p. 129 *the Apostate man* (line 24), i.e. Richard Lalor Sheil, who wrote *The Apostate*, produced at Covent Garden in 1817. The new tragedy was *Evadne*.
Jane Porter (line 25). Her play was *Switzerland*.
p. 130 *Johanna Southcott* (lines 31–2). The notorious eighteenth-century mystic.
Gifford (line 32). William Gifford, thought (mistakenly) to be the writer of the hostile reviews. They were written by J. W. Croker.

NOTES

p. 131   *Carlile* (line 1). Richard Carlile, was sentenced to three years' imprisonment and fined for reissuing Paine's *Age of Reason* and another proscribed book, on deism.
John Snook (line 17). Aged 11 when Keats knew him, he lived to be 79.
Mr Way (line 19). Lewis Way, who bought Stansted Park with part of a huge and unexpected inheritance.

p. 132   *Mr Lewis* (line 7). A Mr Lewis was "very kind to Tom all the summer" of 1818, and was "very assiduous in his enquiries" about the George Keatses. He gave Keats "some American papers" in December 1918.
the Westminster electors (lines 10-11). On 3 January Keats had written to George that "There is a letter today in the *Examiner* to the Electors of Westminster on Mr Hobhouse's account. In it there is a good character of Cobbett". Hobhouse (later Baron Broughton) was seeking election. He lost.
the retreat . . . ten-thousand (line 17). The retreat of the ten thousand Greeks described in Xenophon's *Anabasis*. A translation by Edward Spelman was among Keats's books.
Silenus (line 34). The drunken attendant on Dionysus (Bacchus).
immortality . . . claret (lines 35-6). Ariadne, deserted by Theseus, was married by Dionysus, who set immortally among the stars the crown he gave her on marriage.

p. 133   *the lady . . . Hastings* (lines 5-6). "Beautiful Mrs Jones", Reynolds called her. She figures in the share-out of Keats's books made by Brown in 1821, Lamb's name being crossed out in her favour. Mrs Isabella Jones was befriended by the rich and elderly Donat O'Callaghan, and Keats wrote to George in October 1818 that "she has always been an enigma to me", and described her sitting-room in 34 Gloucester Street, Queen's Square. Woodhouse said she suggested the subject for "The Eve of St Agnes".
My poem (line 15). *Endymion.*

p. 134   *no grove . . . Taylor's* (lines 33-4). Jeremy Taylor (1613-67) wrote *The Golden Grove*.

p. 136   *15-2* (line 4). A score in cribbage.
I would not . . . have her (line 17). Herny Wylie married the lady within the year, and the piece of bride-cake sent to Keats was lost.
St Luke's (line 20). A mental hospital.
The nothing . . . velocipede (line 36). The bicycle was invented by Baron von Drais and was first seen in London in February 1819.

LETTERS OF JOHN KEATS

p. 137   *A handsome . . . guineas* (line 3). The first bicycle was modelled on the horse.
fly-blown . . . review-shambles (line 14), cf. *Othello*. Act IV, Scene ii, line 65.
the Queen's mourning (line 17). Queen Charlotte, d. 17 November 1818.
[*18th September 1819* (line 29). As this paragraph indicates, Keats left the previous two chapters (from "On Monday", p. 135) out of his February letter, and sent the passage later.

p. 140   *I have . . . morning* (line 19). Letter no. 33.
Mr Monkhouse (line 25). Thomas Monkhouse, cousin of Wordsworth's wife, at whose house he and Keats met.

p. 143   *I do . . . nothing* (lines 17–18). This day, however, Keats had £60 from Abbey.
Hodgkinson (line 24). Abbey's junior partner, with whom George quarrelled and whose name Keats could not "bear to write".
I should not . . . two (lines 29–30). This remark may be Abbey's or Keats's. The speech commas are not closed. Hodgkinson was doing well seven years later.
Hilton (line 31). William Hilton, whose chalk drawing of Keats is famous, and whom Woodhouse commissioned to paint the portrait now in the National Portrait Gallery.

p. 145   "*We have . . . heart*" (line 26). See "The Old Cumberland Beggar".
p. 146   *Milton's lines* (line 18). *Comus*, line 475.
p. 147   "*whole . . . casing air*" (lines 23–4). *Macbeth*, Act III, Scene iv, line 23.
p. 148   *put . . . and me . . .* (lines 3–4). One can only guess what Keats intended to write.
Wells and Amena (line 5). Keats never forgave Charles Wells for sending Tom in 1816 mock love-letters signed Amena Bellefila, transparent as the joke was.
Sir John Leicester's gallery (lines 27–8), at his Berkeley Square house, at times open to the public.
Northcote (line 28). James Northcote, artist and writer.
it is to be published this morning (line 35)—by Taylor and Hessey.

p. 149   *The Bold Stroke for a Wife* (line 1). By Susannah Centlivre, d. 1723.
the same . . . commoners (line 14). After "spoiling" and "education" the boy became an M.P. and a knight.

p. 152   *Lord Mansfield's park* (line 33). Kenwood.
p. 154   "*Sometimes . . . with Browns*" (lines 15–16), cf. *The Tempest*, Act II, Scene ii, line 12.

NOTES

p. 156   *a cold pig* (line 12). A dousing.
p. 157   *a little notice* (line 6). The *Examiner* published it.
        Florimell (line 10). See *The Faerie Queene*, Books III–V.
        Archimage (line 14). See *ibid*, Book II.
        Barbara Lewthwaite (line 17), the maiden in Wordsworth's "The Pet Lamb".
        Alice . . . Foy (line 18). See Wordsworth's "The Idiot Boy".
p. 158   *the panorama* (line 7). A display put on in Leicester Square in connection with Franklin's first Arctic expedition.
p. 164   "*a poor forked creature*" (line 3), cf. *King Lear*, Act III, Scene iv, line 110.

LETTER 37

p. 171   *my old lodgings* (line 4). With the Bentleys, 1 Well Walk.
        a friend with ill health (line 9). Rice.
p. 172   *a versifying pet lamb* (lines 26–7). cf. "Ode on Indolence" vi.
        Elisha's ravens (line 35), Elijah's, See I Kings, Chapter XVII, verse 6.

LETTER 38

The earliest extant letter to Fanny Brawne, who from now on dominates the correspondence.

p. 174   *Pam* (line 11). The Jack of Hearts, highest trump in the game loo.
        Some lines (line 18). They are misquoted from Massinger's *Duke of Milan*, Act I, Scene iii.

LETTER 40

p. 178   *I will . . . at most* (line 11). It was 10 September before Keats went to London, and he left on the 15th without seeing Fanny.

LETTER 42

The first part of the letter is missing.
p. 180   *good . . . lodgings* (lines 3–4). In Colebrook Street.

LETTER 43

p. 182   *Idalia* (line 13). Idalium, a town in Crete, was sacred to Venus, and one of her "surnames", taken from it, was *Idalia*.

LETTER 44

p. 183 *August 25th.* A mistake, since the postmark is 24 August.

LETTER 45

p. 185 *William of Wickham* (line 9). William of Wykeham, Bishop of Winchester, added to the building in 1394.
whither . . . with him (lines 22-3). Keats returned to London in early October but not to Wentworth Place.

LETTER 46

p. 187 *8 Duke Street, Bath.* Reynolds was staying with Woodhouse in Bath.
"*keepen in solitarinesse*" (line 5). "The Eve of St Mark", line 106.
p. 188 *I composed upon it* (line 9). The poem was "To Autumn".
"*Hyperion*" (line 15). Keats is referring here to the revision called "The Fall of Hyperion".

LETTER 47

p. 190 "*not quite hob nob*" (line 3). "The Idiot Boy", line 289.
Sed thongum . . . la (line 18). A clever, punning adaptation of Virgil's *Eclogues*, III, line 79.
p. 191 "*Hyperion*" (line 19). i.e. "The Fall of Hyperion".
p. 192 *induction* (line 28), to "The Fall of Hyperion".
p. 193 *Undine* (line 14), a translation from the German by George Soane, of "a melo-dramatic romance in two acts".
All the . . . I write" (lines 26-8). It has been suggested that Keats intended to write "unposted" not unpoeted and had in mind the storm in *King Lear*, especially the line "unbonneted he runs".
p. 194 *agrest* (line 8). A word Keats made up, possibly from Latin *ager*, a field.
sylvestran (line 26). Another coined word, based on silvan.
otiosus-peroccupatus (lines 26-7). Meaning something like "lazy-most-busy". Keats is coining in Latin now.
old Bramble etc. (line 28). Keats is referring to Smollett's *Humphrey Clinker*, and inventing additional material about characters in it, Matthew Bramble, Mrs Clinker, Tabitha Bramble and Chowder her dog.
p. 195 *Cupid and Veney* (line 6). *The Spectator*, 11 March 1712, printed a letter supposedly from a lady "in a modish state of indifference between vice and virtue", who "sent to borrow Lady Faddle's Cupid for Veny".

NOTES

LETTER 52

p. 199   *an illness . . . Thursday* (lines 2–3). See *Introduction*, pp. 12–13.

p. 200   *the late King* (line 3). George III died on 29 January.
         Peter Pindar (lines 4–5). i.e. John Wolcot, the satirist, died on 14 January.

LETTER 53

p. 201   *the brickmakers* (line 3). There were many brick-kilns in the fields north of London.

LETTER 58

p. 205   "*last infirmity . . . minds*" (lines 23–4), see "Lycidas", line 71.

LETTER 68

p. 215   "*true as . . . simplicity*" (lines 18–19), see *Troilus and Cressida*, Act III, Scene ii, line 176.

LETTER 71

p. 217   During this month Severn wrote a letter to Haslam in which he gave an account of Keats's condition:

> My dear Haslam,
>   I have been away from home until Monday—on a face-making expedition —so that your letter has been to Hampton Court, Teddington and Richmond before I received it—it shall be done as you say—next week.
>   Poor Keats has been still nearer the next world—a fortnight back he ruptured a blood-vessel in the chest—I have seen him many times—particularly previous to this accident—once since—and it will give you pleasure to say I think he will still recover. His appearance is shocking and now reminds me of poor Tom, and I have been inclined to think him in the same way— for himself, he makes sure of it, and seems prepossessed that he cannot recover. Now I seem more than ever *not* to think so and I know you will agree with me when you see him. Are you aware another volume of poems was published last week in which is—"Lovely Isabel—poor simple Isabel". I have been delighted with this volume and think it will

even please the million. Keats has been for some time at Leigh Hunt's on account of the attention he requires. Most certain his body cannot be in better hands—but for his soul—altho' I can see in Keats such a deep thinking, determined, silent spirit—that I am doing him the greatest injustice to suppose for a moment that such a man as L-H— can ever taint him with his principles *now* or even school him with his learning. I think the house is 13 Mortimer Terrace, Kentish Town—it is only a few doors from Keats's lodging (2 Weslyan Place). I shall continue to visit Keats very much at every opportunity, perhaps twice a week.

Now about your "dearer self"—I am quite ashamed that I have not succeeded; the white satin gown looks most vile after all my trouble. Now if I may be favoured with a sitting I will succeed—to this purpose I think I can manage. Some day next week I shall be going to Deptford Dock Yard—say Thursday. Now I can call on Mrs H—and regain my lost favour. Present my respects, and say that from any silk dress I can paint white satin—it is merely the light and shade and the form I want. I met your servant on Monday but I could not return from the East India Dock Yard in time to call—try to see me.

Sincerely yours,
Joseph Severn

LETTER 74

p. 221   (*I do not write this till the last* . . .) referring to the words "My dearest girl". Keats was living among Leigh Hunt's numerous family. As far as we know it it the last letter he wrote to Fanny Brawne.

LETTER 75

p. 223   *an invitation from Mr Shelley* (line 1). Shelley's letter is given here. Keats's reply is Letter 79.

Pisa, July 1820

My dear Keats,

I hear with great pain the dangerous accident that you have undergone, and Mr Gisborne who gives me the account of it, adds that you continue to wear a consumptive appearance. This consumption is a disease particularly fond of people who write such good verses

NOTES

as you have done, and with the assistance of an English winter it can often indulge its selection; I do not think that young and amiable poets are at all bound to gratify its taste; they have entered into no bond with the muses to that effect. But seriously (for I am joking on what I am very anxious about) I think you would do well to pass the winter after so tremendous an accident in Italy, and (if you think it as necessary as I do) so long as you could find Pisa or its neighbourhood agreeable to you, Mrs Shelley unites with myself in urging the request, that you would take up your residence with us. You might come by sea to Leghorn (France is not worth seeing, and the sea air is particularly good for weak lungs) which is within a few miles of us. You ought at all events to see Italy, and your health which I suggest as a motive, might be an excuse to you. I spare declamation about the statues and the paintings and the ruins—and what is a greater piece of forbearance—about the mountains, the streams and the fields, the colours of the sky, and the sky itself.

I have lately read your *Endymion* again and ever with a new sense of the treasures of poetry it contains, though treasures poured forth with indistinct profusion. This, people in general will not endure, and that is the cause of the comparatively few copies which have been sold. I feel persuaded that you are capable of the greatest things, so you but will.

I always tell Ollier to send you copies of my books. *Prometheus Unbound* I imagine you will receive nearly at the same time with this letter. *The Cenci*—I hope you have already received—it was studiously composed in a different style "Below the good how far! but far above the *great*". In poetry *I* have sought to avoid system and mannerism; I wish those who excel me in genius, would pursue the same plan.

Whether you remain in England, or journey to Italy, believe that you carry with you my anxious wishes for your health, happiness and success, wherever you are or whatever you undertake—and that I am,

Yours sincerely,
P. B. Shelley

LETTER 78

p. 225   This letter appears in Brown's *Life of John Keats*, with names suppressed as here.

LETTER 80

p. 227 "*Lucy Vaughan Lloyd*" (line 12), i.e. "The Cap and Bells".

LETTER 81

p. 228 The *seal-breaking business* (lines 4–5), see Letter 75.
"*turning a neuk*" (line 25), see Burns, "To Miss Ferrier".

LETTER 82

p. 229 *a friend* (line 5), i.e. Fanny Brawne, who wrote the letter.

LETTER 83

p. 230 *am very provoked . . . Chichester to-day* (lines 13–14). While the *Maria Crowther* was held up at Portsmouth by adverse winds Keats spent his last night in England with the Snooks of Bedhampton. John Snook was married to Letitia, C. W. Dilke's sister. Keats heard that Brown was visiting Dilke's parents in Chichester only 10 miles away.

LETTER 86

pp. 233-4 This letter appears in Brown's *Life of John Keats* with the names suppressed as here.

* * *

In February and March 1821, Severn wrote the following two letters which give a first-hand account of Keats's last days in Rome. The second is to John Taylor:

Rome, Feby. 22nd 1821

My dear Haslam,

O! how anxious I am to hear from you—none of yours has come—but in answer to mine from Naples—I have nothing to break this dreadful solitude—but letters—day after day—night after night—here I am by our poor dying friend—my spirits—my intellects and my health are breaking down—I can get no one to change me—no one will relieve me—they all run away—and even if they did not, poor Keats could not do without me—I prepare everything he eats—

NOTES

Last night I thought he was going—I could hear the phlegm in his throat—he bade me lift him up in the bed—or he would die with pain—I watched him all night—at every cough I expected he would suffocate—death is very fast approaching for this morning by the pale daylight—the change in him frightened me—he has sunk in the last three days to a most ghastly look—I have these three nights sat up with him from the apprehension of his dying—Dr Clark has prepared me for it—but I shall be but little able to bear it—even this my horrible situation I cannot bear to cease by the loss of him—As regards money, my dear Haslam, you will have known that the kindness of Mr Taylor sets me quite easy—

I have at times written a favourable letter to my sister—you will see this is best—for I hope that staying by my poor friend to close his eyes in death—will not add to my other unlucky hits—for I am still quite prevented from painting—and what the consequence may be—Poor Keats keeps me by him—and shadows out the form of one solitary friend—he opens his eyes in great horror and doubt—but when they fall upon me—they close gently and open and close until he falls into another sleep—The very thought of this keeps me by him until he dies—and why did I say I was losing my time—the advantages I have gained by knowing John Keats—would to gain any other way have doubled and trebled the time—they could not have gained—I won't try to write any more—the want of sleep has almost taken away the power—The post is going so would try—Think of me dear Haslam as doing well and happy—as far as— — — — will allow.

Farewell—God bless you—
Sincerely—
J. Severn

I will write by next post to Brown—a 2nd letter has just come from him—

Rome, March 6th 1821

My Dear Sir,

I have tried many times to write you—but no—I could not: it has been too much for me to think on it—I have been ill from the fatigue and pain I have suffered—the recollection of poor Keats hangs dreadfully upon me—I see him at every glance—I cannot be alone now—my nerves are so shattered—These brutal Italians have nearly finished their monstrous business—they have burned all the furniture—and are now scraping the walls—making new windows—new doors—and even a new floor—You will see all the miseries attendant on these laws—I verily think I have suffered more from their cursed cruelties—than from all I did for Keats—These wretches have taken the moments when I was suffering in mind and body—they have enraged me day after day—until I trembled at the sound of every voice—I will try now once more to write you on our poor Keats—you will have but little for I can hardly dare to think on it—but I will write at intervals—and pray you to take it as my utmost endeavour—when I am stronger I will send you every word—the remembrance of this scene of horror will be fresh upon my mind to the end of my days—

Four days previous to his death—the change in him was so great that I passed each moment in dread—not knowing what the next would have—he was calm and firm at its approaches—to a most astonishing degree—he told me not to tremble for he did not think that he should be convulsed—he said—"Did you ever see anyone die"—No—"Well then I pity you poor Severn—what trouble and danger you have got into for me—now you must be firm for it will not last long—I shall soon be laid in the quiet grave—thank God for the quiet grave—O! I can feel the cold earth upon me—the daisies growing over me—O for this quiet—it will be my first"—when the morning light came and still found him alive—O how bitterly he grieved—I cannot bear his cries—

Each day he would look up in the doctor's face to discover how long he would live—he would say—"How long will this posthumous life of mine last"—that look was more than we could ever bear—the extreme brightness of his eyes—with his poor pallid face—were not earthly—

These four nights I watched him—each night expecting his death—on the fifth day the doctor prepared me for it—23rd at 4 o'clock afternoon—The poor fellow bade me lift him up in bed—he breathed with great difficulty—and seemed to lose the power of coughing up the phlegm—and immense sweat came over him so that my breath felt cold on him—"Don't breathe on me—it comes like ice"—he clasped my hand very fast as I held him in my arms—the mucus was boiling within him—it gurgled in his throat—this increased—but yet he seemed without pain—his eyes looked upon me with extreme sensibility but without pain—at 11 he died in my arms—The English Nurse had been with me all this day—this was something to me—but I was very bad—no sleep that night—The next day the doctor had me over to his house—I was still the same—These kind people did everything to comfort me—I must have sunk under it all—but for them—On the following day a cast was taken—and his death made known to the brutes here—yet we kept a strong hand over them—we put them off until the poor fellow was laid in his grave—On Sunday the second day, Dr Clark and Dr Luby with an Italian Surgeon—opened the body—they thought it the worst possible consumption—the lungs were entirely destroyed—the cells were quite gone—but Dr Clark will write you on this head—This was another night without sleep to me—I felt worse and worse—On the third day, Monday 26th, the funeral beasts came—many English requested to follow him —those who did were Dr Clark and Dr Luby, Messrs Ewing—Westmacott—Henderson—Pointer—and the Revd Mr Wolf who read the funeral service—he was buried very near to the monument of Caius Cestius—a few yards from Dr Bell and an infant of Mr Shelley's. The good hearted Doctor made the men put turves of daisies upon the grave—he said—"This would be poor Keats's wish—could he know it"—I will write again by next post but I am still in a poor state—farewell.

Josh. Severn

—The expense I fear will be great—perhaps £50—I owe still on the Doctor —I have not received the £50 you mention, at least Tolonias have had no notice of it—The Doctor pays everything for me and would let me have any money I need.

INDEX OF LETTERS

Recipient	Date of Letter	Letter No.	Page
Bailey, Benjamin	28–30 October 1817	6	56
	3 November 1817	7	60
	22 November 1817	8	64
	13 March 1818	14	80
	10 June 1818	18	94
	14 August 1819	42	180
Brawne, Fanny	1 July 1819	38	173
	8 July 1819	39	175
	15 July 1819	40	176
	25 July 1819	41	178
	16 August 1819	43	181
	11 October 1819	49	196
	13 October 1819	50	197
	(?) 10 February 1820	54	201
	(?) February 1820	55	202
	(?) February 1820	58	205
	(?) 24 February 1820	59	206
	(?) 27 February 1820	60	206
	[date unknown]	61	207
	(?) March 1820	62	208
	(?) March 1820	64	209
	(?) April 1820	65	210
	(?) late May 1820	67	212
	(?) June 1820	68	213
	(?) June 1820	70	217
	(?) 5 July 1820	71	217
	(?) early August 1820	74	221
Brawne, Mrs	24 October 1820	84	232

Recipient	Date of Letter	Letter No.	Page
Brown, Charles	23 September 1819	48	195
	14 August 1820	78	225
	(?) August or September 1820	80	227
	30 September 1820	83	230
	1 November 1820	85	233
	30 November 1820	86	235
Clarke, Charles Cowden	9 October 1816	1	47
Haslam, William (from Joseph Severn)	July 1820	Notes	253
,, ,, ,,	February 1821	Notes	256
Hessey, J. A.	8 October 1818	27	118
Jeffrey, Sarah	31 May–9 June 1819	37	171
Keats, Fanny	10 September 1817	5	53
	2–5 July 1818	20	99
	19 August 1818	24	115
	25 August 1818	25	116
	16 October 1818	28	119
	26 October 1818	29	120
	30 November 1818	31	122
	27 February 1819	33	123
	13 March 1819	34	124
	1 May 1819	35	126
	28 August 1819	45	185
	6 February 1820	52	199
	8 February 1820	53	200
	19 February 1820	57	204
	20 March 1820	63	208
	4 May 1820	66	210
	5 July 1820	72	219
	22 July 1820	73	220
	13 August 1820	75	222

INDEX OF LETTERS

Recipient	Date of Letter	Letter No.	Page
Keats, Fanny	23 August 1820	81	228
	11 September 1820	82	229
Keats, George	15 April 1817	3	48
	(?) 21 December 1817	9	67
	13, 19 January 1818	10	69
and Georgiana	14 February–3 May 1819	36	128
Keats, Tom	15 April 1817	3	48
	(?) 21 December 1817	9	67
	13, 19 January 1818	10	69
	25–27 June 1818	19	96
	3–9 July 1818	21	105
Reynolds, J. H.	17 March 1817	2	48
	17–18 April 1817	4	50
	3 February 1818	11	71
	19 February 1818	12	76
	14 March 1818	15	83
	9 April 1818	16	86
	3 May 1818	17	88
	11–13 July 1818	22	110
	(?) 22 September 1818	26	117
	24 August 1819	44	183
	21 September 1819	46	187
Rice, James	14–16 February 1820	56	203
Severn, Joseph	(*see* Haslam, William; Taylor, John)		
Shelley, Percy Bysshe	16 August 1820	79	226
(to Keats)	July 1820	Notes	254
Taylor, John	27 February 1818	13	78
	24 December 1818	32	123
	17 November 1819	51	198

Recipient	Date of Letter	Letter No.	Page
Taylor, John	(?) 11 June 1820	69	216
	13 August 1820	76	223
	14 August 1820	77	224
(from Joseph Severn)	6 March 1821	Notes	258
(from Richard Woodhouse)	November 1818	Notes	246
Woodhouse, Richard	27 October 1818	30	121
	21 September 1819	47	189
(to John Taylor)	November 1818	Notes	246
Wylie, Mrs James	6 August 1818	23	113